"When I was researching nineteenth century abortion history, I found many books filled with rhetoric and few that emphasized the reality women faced; only one book quoted extensively from women themselves. *Real Choices* is a much-needed book, filled with quotations that ring true today and will be useful to historians a century from now."

MARVIN OLASKY, PROFESSOR
THE UNIVERSITY OF TEXAS

"Real Choices provides a crucial understanding of the pressures women contemplating abortion face. This study is a great contribution to those who want to bring about an abortion-free America."

THOMAS A. GLESSNER, ATTORNEY
PRESIDENT, NATIONAL INSTITUTE OF FAMILY AND LIFE ADVOCATES

"Those of us in the pro-life movement are so often wrongly accused of caring little for the problems women in a crisis pregnancy face. *Real Choices* gives an excellent accounting of the great difficulties that a woman presented with a crisis pregnancy must deal with, more often than not, alone. Frederica Mathewes-Green expertly examines the reasons women feel compelled to undergo an abortion, and how we as prolifers can better help them. *Real Choices* is must reading for all committed pro-lifers."

REPRESENTATIVE HENRY J. HYDE,
UNITED STATES CONGRESS

"At last, the truth is becoming clear: If we want to help women in crisis pregnancies, we must not only defend babies—we must support women as well. It's time to step over the line that has been drawn in the sand, to stretch out our arms, and to reach out to women in crisis with positive *Real Choices.* For they are not the enemy, but possible victims. Only through love can we lead them safely out of the war zone, provide the support they need, and equip them to face the challenges that lie ahead. Frederica Mathewes-Green's book does more than point us in the right direction; it blazes a new trail for the pro-life movement."

MARY CUNNINGHAM AGEE, FOUNDER/EXECUTIVE DIRECTOR
THE NURTURING NETWORK

"Perhaps the sometimes shrill rhetoric on both sides of the culture wars has dulled many to the needs of real people struggling with the abortion issue. Frederica Mathewes-Green has assembled a highly readable, compassionate compendium of real voices and a vigorous, compelling perspective on how to equip women to make a real choice: for life."

ELLEN SANTILLI VAUGHN, CO-AUTHOR
THE BODY

"In a literate and wide-ranging work, Frederica Mathewes-Green has surveyed abortion from a neglected perspective: the women who have experienced it first hand. What emerges is a realistic and personal portrayal of what abortion has wrought in America and what can be done about it, with evident respect for women and for the fragility of human life."

HELEN ALVARÉ, DIRECTOR OF TRAINING AND INFORMATION
SECRETARIAT FOR PRO-LIFE ACTIVITIES, NATIONAL CONFERENCE OF CATHOLIC BISHOPS

"Too frequently, those who promote the right to abortion under the banner of 'pro-choice' have been caught up in slogans and rhetoric that distort reality. For objective insight into understanding choice, look at Frederica Mathewes-Green's *Real Choices.*"

JOHN CARDINAL O'CONNOR
ARCHBISHOP OF NEW YORK

"Those who read this book will have a deeper understanding of the 'real' reasons women chose abortion. The testimonies help you feel the uncertainty, distress, and anxiety that these women and young girls experienced as they faced unplanned pregnancies. These teens and women would have made different decisions if they had been given 'real' choices based on the love and compassion our Lord Jesus offers for them and for their unborn children."

DR. E. JEAN THOMPSON, president
INTERNATIONAL BLACK WOMEN'S NETWORK; HARVEST CHURCH INTL.

"When someone with a feminist, pro-peace background writes an excellent pro-life book devoted to expanding women's choices, all the stereotypes are scrambled and everybody ought to listen."

RON SIDER, PRESIDENT
EVANGELICALS FOR SOCIAL ACTION

REAL CHOICES

OFFERING PRACTICAL LIFE-AFFIRMING
ALTERNATIVES TO ABORTION

FREDERICA
MATHEWES-GREEN

MULTNOMAH BOOKS · SISTERS, OREGON

REAL CHOICES
published by Multnomah Books
a part of the Questar publishing family

© 1994 by Frederica Mathewes-Green

International Standard Book Number: 0-88070-678-3

Cover photos by Mike Houska
Cover design by David Uttley

Printed in the United States of America

Library of Congress Cataloging-in-Publication Data
Matthewes-Green, Frederica.
    Real choices: understanding the needs of women in unplanned pregnancies/by
Frederica Matthewes-Green.
        p.   cm.
    "Commissioned by the National Women's Coalition for Life"--Introd.
    ISBN 0-88070-678-3: $8.99
    1. Abortion--Moral and ethical aspects. 2. Abortion--United States. 3. Pro-life
movement--United States. 4. Pregnancy, Unwanted--United States. 5. Pregnant
women--United States--Case studies. 6. Pregnant women--Services for--United States.
I. National Women's Coalition for Life (U.S.)   II. Title.
HQ767.15.M37   1994   94-37492
363.4'6--dc20   CIP

95 96 97 98 99 00 01 — 10 9 8 7 6 5 4 3 2

To Gary,
a.k.a. Father Gregory,
with love on our twentieth anniversary.
Axios!

CONTENTS

FOREWORD

Could there be a more severe distortion of a woman's identity than for her to turn against her own child? Could there be a more severe distortion of a man's identity than for him to reject the woman he's made love with and to abandon the child he has fathered? Has the spirit of the age ever been more hostile toward women than in our present abortion culture?

Someone might say, "Wake up, my friend. It's the nineties. That's just the way it is." But that's not the way it's supposed to be.

To look at the reasons why women have abortions is to look at cultural disintegration. We see hostility, not only to children, but to what is essential to the fulfillment of feminine and masculine identity. We are witnessing a generation of cultural widows separated from husbands by abortion, children separated from fathers by abortion, and men emasculated by abortion as they give assent to the killing of their own children.

Thankfully, Frederica Mathewes-Green has turned the abortion debate right side up by identifying why women give in to abortion and what it will take to break this cycle of abuse against them and their children. *Real Choices* describes in intimate detail why women resort to abortion and what it is that will empower them to choose life. *Real Choices* is a landmark work, taking a major step toward resolving the most divisive and pressing issue of our time.

Guy M. Condon, President
Care Net

ACKNOWLEDGMENTS

The history of pro-life efforts to help women find alternatives to abortion stretches back over twenty-five years. In this book I stand on the shoulders of more people than I can count, much less thank.

First kudos must go to Jeannie French, the mother of the Professional Women's Network, the National Women's Coalition for Life, and baby Will. The prayers of Mary Bernadette sustained the project throughout.

There is no way to adequately thank the women who participated in the listening groups. Their willingness to expose deep hurts will help other women for years to come.

City coordinators worked hard to organize listening groups and press conferences: Teri Reisser, Right to Life League of Southern California (Los Angeles); Marilyn Kopp, Feminists for Life (Cleveland); Jeannie French (Chicago); Susan Gibbs, Feminists for Life (Washington, D.C.); Leslie Ann Johnson, Concerned Women for America (Phoenix); Valerie Schmalz and Suzanne Corral, Feminists for Life (Tampa); and Barbara Thorpe and Leila Little, Women Affirming Life, Inc. (Boston).

Constructing the Pregnancy Care Center Director's Survey was a challenge for this author, whose chronic impulse in writing is, "Oh, it wouldn't hurt to make it a little longer." Jim Rogers and Amy Miller gave invaluable professional guidance at the beginning of the project, and to Amy belongs the credit for processing the data and producing the final report. In addition to Jim and Amy, wise heads who reviewed and commented on the initial survey include Mike Baselice of the Tarrance Group, Denise Cocciolone of the National Life Center, Anne Granger of the

Nurturing Network, Cheryl Jakubowski of Care Net, and Susan Olasky.

Headquarters of pregnancy center chains received boxes of accurately counted and collated surveys, brochures, and return envelopes thanks to the superior talents of my husband, Gary Mathewes-Green, and our sons David and Stephen. Daughter Megan made an even more extensive contribution to the project in her role as mom's research assistant.

My debt to Marvin and Susan Olasky may be gauged by the embarrassing frequency with which I quote them. The burden of my indebtedness is lightened by the sheer fun of our friendship. I am grateful for Guy Condon's purity of vision, which has illuminated my understanding of this field. Mary Cunningham Agee has consistently encouraged me with affirmations far more generous than I deserve.

Mary Beth Seader, June Ring, Tom Glessner, Peggy Hartschorn, Cheryl Jakubowski, and Denise Cocciolone have been indispensable sources of help and information. David Reardon generously lent his case studies. Many pregnancy care centers wrote, offering to help any way they could.

The members of Holy Cross Orthodox Mission have been a source of spiritual and material support in more ways than I can number. May God grant you *all* many years.

The year 1994 marks two important 20th-anniversaries for me: on May 18 I married my sweetheart Gary, and on June 20 I committed my life to the Lord Jesus Christ. Of all the blessings for which I am grateful, these two top the list, both fountains of other blessings for decades past and to come. Grateful to Jesus, who gave me Gary and every other good thing, "like the thief will I confess thee: remember me, O Lord, in thy kingdom."

INTRODUCTION
ABOUT THE REAL CHOICES PROJECT

A COALITION IS BORN

In early 1992, an assembly of abortion rights groups announced plans to stage a march on Washington, D.C. The purpose of the march was to celebrate the freedom abortion allegedly brings, and to voice the enthusiasm women are purported to feel for the procedure. America was being reminded once again that, if you're not in favor of abortion, you're not a real woman.

Real woman Jeannie French, a health-care executive in Chicago, was as annoyed by these prospects as the rest of us. Unlike the rest of us, she did something about it. French, a self-starter who founded a Students for Life group when she was a student and the pro-life Professional Women's Network when she became a professional (a hospital vice-president at the age of 23), began contacting pro-life organizations that were predominantly female. Her goal: to launch a pro-life women's coalition that would dwarf abortion-advocacy groups pretending to represent all women, one that would demonstrate how deeply runs the opposition to abortion among American women.

On Friday, April 3, 1992, the National Women's Coalition for Life made its debut at the National Press Club in Washington, D.C., slipping in just two days before the abortion-rights march and stealing some of its thunder. French's dream of a pro-life women's coalition had come true.

Today that Coalition numbers fourteen groups, with a combined membership of over 1.3 million. No abortion advocacy group can claim a membership figure anywhere near it; the National Organization for Women, for example, is less than one-fourth its size. NWCL is a diverse coalition, ranging from Feminists for Life to the National Association of Pro-Life Nurses, from the International Black Women's Network to Capitol Hill Women for Life. (At the press conference a representative of a liberal group said of a more conservative leader, "We should sing, 'You say tomato and I say tomahto.'")

Two hundred fifty thousand women who have had abortions are members of the Coalition, represented by three organizations: Women Exploited by Abortion, American Victims of Abortion, and Victims of Choice. Two organizations, Life After Assault League and Fortress International, represent people who have experienced, or were conceived in, rape pregnancies.

The Coalition continues to grow. Individuals should contact one of the Coalition's member groups (see Appendix A); there is no mechanism to join directly. Organizations applying to join must be primarily for women (this is why a group like National Right to Life Committee is not a member) and must have membership rolls (this is why a group such as Care Net is not a member). Consideration is being given to establishing an affiliate status for groups outside these guidelines.

REAL CHOICES, THE COALITION'S FIRST MAJOR PROJECT

Not long after the initial press conference, French had her next brainstorm. In a conference call she presented her idea: why don't we hold hearings across the country to allow women who have had abortions to talk about their experiences, to explore the pressures and problems that lead to the decision to have an abortion. Can we identify these problems and assess our ability to solve them? Where can we do a better job? Even if abortion is legal, aren't there things we can do to reduce consumer demand for this deadly product?

This idea prompted a flood of suggestions. We should talk to pregnancy care centers and build on their expertise. We should look at barriers to adoption, and at child support payments, and at the role of welfare. While focusing on the needs of the woman who is already pregnant, we should say a word about preventing those pregnancies in the first place.

It quickly became apparent that the scope of the project could snowball out of control. I was appointed director of the project, and French and I worked together to bring it down to manageable size. We planned a research project that would take roughly a year to complete and, to avoid burdening Coalition members who had tight budgets, found outside funding. The results of this project, which French named "Real Choices," you hold in your hands today.

HOW REAL CHOICES' RESEARCH WAS DONE

Pregnancy Care Center Survey

When one asks, "Why do women have abortions? What makes continuing a pregnancy hard to do?" an obvious source for the answer springs to mind: the nation's pregnancy care centers. The staff and volunteers in these storefronts are the ones who, day after day, are looking at the problems pregnant women have and trying their best to solve them. They are the experts.

In order to tap into this wisdom, we constructed a survey with the assistance of professional statisticians, pollsters, and pregnancy care specialists. Major pregnancy center chains like Care

Net, Birthright, Bethany, International Life Services, and Heartbeat all distributed the survey to their centers, and we were able to reach many of the independent centers as well; in all, 1860 surveys were sent out.

The survey (see Appendix B) was in some ways uninviting; it was long and, in places, complex. The rate of return for surveys by mail is typically quite small unless significant follow-up is done by phone and postcard. Yet even without this follow-up, the Real Choices survey was returned at a rate of over 10 percent, indicating how willing pregnancy workers are to go the extra mile. Responses to the survey were received by the office of James Rogers, a Professor of Psychology at Wheaton College with extensive experience in statistics and research methodology. His assistant, Amy Miller, entered the data and produced a final report (see Appendix C).

The results were intriguing. In constructing the instrument, we had used as the core a 1988 study by the Alan Guttmacher Institute, an organization associated with Planned Parenthood and which holds a firm stand favoring abortion. This AGI study asked abortion customers to indicate their reasons for abortion, and suggested thirteen categories (see Appendix D); "an attempt was made to include every possible reason for having an abortion," the study's authors say. However, we were able to expand the list to twenty-seven categories, with the addition of items about barriers to adoption, domestic violence, the need for child care or housing, and so forth.

We asked the center directors to indicate which of these situations were encountered most often in their work with pregnant women, and also asked them to indicate which problems were most difficult to solve. To our surprise, the same item rose to the top of each list: "Adoption appears too difficult (practically or emotionally)." While it is unlikely that a pregnant woman would cite this as the reason she has to have an abortion, pregnancy care centers apparently feel that the difficulty of presenting adoption as an attractive option is a major handicap in their work of persuading women to choose life.

This finding suggests that the problems that arise after birth are more daunting than those of pregnancy itself. If the pregnancy alone were the problem, adoption would be no help.

The second most common reason cited was that the husband or partner was absent, undependable, or insufficiently supportive. This was a theme often heard in the post-abortion listening groups as well. The pregnancy center's third and fourth most common problems were that the woman says she couldn't afford the baby now, and that child-rearing would interfere with her school or job situation. Again, both of these concerns deal with her situation after the birth, not during the pregnancy. The fifth most common reason was that the pregnancy would interfere with her school or job situation.

To our knowledge, the only other studies to ask women about their reasons for abortion were two which sought the information only incidentally; their primary focus was on post-abortion stress. Additionally, Mary Cunningham Agee surveyed one hundred post-abortion women asking if they would have preferred an alternative to abortion. The portions of these three studies relevant to our topic appear in Appendix E.

In addition to basic demographic information, the Real Choices survey also asked which resources the center provided and which it needed. For each item in the list of problems, centers were asked to indicate which of their services or resources were used in solving that problem. Finally, the centers were asked two more general questions. The first was, "In your opinion, which are more influential in discouraging a woman from continuing a pregnancy, emotional or practical problems?" The response was a moderate split, with 58 percent citing emotional and 41 percent citing practical concerns.

The response to the second question was more of a surprise. "Would you be willing to work with pro-choice activists to alleviate these problems, if beliefs about abortion were not raised as an issue?" A whopping 79 percent said "yes" to a 21 percent "no." Several wrote in that they were already doing so, for example seeking help from domestic violence or rape activists, even when those resources were not pro-life. For most center directors, the bottom line was helping women continue their pregnancies, and they would not refuse help from someone on the other side of the divide.

Post-Abortion Listening Groups

We also wanted to hear from women who had had abortions, the idea that had sparked French's original vision. We discussed several ways of recruiting participants for these groups, and continually ran into two barriers: participants' need for confidentiality, and the unfortunate necessity of insuring that the group was not invaded by zealots from either side. If the hearings were open to the public, we stood a chance of getting an assortment of curious or angry activists masquerading as post-abortion women, while the women we actually sought would likely find the prospect of a public gathering too intimidating to consider.

We discussed several increasingly-elaborate plans to net a random selection of a city's authentic post-abortion women, but could not in the end devise a method that both maintained confidentiality and screened out infiltrators. In the end, we decided to work through local post-abortion counseling agencies, asking the head counselor to select five to ten women from her clientele. We sought for these groups volunteers who had experienced enough healing to feel comfortable about participating, but we did not require, or even desire, a firmly pro-life stand. The woman's current opinions about abortion were not particularly relevant; what was important was that, at one time, she favored abortion enough to have one. It was that period of time, before the abortion, that we wanted to learn about.

After the Los Angeles group meeting, we made additional efforts to reach women who were not yet pro-life converts, for reasons that will be apparent in chapter 2. In Cleveland and again in Chicago we invited abortion clinics to send participants. In the former city we were told that they really had no one to send; they said, in effect, that "If a woman is having regrets after her abortion, she doesn't come back to us." The representative in Chicago was too wary of the invitation to consider it.

In all I visited seven American cities: Los Angeles, Cleveland, Chicago, Washington, D.C., Phoenix, Tampa, and Boston. The conversations in those groups are recorded in the even-numbered chapters of this book, with a summary of results in Appendix F. These findings differed from the survey results in interesting ways. While four of the five most common problems cited by pregnancy centers involved practical needs, women in the listening groups uniformly talked about pressures in relationships; the abortion was done, each told us, either to please someone or to protect someone. The abortions were done to please the baby's father, who was calling for the abortion in ways ranging from true coercion to passive non-support; to please one or both parents (most often the woman's mother); or to protect the parents, who were thought unable to bear the stress of the pregnancy. No one said she had the abortion because she was afraid her parents would hurt her physically.

Most interestingly, no one said that she had to have the abortion to protect her career or because she couldn't afford the baby, even though those were the sorts of reasons pregnancy care centers cited as most common. In some cases, women insisted that the reverse was true, and that material resources were plentiful. Instead, it was not uncommon for a woman to choose abortion in order to maintain relationships to significant people in her life. The hurt afterwards came when she realized that her unborn child was also a significant person in her life, and that she had shirked her obligation to a child who had no one to trust but her.

Does this focus on relational problems reflect a bias in women who have become pro-life? No, books detailing the abortion decisions of pro-choice women (such as Sue Nathanson's *Soul Crisis*, Carol Gilligan's *In a Different Voice*) echo the theme that abortion is frequently chosen to solve problems in relationships (usually with the baby's father). Current attitudes toward abortion matter little.

Feminist recognition that the spur to abortion is frequently the attitude of the baby's father goes back at least as far as French feminist Simone de Beauvoir. In her 1952 book, *The Second Sex*, she reflected bitterly on male pressure to abort: "It is often the seducer himself who convinces the woman that she must rid herself of the child. Or he may have already abandoned her...sometimes she declines to bear the infant not without regret.... Men tend to take abortion lightly; they regard it as one of the numerous hazards imposed on women by malignant nature, but fail to realize fully the values involved. The woman who has recourse to abortion is disowning feminine values, her values.... Her whole moral universe is being disrupted."[1]

This tacit pro-choice admission of the desperate element to abortion choice is illustrated by the travels of an analogy I included in a magazine article. I wrote, "No one wants an abortion as she wants an ice-cream cone or a Porsche. She wants an abortion as an animal, caught in a trap, wants to gnaw off its own leg. Abortion is a tragic attempt to escape a desperate situation by an act of violence and self-loss."[2] This quote, shorn of its last sentence, popped up a year later in a column by firmly pro-choice columnist Ellen Goodman.[3] Almost immediately it appeared again, this time in Planned Parenthood's *Public Affairs Action Letter*, boxed front-page-center as "Quote of the Week."[4] It then showed up once more as "Quote of the Month" in *The Pro-Choice Network Newsletter*.[5] Apparently there was something about this analogy that struck a nerve; apparently pro-choice partisans could agree with pro-lifers that, no matter what their political differences, abortion was a miserable choice.

The disparity between reasons cited by pregnancy care centers and those cited by abortive women is curious, however. Several explanations have been suggested. Few of the women in these post-abortion groups had visited a pregnancy care center before the abortion; perhaps when the relationship pressures are intense, women don't even make it to the centers, but go directly to abortion clinics. Only those who believe their relationship problems can be overcome will bother going to a pregnancy care center.

Another possibility is that a woman may feel embarrassed about presenting these personal problems to the kindly stranger at the center. She may find it easier to talk about needing an abortion because she can't afford child care, than to say that her boyfriend is threatening to leave her.

Third, we may be encountering one of the mind's tricks: memories of practical problems fade once those problems are resolved, but memories of emotional pain have lingering impact. A woman may well have been distressed by financial and material concerns at the time of the pregnancy, but it is the look in her baby's father's eyes that is seared most deeply into her memory. This is the thing that rises to the top when I ask, "Tell me the story of how you came to have an abortion."

In the end, this disparity is not significant. For nearly every woman, the abortion decision is the result of many reasons, not just one. Relational and practical, emotional and material problems all jumble together in a dense knot, and abortion appears the most efficient—if not the only—way to solve them all.

The Alan Guttmacher Institute study mentioned above takes this view. "Perhaps the most striking finding from this study is not that subgroups of women choosing abortion have a wide variety of reasons for doing so, but that most individual women have several reasons. Ninety-three percent of respondents cited more than one reason for having decided to have an abortion, and on the average they reported almost four." The authors found that social and demographic factors did not predict which reasons women would choose, so that "actions directed toward helping women who are unintentionally pregnant avoid abortion would be most effective if tailored to the individual." Of course, this is what pregnancy care centers do.

Yet the study's authors conclude that "Findings from this survey indicate that eliminating (or even substantially reducing the number of) abortions once women have become unintentionally pregnant will be very difficult, if not impossible, because the reasons women turn to abortion are so numerous and varied." They recommend, instead, improved contraception to prevent these pregnancies.

But for those who see the decision to continue a pregnancy as a matter of life and death such a response is impossible. Instead, as we look at the list of problems, we find that some of them can indeed be solved. Things look very different to the person who says, "It's too hard" than they do to the person who says, "Let's try."

The jumble of problems in a pregnancy is like a pile of pick-up sticks. Pro-lifers and pregnancy care workers will not be able to remove every one of the problems, not in the way abortion can: with smashing finality, flipping over the very table and scattering the sticks in the air. The work of enabling a difficult pregnancy is a careful one of removing sticks one at a time, as many as you can reach, until the whole rolls apart and resolves itself: the impossible becomes something the woman can just envision herself achieving.

It may not even be necessary to solve the problem that the woman indicates is the most important. It may be that dismantling some of the other barriers will be enough to give her the courage to face the bigger challenge. It was striking how frequently women in these groups said, "If I'd only had one other person to stand by me..." They weren't asking for magic solutions. They were asking for a friend.

A second way that this project listened to post-abortion women was through reviewing over five hundred case histories in which women wrote of their own experiences. These results (see Appendix G) dovetailed with those of the listening groups and the pregnancy care centers.

Input from Pro-Choice Advocates

When the Pregnancy Care Center Survey was being drawn up, I became curious about how abortion clinic counselors would answer the same survey. What are abortion clients telling counselors about their reasons for needing the procedure? Would these counselors list the same problems that the pregnancy centers do?

In general, what might we learn about the problems of pregnancy from those on the other side of the abortion debate?

Accordingly, I made a number of attempts to reach out to pro-choice advocates; the resulting files are stuffed with correspondence and notes from phone conversations, and there were even a few face-to-face meetings (see Appendix H). Despite this effort, no useful contact was made; pro-choice advocates offered either cold shoulders or cold feet.

In the majority of cases, invitations netted cold shoulders—no response at all. For example, a letter sent to seven major pro-choice organizations inviting "input" of whatever sort they chose was ignored. In other cases, there was an initial positive response, followed by cold feet—second thoughts and hesitation. Within a given organization some people might be positive while others were negative, depending on individual temperament more than anything else. The eventual outcome, in any case, was the same.

It may have been that the invitation to give input was mistaken as a challenge ("if you're so pro-choice, prove it"), or as a prelude to a joint action project. Neither was the case. We simply wanted to hear whatever they had to say about why women have abortions. It was a rare opportunity for pro-choice advocates to reach listening pro-life ears.

However, if I had received a call from someone saying, "I represent a coalition of a dozen pro-choice groups, with over a million members, and we want your to help with our project," I'd be tempted to say, "I think you have a wrong number." Trust doesn't come easily when a war is over twenty years old. Perhaps, because this project first broke the ice, the next time such an invitation is offered it will be more successful.

HOW TO USE THIS BOOK

Speaking in the name of an organization is a little like trying to maneuver in a dress with a heavy train; the larger the organization, the harder it is to move easily, much less to move in a new direction. The awesome responsibility of saying what thousands, or hundreds of thousands, want to say through you can make anyone tongue-tied.

The National Women's Coalition for Life represents over a million women, members of over a dozen organizations, each with its own particular concerns. It is impossible to speak here for every one of these women except in the broadest terms, a restriction that would be paralyzing. It is important, therefore, to delineate which parts of this project can be fairly described as being done in the Coalition's name, and which parts are opinion for which there is no one responsible but the author.

The Coalition commissioned the research, and so readers are urged to spend time in the Appendixes, encountering the data first-hand and drawing their own conclusions. In addition, the even-numbered chapters which record the conversations in listening groups will put flesh on the bones of the statistical data.

Intervening chapters are my own thoughts on resolving the problems of pregnancy. I admit that I am not a typical pro-lifer. In my college years I was a feminist who strongly favored abortion. The February/March 1973 issue of the leading underground feminist newspaper, *off our backs*, contains both an editorial criticizing the new *Roe v. Wade* decision (too conservative) and one of my movie reviews. My conversion to the pro-life cause a few years later was inaugurated by an essay I read in *Esquire* magazine. This is not every pro-lifer's story.

Only in recent years have I become active speaking and writing on this issue, and some of my colleagues in this cause think my related views—for example, on war and capital punishment—still lean a little too far to the left. My opposition to abortion is based, not on an appreciation of the cuteness of babies and the sweetness of family life, but on a conviction that it is wrong to solve problems with violence. I believe that this principle of non-violence extends even to the evil of bearing a violent or hateful spirit toward our adversaries, whom we are commanded to love. I am sure that I fail so regularly at exemplifying Jesus's pattern of long-suffering love that I make either the principle, or myself, look foolish. I hope it is the latter.

My opposition to abortion also springs from a conviction that it is ugly and degrading to women. Years spent as a natural child-birth teacher, devising my own method of pain relief and becoming a homebirth mom myself, wrought in me a deep conviction that pregnancy and birth are a healthy process that should be, as much as possible, left alone. Pregnancy and birth link together women all over the world and throughout all time; that earthy, vital process is the most elemental symbol of woman's strength. Disrupting it by thrusting tools deep into her body is as obscene as pouring dirty motor oil into a mountain lake. I oppose abortion because it violates women more deeply than rape, a more hideous violation because it brings grisly death into the very house of life.

If I sound like an aging ex-hippie, I am. On the other hand, my insistence on seeking what is healthy in the natural order, as above, leads me to take what some would call very right-wing stands about sexual responsibility and welfare. I believe that some of the things pro-lifers do—for example, treating post-abortion women as helpless victims, or encouraging the use of public assistance, or failing to discourage single parenting—only cause more trouble down the road, because a healthy natural order is not their destination. As I develop these ideas in the pages ahead, I hope readers will find them at worst amusing, and will not assume that they are in any way official positions of the National Women's Coalition for Life.

The final question that usually emerges when abortion is the topic has to do with the speaker's religious beliefs. It is usually assumed that a pro-lifer will be either an evangelical Protestant or a conservative Roman Catholic. I am neither. Although I have learned and gained much from both those traditions since my conversion to the Lord twenty years ago, I am a *khouria* (priest's wife) in the Holy Orthodox Church, that ancient communion which has its roots in the lands and times of the New Testament, and to which over four million Americans belong.

In summary, then, the Real Choices project was commissioned by the National Women's Coalition for Life in order to understand better the problems that cause women to choose abortion. This book offers statistical data that emerged from that research, plus a chance to hear women speak for themselves about their decisions, as well as my own analysis and recommendations. In the course of this work we discovered that women in difficult pregnancies are plagued by numerous problems, both practical and emotional, and that relieving these problems is neither straightforward nor easy. That does not mean that the task is impossible, or that we may shirk the attempt. In the hope that we can make a difference in the lives of the women who face the tragic choice of abortion, this volume offers an alternative: Real Choices.

1. Simone de Beauvoir, *The Second Sex* (New York: Bantam Books, 1952).
2. Frederica Mathewes-Green, "Unplanned Parenthood," *Policy Review*, Summer 1991.
3. Ellen Goodman, "Not 'Choice,' but 'Better Choices,'" *The Baltimore Sun*, September 18, 1992.
4. Planned Parenthood Federation of America Public Affairs Action Letter, September 25, 1992.
5. The Pro-Choice Network Newsletter, May 1993.

The Question about Jean

J ean has been dumped by her boyfriend, an event that still amazes and wounds her. Now she doesn't know where to turn. She's afraid to tell her parents: she sees her mother's face fall with sorrow, her dad turn away ashamed. Her boss has hinted before that a girl who got pregnant would have her work closely evaluated. Her landlord made it clear that the apartment building did not welcome children.

She sits on the side of her bed in the morning, fighting back waves of nausea; she weeps into her hands and feels so frightened and alone. The baby growing inside her seems an evil invader, like a cancerous tumor impudently growing larger every day. Soon it will become obvious, and everyone will know—at the office and at church and in the grocery store—and she'll be the object of pity and the object of scorn, and eternally the object of gossip.

What will happen next?

Over forty-four hundred times a day, stories like Jean's end on abortion tables. Yet for over twenty years the abortion battle has been fought on the harshly-lit stage of political power, disconnected from these intimate narratives of sorrow and loss.

Both sides had strategic reasons to ignore women's personal, complex stories. Pro-life advocates saw their chief role as defending the unborn baby, and so the woman became by default the enemy. Behind the scenes, the pregnancy care movement was reaching out to women in trouble, but their work was under-represented in movement rhetoric. Instead, at the podiums, marches, and TV studios, many trivialized the woman's situation.

Some pro-lifers chided the woman for using abortion "for birth control," as if she frivolously chose this grotesque alternative from a tray of pre- and post-conception methods. Few would intentionally decline a condom in favor of something so painful, awkward, heartbreaking, and hundreds of times more expensive. They charged she only wanted the abortion "for convenience," as if the life-changing tumult of pregnancy and birth were a mere annoyance. Changing a flat tire on a rainy night is more inconvenience than most of us handle gracefully. Some pro-lifers sneered that she only wanted the abortion because she didn't want to damage her career or change her life plans—but a few minutes spent picturing yourself helpless before something that will damage your career and change your life can be a sobering exercise.

It was easy to champion the baby and denigrate the woman in framing the abortion debate. But the more we insisted that the baby's rights were more important than the woman's, the more we made her feel besieged and friendless. We reinforced the message our abortion-rights opponents were murmuring to her: the baby is your enemy, and pro-lifers are advancing your enemy's rights against your own. Sympathetic abortion providers begin to look like her only friends. When she turned toward the comfort of that sympathy, she took her baby with her.

But pro-choice activists were not much interested in getting the woman's story out, either. Abortion was being sold as a civil rights issue, a glorious bid for autonomy and power. There was a terrible danger that, if a woman spoke about her personal experience, she might reveal that it made her sad. Abortion advocates wanted to paint the woman's choice as serious and difficult, but if anyone directly asked her the obvious question—"If it's so freeing, why is it so hard?"—she might blurt, "Because I know it's killing my baby."

Women's stories might also reveal that abortion was often not a free choice but a forced choice, coerced by the threats or coldness of her lover or her parents. That admission would logically require that abortion be revealed as, not a victory, but a capitulation. Women would not be willing to march in the streets with banners reading, "I'm proud I gave in and killed my baby to keep my boyfriend."

Then there was the damaging truth that vanishingly few abortions are done for grave reasons of rape, incest, or to save the woman's life. Most are done for messy personal reasons that wouldn't seem sufficient justification to the Mom-and-Pop households across the country. Abortion was being presented as an isolated life-event, chosen after impartial consideration. In this vision, the elegantly-suited lady puts a finger to her chin and studies the dessert cart: chocolate mousse or creme caramel? Have an abortion or have a baby? Far more often the abortion "choice" was one more symptom of a life in which very little was consciously chosen, very little was under control.

Sometimes the hyperbole about "abortion for convenience" rang uncomfortably true: the women who don't want to get fat, who don't want to quit the party scene, who don't want to miss out on a new bikini next summer. A Baltimore abortion clinic chose for its Yellow Pages ad a photo they think will win them customers: a lithe young woman in a red leotard, lacing up her running shoes. Want to keep trim? Have an abortion!

As the abortion battle progressed, it's lines grew clear: women against fetuses in a fight to the death. Any political battle demands such cleanly defined teams, and each side continued to demand justice at the other's expense. Like a Punch and Judy show, mother and child battered each other on stage, while unseen hands worked them from below.

But in no sane society are women and their unborn children treated as mortal enemies. When they are set against each other, like contestants in a boxing ring, something is wrong with the whole picture. Surely, any society that makes mother and child enemies is slowly committing suicide. This is true both literally— what healthy mammalian population intentionally kills its own offspring?—and symbolically as well. When we institutionalize the violent ripping of a child from her mother's womb, we violate something disturbingly close to the heart of the human story. In the land where women kill their unborn children, every lesser love grows frail.

When circumstances make a woman feel so desperate that killing her own child seems the only way to survive, the problem is not inside her body, but outside it. Abortion adapts the woman's body to her hostile surroundings, bypassing her problems without resolving them. When she becomes pregnant again, or when her sister or daughter becomes pregnant, the same overwhelming pressures will be there to demand another abortion. The stream of women into abortion clinics remains steady at over forty-four hundred per day, a surgical epidemic so mind-boggling that we can cope with it only by ignoring it.

Ignoring it appears, in fact, to be becoming the preferred alternative. Polls over the last few years show that the majority of Americans are convinced that abortion does kill a baby. Pro-life rhetoric along these lines has accomplished about all it can.

For example, at the 1989 conference of the National Abortion Rights Action League, pollster Harrison Hickman mourned, "Nothing has been as damaging to our cause as the advances in technology which have allowed pictures of the developing fetus, because people now talk about that fetus in much different terms than they did fifteen years ago. They talk about it as a human being, which is not something that I have an easy answer how to cure."

Polls confirm Hickman's fears. Since the late 1980s they have consistently shown that Americans believe that the life in the womb is a baby, and are even willing to say that taking that life is wrong. Three-fourth of the respondents to a 1990 Gallup poll agreed that "Abortion is the taking of a human life." In 1992, 73 percent of those polled by Command Research stated that the fetus is a human baby, and "killing is wrong." In a 1989 poll by the *Los Angeles Times*, 57 percent called abortion "murder," a term even some cautious pro-lifers will reject as legally imprecise.

The "It's a Baby!" strategy has succeeded. When we tell America one more time that the life in the womb is a baby, we're answering a question no one is asking.

The paradox is that, even though a majority calls abortion "murder," it is a kind of "murder" that they want legal. The same Gallup poll cited above shows 63 percent of respondents saying the federal government should have no voice in the abortion decision. Nearly three-fourths in the Command Research poll said they opposed society deciding whether a woman should have an abortion. And, in the *Los Angeles Times* poll, one-fourth of those who "generally favored abortion" were also willing to call it murder.

This ambivalence frustrates activists on both poles. While both camps would prefer an ideologically pure victory, average citizens seem willing to tolerate this wobbly détente as long as they don't have to think about it too much.

This was the genius of the pro-choice "Let the woman decide" slogan. After decades of an unpleasant struggle which became increasingly deadlocked, most people just want the issue to go away. "Let the woman decide" gives people permission to do what they really want—walk away from the issue without having to take a stand.

Pro-choice activists had wisely deduced that they were not going to succeed in convincing a majority of Americans to affirm abortion, so they opted for this second best. In terms of practical results, this is as good a victory as any, as it leaves all under the rule of *Roe v. Wade*. The wearying, repetitive abortion battle has been like an endless game of Musical Chairs, participants shuffling in a circle for twenty years. When public patience runs out, the music will stop, and the enduring status quo will win by default. At this point, it looks like pro-lifers will be the ones short of chairs.

So, while neither side was able to turn its program into sweeping federal law, the middle's emerging consensus is to tolerate abortion as a necessary evil, hedged about with restrictions concerning parental consent, waiting periods, and so forth. These restrictions, necessary as they are, may actually have the side-effect of making abortion more acceptable. Statewide liquor laws generally regulate when, where, and how alcohol is sold, but do not restrict adults from buying as much as they like. These laws give the public a feeling that alcohol consumption is under reasonable control. Abortion regulatory laws may have the same impact.

Pro-lifers will not be able to break through this deadlock by stressing the humanity of the unborn; as noted above, that is a question no one is asking. But there is a question they are asking. It is, "How could we live without it?" Their problem is not moral but practical: in this wrecked, off-center world, where women are expected simultaneously to be sexually available and to maintain careers, unplanned pregnancies seem both inevitable and catastrophic. It's too hard to change all of that; it's much easier to change the woman.

People don't really like abortion, but they can't see any other way out. They will adamantly resist passing a law against it until we can convince them that, if such a law were passed, utter chaos would not result. We must show them that unplanned pregnancies can be resolved in life-affirming ways without destroying our already fragile social order.

To answer that question, to show that we can live without it, we must begin to envision how America would look if abortion were gone. What would women do instead of having abortions? What changes might this require in sexual relationships and marriage? Adoption procedures? School and the workplace? Child-rearing?

We began the Real Choices project with the expectation that we would be able to come up with a handy list of problems that needed to be solved. We might find that the most common cited by women considering abortion was how to care for her child and keep her job, for example. The second concern might be getting financial help for child-rearing, for example child support payments. We might find in third place a need for housing during pregnancy.

However after looking at data from a number of different sources it was impossible to arrive at any such consensus. There was seldom a single, compelling, practical reason for the abortion. There was nearly always a complex nest of problems, affecting both her material situation and her emotional well-being.

Yet when we listened to women describe their situations in depth in the listening groups, a surprising theme emerged. In nearly every case, the abortion was undertaken to fulfill a felt obligation to another person, a parent or boyfriend. Our assumption that abortion decisions were prompted by the sort of practical problems—food, shelter, poverty, clothing—which a pregnancy care center could attempt to solve was not borne out. Instead, the woman felt bound to please or protect some other person, and abortion was the price she felt she had to pay.

Pro-choice rhetoric presents the decision for abortion in terms of autonomy. The woman acts alone, choosing for herself what will best empower her. It is her body, her life, her right to decide, and no one else is concerned.

This rhetoric imagines women unfettered, empowered, and free; the women we listened to said instead that they felt isolated, endangered, and sad. Loneliness and fear of abandonment pushed them toward this choice, decked out in its first-person-singular bunting.

The isolationist rhetoric fails to visualize her situation. The woman considering abortion doesn't feel autonomous, but enmeshed in relationships which bind and constrain her decision, now this way, now that. She is not free to choose her course like choosing a chocolate from a box. Her choice will reverberate through many lives, and she fears provoking anger or pain. Naturally the big, walking-around people appear much more daunting to her, while the little, dependent person within exerts a stronger, prior claim of more primal obligation.

When the women described their state in early pregnancy, they often reported feelings of dependency. Many said they felt bewildered and overwhelmed, and found it hard to think clearly or visualize the path ahead. In describing the abortion decision, they might say, "I was led like a lamb to the slaughter. I let other people take charge of my life because I felt out of control." Whether this dependency is exacerbated by the hormone shifts of pregnancy, or due to an impulse to draw in resources and nest, or simply due to being in a difficult and perplexing situation, when this helplessness sets in, women are prone to follow others' advice.

Of course, those others, whether good friends or family, probably do not want to do the woman harm—quite the opposite. It's obvious to them that the pregnancy is causing the woman distress, and the surest way to help her is to get rid of it. Continuing the pregnancy would only bring in more and more life-changing problems, from which abortion can readily set her free. Helping her, they believe, means giving her compassionate encouragement while she does the only thing that makes sense to them. Helping her overcome her ambivalence, reassuring her that it's the right thing to do, is, they believe, the best support they can give.

What can't be glimpsed from the outside is the profound attachment she feels to her own child, an attachment that may seem shadowy and submerged even to her. Yet there is a primitive bond between them. If this were not so, having an abortion would not be any more difficult than having a tonsillectomy. But this secret, invisible bond, submerged from consciousness, is radical in its power, because it is part of the mother-love necessary to the continuance of the human race. No one outside her body can understand it.

There are many practical problems that must be solved in the course of an unplanned pregnancy. But the primary need appears to be to forge connections to other people, people that she can lean on through the difficult months ahead. This cannot be a superficial or faceless support. Women in the listening groups frequently would say, "If I'd only had someone I could count on to stand by me," insisting that they meant someone really dependable, someone who would care for them personally and who wouldn't let them down.

Pro-choice rhetoric leaves her lonely, consoled only by her power to kill. To overcome the forces that drive her toward this tragedy we must explode the shell of her isolation, making her problems our problems, building concentric rings of support from the mother-child dyad outward to all society. The first natural connection is to her own child; to that dyad we add the baby's father to form the smallest unit in the human family; the circles spread to include the young couple's parents, their employers or school officials, and continue outwards to reach adoptive parents, pregnancy care workers, and the larger tax-paying community. It is the human connection that gives her hope, and those connections pave the way to give her help.

Jean's friends are worried. They call each other on the phone, indignant at the unfairness of it all. That jerk just walked away and left poor Jean to suffer. There's no alternative now. As sad as it is, she must have an abortion.

Barbara takes it on herself to drive Jean to the clinic, squeezing her hand and proffering tissues. As they pull up she sees prolifers distributing leaflets on the sidewalk. The sight strikes like a knife. How could anyone be so heartless? Don't they know that she's already upset, that she's suffered enough over this decision?

Barbara parks her car at the curb and comes around to open the passenger door and take Jean's trembling hand to lift her out. The pro-life woman approaches: "You don't have to do this. We can help you. Will you read this leaflet?" The pregnancy care center's phone number is printed under a photo of a mother and child.

What will happen next?

Listening in Los Angeles

os Angeles is a city of cars; I was issued mine at the airport. As I sail down Crenshaw Avenue in the pale morning light I am admiring the trees that line the road, beautiful trees the likes of which I have never seen. They are perfectly shaped, as if posing for a child's coloring book. The trunks are silvery-white, but free of birchy peeling flakes, as smooth as stone; the limbs, lifting bunches of leaves, are like the graceful marble arms of a statue. And what leaves, flipping light and dark green, in overabundant profusion, more leaves than a tree could reasonably hold. I imagine that elves come at night in order to stuff still more leaves into the embrace of those marble arms.

As I speed toward a somber meeting, one where a circle of women will sift through memories of abortions past, the trees offer a contrast of radiant, exuberant femininity: strong, beautiful, voluptuously fertile. No wonder the Greeks envisioned a tree with the soul of a woman: Daphne, fleeing an emotional/sexual aggressor, twists as her conqueror's embrace at last closes around her. Her arms shoot up, fingers into twigs, hair tumbling down brushy with leaves, feet sending roots deep into the loam. Apollo's lips press only against bark. As these trees stand, so might the transfigured Daphne have stood, shoulder to shoulder with her sisters, delivered from the abuse of men. Perhaps the women I go to meet didn't run quite fast enough. The trees march down Crenshaw, glowing jewel-like through the smog.

The pregnancy care center fills several rooms on the first floor of a small building. It resembles most of the two thousand centers scattered across the country: warm wallpaper, sofas, and cheery posters grace a reception room, which leads to a large meeting area, then an intimate counseling room or two. There are racks stuffed with pamphlets and books for loan, and storage rooms with maternity and baby supplies. These centers usually operate on a shoestring—sometimes the director draws a small salary, sometimes not—and offer everything to clients free. What they can offer is whatever they can gather from citizens and businesses nearby: donations of clothing, diapers, formula, medical care, counseling, and volunteer time. It is a neighbor-helping-neighbor effort, in the old American "barn-raising" tradition, organized by people who want to help pregnant women have the resources to choose life.

The five women in the counseling room have gathered today to provide me with a dress-rehearsal. The Real Choices project doesn't officially begin until fall. But at my request a friend has assembled this circle during my visit to Los Angeles, so that I might have a foretaste of what such hearings may be like.

These women are in some ways atypical of the post-abortion population. They are now all firmly pro-life, and active in local pro-life affairs. Two of them are experienced in offering abortion grief counseling; petite, dark-haired Deb says she has counseled over 150 women over the last seven years. These are not women whose grief is raw, nor whose attitudes toward abortion are ambivalent. They have grown relatively comfortable talking about their abortions and eloquent in presenting the unborn's right to life.

When I ask the women to think back to the situation they

were in when they had their abortions, Jill offers that her homelife was relatively positive; she thinks many aborting women come from normal families and Christian backgrounds. Paula chimes in that she was a cheerleader. She is still slim and athletic, with tumbling blond curls. But Becky demurs—she was a victim of sexual abuse, and believes that experience is in the background for many aborting women.

Sexual abuse, she explains, leads you to conclude that "sex is how you know that somebody cares about you. That makes you more aggressive" in seeking the reassurance of multiple sexual experiences. More sexual experiences means more risk of pregnancy, pregnancies begun in situations where there is less likely to be the commitment necessary to sustain a relationship and raise a child. Sexual abuse also made Becky more pliable, she feels; it had been stressed to her that she must "do whatever they tell you to do." In this case, they told her to have an abortion.

Becky says she had at first resolved to have the baby. But her mother took her to a counselor, ordering her to wait in the reception room while the two of them conferred. When they called Becky in, she was told that the counselor and her mother had agreed that Becky should have an abortion. Her mom added, "If you continue this pregnancy, you can't live in my house."

Becky was stunned, but at a loss for alternatives. She had a vague idea that there might be places for rejected pregnant women to go—"there were some Catholic maternity homes, somewhere"—but had neither the resources nor the self-confidence to track down that possibility. She had the abortion. Eight years later, she is still grieving: "I was already attached to that baby." Grieving post-abortion women rarely say "fetus."

Jill becomes indignant at this manipulative counseling. "Those people at Planned Parenthood are so cold," she says, recalling her own experience. "They deny that you have feelings, guilt about what you're doing to your baby. It's like you hit a child with your car and you feel devastated, but they're trying to pass it off, telling you you weren't responsible."

"They play to your impulse to block your feelings, your need to just not think about it," says Martha, tall and slender in a fashionably sleek rayon dress. Martha, an experienced post-abortion counselor, seems so confident and polished that her next statement is a surprise. "I had three abortions in five years," she says. "The first one is socially acceptable, the second one is an embarrassment, and the third one is so shameful you won't admit it to anyone. I had even been counseling for awhile before I'd actually admit to that third abortion." She breaks a rueful smile. In each case, she became pregnant in a situation where a continuing relationship with the baby's father was not possible; she chose abortion over single parenthood or adoption. If the first reaction to the shock of unwanted pregnancy is denial, abortion serves that need better than any more complicated path.

"The point is that, when you're considering abortion, you want to get it over with *as quick as possible*," Martha goes on. "You just don't want to think about it."

Paula says quietly that she thought about it constantly. She was seventeen, engaged to marry the baby's father at twenty-one. But she was from a "good family;" when she told her mom about the pregnancy she was informed, like Becky, that "you have a choice" between her baby and her family.

I reflect ironically that this is not the "choice" that pro-choice partisans imagine. "Freedom of choice" brings to mind the image of a stylish, confident woman considering an array of possibilities, all competing for her approval. "Lose your child or lose your home" is a very different sort of choice, and hardly an empowering one.

Paula recalls crying convulsively on the abortion table. The doctor pleaded with her to stop: "If you don't stop crying we can't do this, because maybe someone's forcing you." She choked back her sobs. But after that she took drugs, found it hard to accept love ("How could anybody love me?") and even attempted suicide three times. Tears form in her eyes.

Jill, sitting next to Paula, squeezes her hand; though they are not close in age, they have become good friends through shared pro-life work. Jill says that her abortion was twenty-five years ago, before *Roe v. Wade*. She was twenty-four, a virgin, when she fell desperately in love with a married man. She was afraid of hurting her parents and so decided to try to have a doctor approve her for an abortion.

"In those days, you had to have a physical or mental reason to have an abortion. As I talked to the doctor in his office, he was sort of fishing around for a reason to approve me. I talked about how upset I was and mentioned that I'd always imagined that if I ever got pregnant, well, I'd just *kill* myself. I was just using the expression, of course, but that was enough for him. He wrote that I had to have the abortion for my mental health."

The abortion had its own impact on her mental health. "For eighteen years, I had to have a drink before I had sex," she confesses shyly. "Otherwise I would just be reminded of the abortion; I would close my eyes and picture awful things. I know it hurt my husband's feelings, but I couldn't help it." (I am reminded of Planned Parenthood founder Margaret Sanger's warning that repeated abortions "can do considerable harm to a woman's sex life" and "may result in frigidity.")[1] It wasn't until a half-dozen years ago that Jill found help to resolve her grief. The couple has two daughters.

Deb says that she now has three daughters, after an abortion at seventeen. She says that for her it was her monthly cramps and the contractions of labor that reminded her most painfully of her abortion. A malevolent voice seemed to whisper in her ear, "Remember how this felt when you killed your baby?"

Her husband was father to all four children. "I'm open with my kids about our life then—it was sex, drugs and rock 'n' roll." She had submitted to her boyfriend's demands for sex: "say yes or I'm gone." Deb had concluded that "without him, I'm nothing" and gave in to that demand, and then gave in again when he "forced me to have an abortion." It seemed like the only alternative—she was a teenager, had no high school diploma, and her boyfriend was facing cocaine charges.

But their lives changed one month after their marriage when they were converted to Christianity. "Self-esteem can't come from anywhere but Jesus," Deb says. "He will love you in spite of your failings, and that never changes. If your self-worth is based on your looks, your parents' love, or the sense that you're great, it will fail. All that will pass."

Martha agrees that God is the source of all healing and strength: "Man comes and goes, but God will never leave you."

I ask, in summary, what was the main reason you had an abortion?

Martha says, "I have to say that I had my abortions for convenience. The reasons were selfish." This surprises me; I've often criticized the charge that women have abortions for convenience. But Jill, Paula, and Deb agree with Martha. No matter what pressures they faced, they refuse to lay the responsibility for the abortion on anyone but themselves. The judgment seems harsh to me in the light of their difficult situations, but they appear to find freedom, even fortitude, in shouldering the burden squarely.

Becky tells me, "I had the abortion mostly because I just didn't love the guy." Martha adds that it's easy for love to become hate toward the person that helped put you in this painful situation.

What, I ask, would have helped you to continue the pregnancy instead of having the abortion?

Becky says that if she had known the facts of fetal development, of how the baby grows in the womb, that would have stopped her. If she had only known that it was really her baby in there, she would have done anything to give it life.

The other women agree vociferously. Knowledge of their unborn children would have weighted one side of the scale more than anything the other side could present. The pain of years of grief now resolved, these women have bonded with their long-dead children, and the maternal urge to protect one's offspring is strong. They cannot imagine anything standing in the way of bringing those children to life.

I am impressed with the light in their eyes, the healing won after such piercing pain, and the wholeness all these women now seem to show. But, at the same time, I question whether their viewpoint is prevalent among women at the beginning of the journey, those just now considering abortion. I am skeptical of the belief that the facts of fetal development alone will be convincing in most cases. I wonder whether, given the original desperate situations, it would have even been sufficient for these women who face me now.

A plaintive post-abortion song is titled, "If I Knew Then What I Know Now." But, of course, no one can import such knowledge backwards into a situation without importing as well the passing years' experience, pain, and maturity. You see your "now" self walking staunchly through those flames, easily outperforming the "then" self who was overwhelmed and frightened and alone.

As I drive away, I am reflecting on what I've learned here. I must take care not to over-populate future groups with pro-life professionals who have thoroughly worked through their grief. I am afraid that they may have forgotten what it is like to be at the beginning of that road. I have also learned that descriptions of *post*-abortion grief and suffering tend to run away with the discussion; that is where the energies of much pro-life research has gone. In these groups I must stress to participants that we will be focusing on *pre*-abortion stress, the factors that contributed to the decision.

My busy day carries me up and down the coast, till I can finally pause for a late lunch with a pro-life lawyer of deserved national renown. We stop at a trendy spot boasting California cuisine, and I ask him about the beautiful trees I saw along the road. Yes, he says, he has them in his yard. I worry that, when all those leaves fall, it's a lot of raking; he says no, they're evergreen. This sounds better and better. What are those beautiful, feminine trees called? Oh, he says. They're some kind of fig tree.

Figs—of all the fruits, the one classically associated with

women, but not in the exalted way I was projecting. I feel the victim of what, in college, we called a "cosmic joke."

1. "Birth Control's 21st," *Time*, 18 February 1935.

## CHAPTER THREE

MEN, PART ONE:
Sex and Pregnancy Prevention

When post-abortion women talk about the reasons for their decision, they talk most often about the failure of the baby's father to be supportive, to fill the father's role. Unexpected pregnancy can raise some breathtaking problems, but a partner's vigilant love has a way of easing them. Imagine a woman discovering a pregnancy in a difficult situation, but her partner saying to her, "I love you, I love our baby, I'll do anything I can to make this family work." On the other hand, imagine a story from one of my listening groups: a married woman with two kids, living in reasonable security, to whom her husband says, "Only ignorant people have more than two kids. I don't want this baby. You have to have an abortion." Which child will survive?

Before tackling the practical problems raised when the baby's father fails his role, we need to get a clearer picture of what this role entails, and what motivates a man to fulfill it. We need to ask also what can be done to limit the numbers of pregnancies begun in situations where the man and woman are unready to take responsibility for a child and whether contraception is the best way to prevent these pregnancies. But even when unplanned pregnancies develop, why should women be so dependent on men's help? Why can't she just tough it out on her own?

Of course, many women do exactly that. But there are two compelling reasons that women find themselves unexpectedly dependent on their men when a pregnancy begins: one physical and one emotional.

To grasp the first reason, it's necessary to step back and take a broader view of human reproduction. Step *way* back. Imagine a zookeeper on Mars, who has built up a pretty thorough collection of earth mammals.

The Martian zookeeper has noted some interesting things about the residents of the human exhibit. In the first place, their young are born alarmingly premature. Other mammalian new-borns crawl to the mother's breast and begin to nurse, but if the human baby were not assisted to do this it would starve. The human baby takes a full year just to walk, an age where—even allowing for proportionate life-spans—other mammals are near adulthood. The baby's ability to communicate in the language of the species is similarly slow to develop; human parents are markedly more frustrated by inability to interpret their baby's cries than are bovine or canine mothers. Most mammals rapidly learn to survive without their mother's care, but a human may take decades of training before he is able to support himself.

The Martian notes that raising a human baby is a lengthy and exhausting process. Unlike the rearing of other mammals, it requires the attention of an adult nearly full-time; without that attention, the species would not survive. It seems that the female is more suited to this intensive labor of child-rearing, both by temperament and by her ability to nurse—an attribute so vital that it gives the mammalian family its name. Child-rearing is so demanding that she has little time to provide food and shelter for herself, and both mother and child are at risk. The mother's arms encircle the child, but a second adult is required to add an outer ring of care around those two.

The child's father seems suited to this role, although not

without ambivalence. The early years post-puberty, in particular, propel human males into an exhausting round of compulsive sexual thinking and (attempted) activity that was described by one as "waking up every morning chained to a maniac." A look at these same males a few years later reveals that most have settled down in monogamous, child-rearing arrangements, although some continue to struggle against a recurrent longing for sexual adventure. What would motivate the males to accept such a trying bargain?

The zookeeper is not surprised that males wind up monogamous. The hand that designed the varieties of life in his zoo consistently reveals exacting care for efficiency and symmetry. It would not have rigged a situation as counter-productive as a female who needs monogamous loyalty to produce the next generation and a male who flees it. Males must inevitably have a need for monogamy as well, although their motivation is not obvious.

The Martian zookeeper has developed some theories about why human males make this bargain. First, at the root, what feels like a sex urge is actually a reproductive urge. It will do the male no good to impregnate many women if these women are barely able to raise healthy children unaided. The children must survive and be strong enough to carry his genes forward one more generation for reproduction to have truly taken place. Secondly, how can he know that the child his mate is raising does in fact carry his own genes, and not some other male's? Ultimately, he can only trust her word. In order to persuade her to mate only with him, he must offer her inducements: shelter, provisions, protection and, perhaps most difficult, his own fidelity in pledge. As he watches the mother nurse their child, he sees his only link to the chain of human life. Without his connection to the two of them, he would free-fall into oblivion.

Is biology destiny? No; we are not prisoners of these roles, and our ingenuity can offer many ways to redesign them. But biology is orderly. It has its own internal logic, and when we tamper with one element of it we must expect another element to fall out of place. The superwoman single-mom with a hot career and a hot date is famously exhausted on her treadmill. This should not be surprising. Disrupt biology's rules and you will find yourself doing things a less-efficient way.

The other thing the Martian zookeeper notes is the heightened sense of loneliness humans display. They carry a burden of self-awareness that other mammals appear to evade, with associated fears of abandonment, rejection, and meaninglessness. They seem to need more complex things from each other than goats do. Even in old age he sees them in pairs, when the impetus of child-rearing is decades past. Gliding over earth's atmosphere in his saucer he observes elderly couples on Florida sidewalks wearing identical clothing. What's that all about?

The Martian is recognizing the profound human need for connectedness, and pregnancy is the icon of human intimacy. The connection an unborn child experiences with her mother is the first any human has of closeness to another person. Because it predates language and self-awareness it is the more profound and ineradicable, though we may be largely unaware of this pull.

Life outside the womb is lonely. We look all our lives for an experience of similar intimacy and safety even though many, as the saying goes, look in all the wrong places. When pregnancy begins, a woman is plunged into an experience of intimacy more profound than any of her adult life; she is knit, literally, to another human, one half-made of her own self. In the same blow she is linked to the child's father, whose half-life lives on as well within her body. Yet this being formed of two halves is more than their sum, a radical third never before seen on earth. She shoots from her parents' bodies like an arrow from a bow, carrying their immortality into the future, beyond the reach of their crumbling arms.

Pregnancy is about connectedness. It spins the wheel tighter, and centrifugal force draws the players together, more aware than ever of their mutual dependence. Pregnancy problems have to do with broken connections: broken trust, fear, loneliness, abandonment.

Abortion-rights rhetoric recognizes the riskiness of trust and urges the woman to rely only on herself—my body, my rights, my decision. This argument twists necessity into a virtue, and offers a wry consolation prize: life as a steely atom, spinning without contact, without the dangerous and tender cloak of skin.

If pregnancy turns a wheel that draws all together, abortion breaks the wheel, spinning the participants out into isolation. It severs at one blow the woman from the child who trusts her, and from the man she wants to trust. As French feminist Simone de Beauvoir wrote, after abortion women "learn to believe no longer in what men say...the one thing they are sure of is this rifled and bleeding womb, these shreds of crimson life, this child that is not there. It is at her first abortion that a woman begins to 'know.' For many women the world will never be the same."[5]

These somewhat philosophical musings lay a necessary foundation for the first topics that must be taken up when reducing the numbers of abortions is discussed: monogamy, sexual responsibility, contraception. Can these pregnancies be prevented, or at least reserved for marriage?

Prevention is indisputably better than cure when it comes to unwanted pregnancy. But deep disagreement reigns over how to prevent. Abortion-rights advocates tend to see contraception as the best solution; pro-life Roman Catholics tend to see it as part of the problem (believing that contraception leads to an "abortion mentality" of pregnancy-free sexual entitlement). Other pro-lifers accept contraception and even use it in their own lives. Nevertheless, they remain skeptical of its ability to universally prevent unwanted pregnancies, suspecting that the causes of these pregnancies are more complex than they initially appear.

Promotion of contraception has been a growing part of the abortion rights movement for a half-dozen years. Some have even changed their names to reflect this: NARAL is now the National Abortion and Reproductive Rights Action League. Subsuming abortion, contraception, and sex education all under the heading of "reproductive rights" seems to be a winning strategy. At a NARAL conference in 1989, pollster Harrison Hickman noted that when respondents were asked, "How should we prevent unplanned pregnancy and abortion among teens?" the answer, "mandatory sex education and greater availability of contraception" won by a 76 percent to 14 percent majority.[2]

Abortion alone never won such applause. This new strategy invites quiet, middle-class citizens to imagine a direct connection between restrictions on third-trimester abortions and a Condom Cop marching into their home and confiscating the pack of Trojans on the nightstand.

Blending abortion and contraception into a reproductive-rights stew enables advocates to attract new interest precisely from those who are queasy about abortion, since more contraception and sex education is supposed to reduce the number of abortions. It sounds reasonable on the surface: women who have abortions got pregnant by mistake, probably because they didn't know about contraception. Tell them, make it available, and there won't be as many pregnancies.

But an attempt to find out how such an improved state of affairs might be achieved reveals a plan that is less than clear. Contraceptives are already widely available; condoms can be purchased for less than the price of a pack of cigarettes at shops in every small town across the land. The existence of this product has not been kept a secret; using a condom is touted nearly as a patriotic act. If anything, education about, access to and effectiveness of contraception has increased dramatically in our generation, yet the abortion rate has remained steady at 1.5 million per year for over a dozen years. What further contraceptive development or promotion is necessary before we see a difference?

Susan Tew of the Alan Guttmacher Institute, an organization concerned with reproductive health research and sometimes associated with Planned Parenthood, was invited to explain to prolifers why increased contraceptive research and sex education are important. Tew pointed to two problems: "not enough choices" for the various phases of a woman's reproductive life, and reluctance to use contraceptives due to misunderstandings about risks.[3]

As an example of the first problem, Tew cited the paucity of methods offering "dual protection": "Condoms don't provide protection against pregnancy as well as the pill does; pills don't provide protection against sexually transmitted diseases as well as condoms do." When asked to fantasize about an ideal contraceptive method that would improve on these flaws, Tew pointed out that the new female condom is expected to provide protection comparable to the standard condom. (The improvement here is that the woman is in control of whether the device is used. The product will be marketed under the name "Reality," as in, one supposes, "Get real, *he's* not going to use a condom.") There are no statistics yet on how acceptable women find this method; as with other barrier methods, there are discouraging problems with aesthetics.

Overall, Tew granted, there is "relative accessibility" of a range of contraceptive methods. She added that Natural Family Planning, a method promoted by the Roman Catholic Church and which utilizes observation of the woman's fertility cycles to avoid or achieve conception, is "a fine, a very good method for some people," particularly those who are older and in stable relationships. "They can do very well as far as protection is concerned and are very happy," Tew said.

The second problem, Tew said, was one of "attitudes and knowledge;" many people mistakenly believe that with contraception "the health risks are higher and the benefits are lower" than they really are. She volunteered that it was hard to judge the effectiveness of sex education, since there are so many different varieties that they cannot be compared. It cannot be decisively stated, she said, that sex education does or does not prevent unintended pregnancy; "a lot of different attitudes dictate contraceptive behavior."

Sex education may, in fact, boomerang. Between 1971 and 1988, the federal Title X program spent $2.1 billion on family planning education and contraceptive services; during that period, births to unwed teens increased 61 percent.[4] "Instead of the expected reduction in teenage pregnancies, greater adolescent involvement in family-planning programs was associated with significantly higher teenage pregnancy rates."[5] Family planning programs may not have caused this increase; too many other possible causes are at play. But one thing's for sure: they didn't prevent it.

The image of a magical contraception/education army marching down and eliminating unplanned pregnancies dissipates rapidly. The problems are more complex than that. When contraceptives are available but are not used a whole host of new questions arises: an Alan Guttmacher Institute study indicates that 49 percent of women having abortions were using no form of family planning.[6]

Are people simply ignorant of contraception? At one Real Choices press conference, a reporter asked whether the women in our listening groups were saying that what they had needed most was information about contraception so they wouldn't have gotten pregnant in the first place. This assumption is broadly held, yet is startlingly unrepresented by reality.

Washington Post reporter Leon Dash bore witness to this. When he began his series of articles on teen pregnancy among inner-city blacks, he assumed that the phenomenon "grew out of youthful ignorance both about birth control methods and adolescent reproductive capabilities...I was wrong on all counts."[7] Dash found that, while every conception story was initially presented as a case of contraceptive ignorance or misuse, these stories were myths developed in the name of acceptability. In actuality, the teens were well aware of the where and how of contraception. They deliberately chose pregnancy for various reasons: to prove adulthood, to win peer approval, to have someone to love. Another lesson with a condom and a banana would not resolve those more complex needs.

Rachel MacNair, past president of Feminists for Life of America, says that two elements are necessary for a contraceptive solution to reduce the numbers of abortions. The first is that the sexual experience must be voluntary and unpressured, if she is to be able to plan for the use of contraception. Germaine Greer alludes to the necessity of this condition: "Abortion is the last in a long line of non-choices that could begin at the very beginning with the time and the place and the manner of love-making. How does a woman come to be having unprotected sex of the kind that could expose her both to HIV infection and pregnancy? Perhaps, but only perhaps, because she wanted to."[8]

The second element MacNair lists, which points to Dash's findings above, is that the pregnancy must be clearly involuntary, and not secretly or subconsciously desired. Feminist theorist Naomi Wolf writes that all the people she knows who use contraception carelessly are educated and financially secure. In some cases the unplanned pregnancy was caused by heedlessness, in others "both the men and the women were grazing the edge of destiny almost for the sake of the ride, flirting a little with the idea of parenthood, or forcing a psychodrama in the relationship."[9]

The Martian zookeeper has ample cause to be perplexed. People "don't want" to have unplanned pregnancies, contraception is cheap, available, and more effective than nothing—but humans often choose not to use it. The initial theory that we could end abortion by flying over the country in a helicopter and tossing condoms out with a snow shovel seems doomed to fail.

Pro-life sentiment is far from uniformly anti-contraception. But even among those who personally use such methods there is persistent skepticism about the ability of those methods to solve the problem. Contraception tries to fix physical problems in unreal isolation, without consulting the hearts that drive the bodies.

Unreckoned with in the contraceptive strategy—indeed, nearly unrecognized in twenty years of sexual revolution—is the distinctive character of women's sexuality. As feminist poet Adrienne Rich writes, "The so-called sexual revolution of the sixties [was] briefly believed to be congruent with the liberation of women...It did not mean that we were free to discover our own sexuality, but rather that we were expected to behave according to male notions of sexuality."[10]

The feminist movement bought the *Playboy* philosophy of sex without consequences, instead of discovering what women really want. Continuing her argument above, Greer says, "Women's desire for affection and closeness usually has to be translated, more or less unconsciously, into desire for sex." As the old cliché has it, girls give sex in order to get love; boys give love in order to get sex. The sexual revolution flooded the market with "free sex," so that its trading equivalency in square units of love was radically depreciated.

Women are getting less and less durable love in return for sex, and some are suspecting they made a bad bargain. A poignant indicator is the finding that 84 percent of sexually active young teen girls, when asked what topic they wanted information about, checked, "How to say no without hurting the other person's feelings."[11] Likewise, 83 percent of sexually experienced upperclassmen at inner-city high schools said that the best age to begin having sex was older than they had been.[12]

Little girls have been catapulted into experiences they can't handle and don't enjoy (young teen boys not being known for their sensitivity as lovers) by the adult insistence that they're going to do it anyway. This insistence, one teen girl tells me, rings like a command: you *will* have sex—it's the law.

For adult women, the benefits of "free sex" have not been better. The consumer culture, which has found sex to be the magic bullet that sells anything, promotes compulsive, nearly compulsory sexual activity as the norm. As sexuality is snipped from the fabric of personhood and isolated as sheer mechanical act, severed from context and emotional ties, women are lonelier than ever. The self-help shelf in any bookstore is crowded with titles explaining How to Keep Your Man, How to Get Over Your Man, and How to Learn to Trust Men Again. Apparently this is a boom market.

Conservatives have a plan for preventing unplanned pregnancies, but it doesn't center on contraception; instead, it is concerned with responding more accurately to women's trust-based sexuality. Taking into account her need for emotional security, plus the indications that child-rearing requires two parents, strategists have cooked up a notion to cover all bases. They call it "marriage."

The very term is enough to provoke sneers among the elite. Marriage can't be the answer; it disappoints, is imperfect, demands annoying sacrifices, limits one's range of sexual adventure. The preferred way of stating this is "Ozzie and Harriet is a myth," an oddly naive protest. Those who are startled to find that marriage isn't like a chuckling '50s sitcom are going to be disappointed to realize that clapping their hands doesn't make Tinker Bell fly, either.

But it is currently fashionable to see the nuclear family as the repository of evil. New York senator Daniel Patrick Moynihan has described a modern impulse to sanitize "deviancy" and condemn the conventional, particularly the family. Thus we hear that "96 percent of families are dysfunctional,"[13] an item of statistical absurdity comparable to "96 percent of humans are too short."

The nuclear family is not a wacky new untested idea, prone to damage participants virtually every time. There are many centuries of evidence showing how the concept works in practice: pretty good, usually resulting in the survival and success of a new generation, humankind's first responsibility. Bonuses of companionship, romantic love, pleasure and joy sometimes appear as well.

In comparison, an ethic of sexual freedom, where one in four pregnancies ends in abortion and the numbers of children in single-parent homes keeps rising, fails this goal like clockwork. Indicators for sexually transmitted disease, divorce, abandonment, impoverishment of women and children, unwed motherhood, and abortion are at record levels; the heartbreak index is at an all-time high. Despite all this pursuing of happiness, Americans appear to be, by every reasonable standard, markedly more unhappy. The flip side of freedom is loneliness.

Those who sold the sexual revolution as a blessing for women turned out to be no friend of womankind; those who opposed it turned out to be no enemy. There may be a reason why the feminist movement arose on the left, not the right: men on the left are harder on women. Left-wing men expect women "to behave according to male notions of sexuality," while men on the right, especially Christians, generally uphold woman-friendly notions of chastity, fidelity, life-long marriage, and so forth. Every few years a study comes out showing, to general amazement, that devoutly religious married women report the highest levels of sexual satisfaction. Maybe it shouldn't be so hard to figure out.

The sexual revolution made the promise that we were entitled to fun without consequences, but that was nonsense along the lines of "You can eat banana splits all day without gaining weight." In real life, actions have consequences, and they can't be warded off by crying, "Hey, no fair!" If it hurts enough, we can stop now.

But these are not matters for public policy. We cannot pass laws to induce people to behave responsibly and honor their commitments. Such self-sacrificial changes come only when people have determined that the course that promised pleasure is instead bringing pain. Changing behavior comes from changing minds, which can be a sometimes easy, sometimes impossible task.

In April 1991, the moderate-left Progressive Policy Institute sponsored a forum titled "Fortifying the Family," which presented the daring idea that children are better off with two parents.[14] Backed by impressive statistics, T. Berry Brazelton, Barbara Whitehead, William Galston and others eloquently argued children's need for intact families.

I sat near a woman who carried a journalist's notepad and who was not having fun. She passed the morning scowling at the floor, tapping her pencil, tapping her foot, and emitting derisive snorts. When others applauded, she hugged her legal pad to her chest. She had apparently made choices in her life that did not follow the proposed direction, and as a result was not feeling adequately affirmed. When the question period began, she confessed herself "nervous" at the promotion of two-parent families, and informed the crowd that "Ozzie and Harriet is a myth."

How do you think her news story read?

We often plead for stable marriages on the basis of the good they do children, but children are not the ones we need to convince. Kids already know that they want both a mommy and a daddy. The harder task is convincing grownups who may have made life-choices that they feel compelled to defend, who, when they hear the two-parent model celebrated, feel scourged as failures. How can we expect the elite of the media, education, and government to promote values they are unready to meet?

It is hard to gain public approval of any moral conviction in such circumstances. For example, the idea that teens should be taught to abstain from sex before marriage is attacked, not by teens, but by adults; they protest that expecting abstinence is unrealistic. One imagines they are speaking from current personal experience. They may also be feeling something like the sting of personal insult. A public-school teacher who taught a class on abstinence outside marriage got angry calls from her students' parents: "Don't teach my kids to judge how I live!"

The well-being of children is urgently dependent on restoring the two-parent family, and so far reformers have mostly emphasized the threat: stay together or you'll damage your kids. But there is a promise as well: the inherent joy and goodness possible in marriage, the love that makes the couple the beating heart of a two-parent home.

The image of marriage has been so distorted that it will take some work to recover. Currently there are only two varieties of couple-family our culture can imagine: shiny-glib TV show heaven, or grim, abusive horror-show hell. Real marriage, marriage that lasts, is neither.

If Tolstoy is right that "happy families are all alike," perhaps they are alike in not expecting to be happy all the time. Perhaps they expect to meet problems and disappointments and take them in stride. In real marriage—not the TV/horror-show versions— the dishes get dirty, the wife gets plump, the husband gets bald, and everyone gets grumpy at least occasionally. In the course of a lifetime together, everyone will need forgiveness, and happy families learn that giving it is the best way to insure receiving it in return.

Why put up with these annoyances? For one thing, it is far worse to be alone. The world is too big and we are too small to make it through without being trampled. The bravado of individualism is false; we can never be free enough to be all-powerful, but we can be free enough to be lost. We warm our hands together at the night fire. Behind the other's back we see, behind our own back we know, the dark wilderness broods.

"It is not good for man to be alone," but it is also positively good to be together. The light you loved in your lover's eyes at the beginning grows more compellingly beautiful through the years. You meet those eyes in worship, in passion, in anger, in tears, over the baby's bassinet, over your father's casket. There is no substitute for the years, the life-time work, of looking into those eyes. Gradually, you see yourself there; gradually, you become one.

Our shallow consumer culture chants that we want to wake up next to someone sexy tomorrow morning. In the quiet of our hearts we know: we want to wake up next to someone kind, fifty years from tomorrow morning.

When sexual activity is kept within the bounds of life-long commitment, babies are more likely to survive and women more likely to feel secure and loved. The person unconsidered in this scenario is the man, the father of the child. What's in it for him? Don't men's desires run to sexual adventuring, spurning hearth and home?

In a tony seafood restaurant in the suburbs of Washington, D.C., our dinner business meeting is running late. As we hammer out the course of a proposed magazine article, three male leaders of the pro-family movement are trying to convince me of the persistence of male sexual incorrigibility. Men are shallow, self-centered, and interested only in the next exploit, they tell me. They will inevitably use women and dump them without a backward glance. "Men just want to do it and run," one states bluntly.

I look at three tired faces, winding up another long workday. In three suburban homes, these men's wives are tucking in nine children and ending busy workdays of their own—days they could spend at home because their husbands are still wearing ties at 9:00 P.M.

I think about sheep in wolves' clothing. I ask my dinner companions why, if they are such barely restrained fiends, they are going home tonight instead of running off with a perky office intern. They register surprise. Because the risks are too high and the benefits too low. Because they delight in their homes and children. Because they feel pride in protecting and providing. Most of all, because they love their wives.

The Martian ponders the white-haired man on the sidewalk. He is baking in the Florida sun, waiting outside the craft shop while his wife gathers materials to make another ceramic doll. His lime-green polo shirt and white slacks match her own.

His children are grown, his youth is gone, twenty thousand days and night of marriage have flown past. His days of power, of protecting and providing, have slipped away. He waits quietly in the sun, a little drowsy. There is no reason on earth for him to be there but one.

1. Simone de Beauvoir, *The Second Sex* (New York: Alfred A. Knopf, Inc., Bantam Books, 1952).
2. Harrison Hickman, "Framing and Selling the Pro-Choice Message," (cassette tape), National Abortion Rights Action League Conference, Washington, D.C., 1989.
3. Susan Tew, Assistant Director of Communications and Development, Alan Guttmacher Institute, personal interview with the author, April 28, 1994.
4. Congressional Budget Office, Sources of Support for Adolescent Mothers, September 1990, cited in "A Decade of Denial," a report of the Select Committee of Children, Youth, and Families, 102nd Congress (Minority Dissent).
5. Zelnik and Kantner, 1979, cited in "A Decade of Denial."
6. Stanley K. Henshaw and Jane Silverman, "The Characteristics and Prior Contraceptive Use of US Abortion Patients," Family Planning Perspectives, Vol. 20, No. 1, July/August 1988, 158 ff.
7. Leon Dash, *When Children Want Children* (New York: Morrow, 1989). Quoted in Susan and Marvin Olasky, *More Than Kindness* (Wheaton, Ill.: Crossway Books, 1990).
8. Germaine Greer, *The New Republic,* October 5, 1992.
9. Naomi Wolf, *Fire with Fire* (New York: Random House, 1993), 130.
10. Adrienne Rich, *Of Woman Born* (New York: W.W. Norton & Co., 1976), 73.
11. Marion Howard and Judith B. McCabe, "Helping Teenagers Postpone Sexual Involvement," Family Planning Perspectives, January/February 1990, 22; cited in "A Decade of Denial."
12. Jonathan Fielding and Carolyn Williams, "Adolescent Pregnancy in the United States," American Journal of Preventive Medicine, Vol. 7 No. 1, 1991; cited in "A Decade of Denial."
13. Attributed to pop therapist John Bradshaw; cited by Barbara Dafoe Whitehead, "Dan Quayle Was Right," *Atlantic Monthly,* April 1993.
14. See, e.g., Paul Taylor, "Conferees Urge Spending, Tax Policies to Reinforce US Families," *Washington Post,* April 13, 1991.

## CHAPTER FOUR

Listening
in Cleveland

O n a cool night in early fall, nine women file into a pregnancy center on the outskirts of Cleveland. Mary, the cheerful center director, has a pot of coffee ready, and a popular downtown restaurant has donated a rich chocolate cake. It's hard to top chocolate for comfort food.

The large group—some friends, some strangers—settle into the ring of sofas and chairs in the large conference room, and forks poke at the solid slices of cake. I begin the discussion by recounting an image that came up in a meeting that afternoon. As I had described the difficulty of solving pregnancy problems, a city official had grown thoughtful. "I don't mean this to sound dehumanizing," he said, "but it reminds me of how we deal with abandoned buildings. We get a complaint that a building or house is standing empty; it's an eyesore, dangerous, attracts vermin, maybe even drug dealers. Well, what do we do?" He brushed off his palms briskly against each other. "We tear it down. It solves all the problems at once. Now, we could do a search and locate the owners, compel them to take responsibility, or failing that auction the property, recover its use that way...but, no, that's too much trouble." Once again his palms slapped against each other dismissively. "It's easier to tear it down. But in the process you destroy the very fabric of the community."

The women in tonight's group nod their heads reflectively. It's true for them: abortion's appeal was that it could wipe out all the problems at once. Anna says that, when she thinks back to her situation and the "woulda-coulda-shoulda"s start up, she knows she really needed only one thing to solve all the problems: "the guy." The need was not for money or health care, but for a faithful man to stand by her. She was divorced and "looking for love in the wrong places;" when she got pregnant, she was afraid that "if I have this child, he will leave me." She had the abortion, and he left her anyway.

Annette, an animated brunette with Italian blood, says that in her case the man would have stayed, but he wasn't someone she could lean on. "He wasn't a good provider; he didn't have a job. I was the provider and breadwinner." Bright and energetic, Annette looks capable of winning any bread that might be required. She is annoyed with herself for being "led like a sheep to the slaughter" and going along with the abortion. She feels that she was told that "this is what you do in this situation" and was "clueless" about any other alternative. She wishes she had known about pro-life organizations, or pregnancy care centers like this one, that could have helped her out.

Eunice, sitting next to Anna, chimes in with her own story. She had been married a short time, and became unexpectedly pregnant. "My husband shut down. He said, 'I don't want it.' I was so afraid of being alone and abandoned. So I went to the abortion clinic, hoping for some kind of counseling, but they only told me what physical effects to expect afterwards."

She voices the secret hope many aborting women harbor: "When I was at the clinic waiting for the abortion, I kept hoping my husband would show up. I kept hoping he would come in and say, 'Don't do this! I changed my mind!'" But he didn't show up. The marriage grew tense, and they divorced a few months later.

Eunice and Anna are not unusual in seeing their relationship with the baby's father break up after the abortion; it happens roughly half the time.[1] A post-abortion counselor described the mechanism this way: after the abortion, the woman normally has conflicting feelings and a desire to talk out what has happened. But the more she talks, the more her partner withdraws. He feels accused and guilty. Didn't they agree it was the best thing to do? Why does she have to keep hashing it over? The more he withdraws, the more angry she becomes. Why can't he be there for me when I need him? The relationship starves in silent recrimination, denial and pain.

But Eunice's story concludes with a surprising twist. Her husband is remarried and has become very active in the pro-life movement. Recently she arranged to meet him outside an abortion clinic. While other pro-lifers prayed and sang, the two of them spoke to women entering the clinic, telling their story and their regret. Three of the women they encountered decided to give birth to their babies instead of having abortions.

Kate, across the room, comes in with her own story. Like Eunice, she was married when a pregnancy disrupted her life. It was a long time ago, nineteen years earlier; her experience was different from that of the younger women here, though the aftermath was much the same. Kate and her husband already had two children; when this new pregnancy began he protested that he didn't want any more kids, that his health couldn't take raising another one. Kate deeply longed to have the child, but felt that she had no right to those feelings. A nurse-friend set up the abortion, and arranged for the regulation approval of three doctors.

Kate walked through those days feeling alone; she says, "Nobody asked me, 'Is this really what you want?'" At last she was on the table in the operating room. "I was hoping and praying that someone, my husband, would come in and stop it from happening. But he was totally opposed to what I wanted to do. I felt like I was just being selfish, wanting the child; it was too much of a burden on his health." I ask how her husband's health is now;

she responds that he's fine, but he isn't her husband anymore. He left her a few years ago.

Kate goes on, recalling the abortion. "They had told me it was just a clump of cells, but I was very upset. As soon as I woke up from general anesthesia I started vomiting. I became very sick. But I couldn't find anybody to talk to; everyone would just pat my hand and say 'Get over it.' But I was so upset, deep inside. I remember that the first thing I said to my husband after the abortion was, 'But what about God?'"

Annette picks up on Kate's pre-abortion isolation, which echoes her own. "Even just twelve or thirteen years ago, when I had my abortion, there weren't any pro-life groups around to help you or teach you about how much you were going to suffer afterwards. At any rate, I didn't know about them."

Kate goes on: "Everybody told me I should be relieved and happy. Well, maybe their problems were solved, but my problems weren't solved. I couldn't stand to say or even hear the word 'abortion' for years afterwards."

Eunice adds, "They tell you you'll just have a little teariness. That it's hormonal, like post-partum blues. That this is normal."

Cathy has been keeping quiet, but now speaks up to defend clinic counseling. "Yes, I was sad; I was already crying before they put me to sleep. But I can't say that the clinic didn't give me good counseling. They tried hard to make sure that this was what I really wanted. I had two sessions with the counselor, and they had a separate session with my boyfriend, too."

This sparks some dissent. "Well, for me it was like a cattle call," Rochelle put in. "They had all of us women there in a group for our abortions. We went around the room one at a time, and they made everyone give the reason she was having the abortion. And no matter what we said, they went, 'Oh, we understand.' Then they said, 'Now it's time to go in.' They gave us no information about fetal development or other options."

Annette sides with Rochelle. "It was like a tea party. Everybody gave her reason, like, 'I forgot to take my pill.' And the leader would go, 'Oh my!' It felt so unreal, so phony."

"Well, they talked to me a lot," says Cathy. "I saw a film on the abortion procedure, and they talked to me about adoption. I feel like they did a good job in that way."

I ask what led up to Cathy's decision to have an abortion. "I was in an unusual situation, I guess. It seems like most of the time people have abortions when they're young, but I was thirty-seven. I'd already been married and divorced, and I thought I was sterile. I wasn't a kid. But I had the abortion because I was afraid for my father to find out that I was pregnant. You see, I was in an interracial relationship, and I knew it would kill my Dad just to know I was dating a black guy, much less having a baby with him. So I had the abortion because I was scared of my father—even at my age.

"The guy was more supportive than a lot of men are—that is, he offered to adopt the child and raise it himself. But he didn't offer to marry me. I was afraid that he would abandon me, that my friends would reject me, and of course my dad—it was just too much. I had the abortion on a Thursday and we broke up the following Wednesday. I just fell apart. I thought I was having a nervous breakdown, and I thought it was because of the breakup. Only later I realized it was because of the abortion.

"You know, physically the abortion was no big deal. But if I'd known how much it would break my heart..." she trails off.

There's a pause of silence as faces turn inward. Rose bursts out with a passionate plea: "It's women who have to bring this to light. I feel very strongly about this. No one else is going to tell the truth—we have to tell our own experience. It was NancyJo Mann, a dozen years ago, who was the first one to come out and talk about how much her abortion hurt her, and she founded Women Exploited By Abortion. More and more women have come out ever since. We have to tell the truth about it, because if women don't know they'll go to any lengths to have one. I know I would have had an illegal abortion; I would have done it to myself."

"Making it illegal won't stop it," put in Lee, sitting beside her.

I ask Rose what anyone could have done to help her not have had her abortion. For example, could anything this pregnancy care center offers have made a difference? Or are the resources offered here mostly material and practical, whereas her needs were emotional?

"They were mostly emotional and family problems," she says. "A pregnancy center would have had to have the gift of pulling out my underlying problems. Because the ones on top—that I'd have to lose my boyfriend and give up college—weren't the real reasons. The real problems were within me, and the pregnancy was just a symptom of how chaotic my life had become—so many problems, including sexual abuse. If someone was going to help me, they'd have to get down to where I was really hurting, but I wouldn't have been able to articulate that.

"I had two abortions, nine months apart. I had full knowledge of what I was doing; the day of my second one I wrote in my diary, 'Today I'm going to kill my baby.' I didn't care about myself or my baby. I was just filled with cold, hard despair. So any kind of financial help or medical help wouldn't have made any difference. The only possibility might have been family intervention. That might have helped."

"So many times the parents are tangled up in this," murmurs Anna.

"I was living a lie," Rose goes on, "both to my family and myself. To continue the pregnancy I would have had to be honest about who I was, and I hadn't hit rock bottom yet. I guess the bottom line was lifestyle—I wasn't ready to give up having *fun*.

"But I felt regret as soon as it was over. I remember the woman next to me was crying, saying, 'That's the last baby I'll ever have the chance to have.' We were in the recovery room, all of us, just quietly sniffling. We were sitting around drinking tea and nibbling cookies and we'd all just killed our babies. It was like waking up to insanity."

"How can people be pro-choice?" Eunice bursts out. "Don't they know it's wrong? When my ex-husband and I were counseling outside the clinic that day, the people going in wouldn't even look at the pro-life posters. They *do* know it's wrong, deep inside."

"Sometimes it's prejudice behind it," asserts Annette. "My mom says, 'I'm personally opposed, but it's great for *some people*.' My dad grumbles about 'babies that got no business being born.' They both think my abortion was a good thing—that abortion liberates you, sets you free to continue your life. 'Having a baby could ruin your life.' But you know what? *Not* having my baby has ruined my life."

"They do know it's a life," surmises Rochelle. "They just think that the mother's life is more valuable. They don't think of trying to help both the mother and the baby."

Rose reaches for a more generous assessment. "I believe that many abortion clinic workers are trying to be compassionate. They think they're helping women. But true compassion is being willing to walk with someone through pain. Having that child is going to be difficult. It will involve sacrifice. They're not willing to go through that with you, to say, 'I will suffer with you.'"

Lee is angered by this talk. "Everyone's just worried about who's right and who's wrong. Well, I went to one of those pregnancy care centers before my abortion. I didn't feel compassion. First of all, they *lied* to me." Some of the women recoil, shocked. "When I called I asked, 'Do you do abortions?' They said, 'Yes, we'll help you have an abortion or have a baby.'" Lee is asked where and when: in 1986, at another pregnancy care center here in Cleveland. There used to be a small chain of pregnancy care centers that advocated this sort of duplicity in order to get women in for counseling; perhaps this center was part of that chain. Tactics like this are roundly denounced by the vast majority of pregnancy centers.

The situation did not improve when Lee arrived at the center. "When I figured out what was happening, I got so mad and upset, I was just crying and pacing in circles. This woman was talking God at me, showing me pictures of fetuses, threatening to show a video. My resentment just shot *up*." She slaps a palm, hard, against her leg. "I didn't feel any compassion or support. They were just shoving Jesus at me. The only God I knew was a punishing God, so the religious stuff was not good news. At least in the abortion clinic they gave me compassion.

"The night before the abortion I prayed for my baby's soul. I asked God to take care of it. I knew my baby was going to heaven. But those signs outside clinics are disrespectful. It hurts me to see it. You should encourage people, but this is a big turnoff. Who are you to point a finger and judge me?"

Eunice, who had earlier told her glowing story of converting women outside a clinic, looks down. "I know there are problems with it," she says. "For example, there were other doctors in the building besides the abortionist the day I was out there. People were embarrassed to go in past us to see the other doctors. But I guess," she concludes, "it still seems worth it to me. It's the last chance we have to reach people. It should be an offer of hope—not judgmental or rude."

I ask Lee about the situation leading to her abortion. "I was partying, drinking, and in a crazy, sick, abusive relationship. The guy walked out when I got pregnant. I had the abortion because I was scared, running on my fears.

"But I did it mostly because of my mom. She was working to raise us single-handed, holding down a job, she was just trying so hard and was so tired. And there I was, running wild. How could I do this to her? How could I bring home a baby too?" As Lee recalls her mother's sacrifice, she looks close to tears.

I ask if anyone would like to add anything about the reason for her abortion, or what might have helped her take a different path.

"In my case, it was low self-esteem," says Eunice. "I thought, 'This is just like something you *would* do. It's just the kind of person you are.' I was a horrible person, real mean to a lot of people." It's hard to picture; she seems demure and sweet as she perches, petite and pretty, on the sofa.

Anna says, "Sometimes I wonder who did I really hurt, who was I really trying to hurt, when I had the abortion? Maybe I was punishing myself. But I think that if I had heard my baby's beating heart, it would have turned me around. Had I seen that baby's form, like on a sonogram, I could not have had that abortion."

Annette disagrees. "I knew all about fetal development; I was a biology major at a Catholic college, so I knew all the facts and all the church teachings too. A place like this giving me that information wouldn't have made any difference. But I did feel that need to know about my *own* baby. When I was on the table at the abortion clinic the one thing I asked the nurse was, 'Tell me if it was a boy or a girl.' She hesitated and said, 'We won't be able to tell.' I could read it like it was written across her face: Because the pieces will be too small. Because it will be ripped to shreds.

"I really didn't want to have an abortion. When I found out I was pregnant, I told my boyfriend, and we both wanted to have the baby. He told his family and everything looked fine. But my mother went into shock. 'It was a mistake—you have to finish college—I'm afraid of what your father will do—' The one constant in my upbringing had been, 'Don't ever come home pregnant.'

"Mom finally told me that if I had the baby, *her* marriage couldn't take it, my father would leave *her*. Even though I could see lots of ways to have the baby and make ends meet, my mom kept up this constant pressure, and eventually I gave in. Just like a lamb to the slaughter—okay, Mom, take care of it." Annette throws her hands in the air, disgusted with herself.

It's getting late; we should close and let folks go home. Several of the women turn toward Ruth, a small Hispanic woman sunk into the sofa. "You haven't said anything yet!" they beam at her encouragingly. When Ruth came in at the beginning of the evening she seemed cheerful, but I've been watching her gradually withdraw as the evening passed. Now, as she shakes her head, I hasten to say, "She doesn't have to say anything if she doesn't want to," and with a thin smile she confirms, "I don't want to."

I point out that many of the women tonight have said that they had the abortion primarily to please or protect their mother or, in Cathy's case, her dad.

Cathy comes back out of her silence now and says, "There's one more thing about my dad. He died last summer—that is, he got so sick that he was in the hospital, and I had to be the one to make the decision to take him off life support. That was the hardest thing of all." She begins to cry. "I felt like, first I killed my baby, and now I killed my father." As she sobs, the group breaks up; some move to hug her, while others embrace each other and say good-bye.

Mary, the center director, and I meet in the small kitchen to wrap the leftover cake and wash coffee mugs. "How did it go?" she whispers. "I think it went really well," I respond, "but I'm worried about one person—Ruth. She just withdrew and didn't say a word all evening. I feel terrible about it. I hope the evening wasn't too hard on her."

A moment later Ruth comes in. Now she's smiling shyly. "I wanted to ask you something," she says, "is that okay?" I assure her it is as she hesitates. "Is it normal to not remember anything about your abortion?" she asks, still smiling hopefully. I am taken aback.

"You mean, you don't remember anything at all?" I ask, and she nods. "You mean," I try again, "you remember before and after the abortion, but from the time you went to the clinic, it's just a blank?"

"Yes," she says, still looking to me for reassurance. "Is that normal?"

I have actually never heard of this before, and I'm pretty sure that, whatever it is, it's not precisely *normal.* But I don't want to tell her that, not when she appears so vulnerable. "Yes," I say, "I think that happens sometimes. You're in post-abortion counseling, right?" She nods again. "I think that, as you go along, the memories will come back gradually. Don't worry about it, and let your counselor help you look at those memories as you're ready."

Ruth is reassured, and goes out after thanking me with a hug and kiss. I later learn that Ruth's experience is not uncommon: psychogenic amnesia is one symptom of Post-Traumatic Stress Disorder that some post-abortion women share.[2]

As we drive away from the center, the black night is swirled with stars. Memories come out of blackness, amazing in their potency, sometimes humming below the surface and tamed, sometimes knocking the sobs out by main force. I think of how the women came in tonight, each with her memories captured inside; over the course of the evening they spilled them out, mixing and overlapping, prompting other memories across the room. A large group like this is hard to manage; no one gets to say everything she wants to, in just the right order and the way she wants. Ruth couldn't say anything at all. We end up with a jumble of memories, of sorrows, broken fragments of life-stories.

Once more I feel awe at my role in these tender gatherings, the stranger who breezes in juggling memories, juggling hearts. I am touched that these women would come here trusting enough to share such intimate pain, and go home again, in many cases, to loneliness. All I could give them was some chocolate cake. As we speed through the silent streets to the other side of Cleveland, the heavy slab of leftover cake weighs on my lap, the aluminum foil twinkling in the dark.

1. "In 50% of the cases, the abortion was quickly followed by disruption and termination of the relationship with the man involved." Research by Mary K. Zimmerman in *Passage Through Abortion* (1977), cited by David Reardon, *Aborted Women: Silent No More* (Westchester, Ill.: Crossway Books, 1987), p. 45. Open Arms Abortion Information Survey (Appendix E) found that 52 percent of relationships broke up.

2. Anne Speckhard and Vincent Rue, "Complicated Mourning: Dynamics of Impacted Post-Abortion Grief," *Pre- and Perinatal Journal,* 8(1), Fall 1993.

MEN, PART TWO:
The Artifical Husband

W hen the hotline phone rang, the pregnancy center counselor was ready. The client on the other end talked in detail about her pregnancy, her situations at home and at work, all the elements that made having a pregnancy now less than ideal. The counselor went over some of the ways the center could meet the woman's needs with material aid and emotional support. She wound up with a summary question: "Tell me—when you imagine yourself continuing this pregnancy and having this baby, what do you need the most?" The woman laughed: "Honey, I need a *man!*"

The ideal cure for the problems a pregnancy presents is a husband. When he is providing the household's financial security, the mother does not face the simultaneous challenges of full-time child-rearing plus full-time employment. She doesn't have to fret about finding child care so she can keep her job, choosing between bad care that she can afford and good care that she cannot, with neither meeting the need of mother and child to be together.

Providing a substitute for the father in pregnancy and child-rearing is like providing a substitute for the human hand. A dexterous, light-weight prosthesis with some grasping abilities is better than nothing, better than a hook, better than last year's model prosthesis. But the most advanced artificial hand that researchers can dream up will always be blunt and clumsy compared to the flexibility, warmth, and sensitivity of the original. It is better not to lose your hand.

It is better not to lose your man. Besides the glaring need for protection and provision after the birth, the mother needs help with the incessant round of newborn care. She needs someone who will bring her the baby dry-diapered for some of the night feedings, who will walk the crying child when she's at her wits' end, who will murmur comfort to her fears that she's doing everything all wrong. She needs someone who will love her baby as wildly as she does and defend it with as much passion. The kindness of strangers cannot do this.

During pregnancy she needs someone who will worry about her like she worries about the baby. She needs an encourager when the tides of hormone-laced emotions throw her against the rocks. She needs someone to reassure her when her body goes through changes that, especially in a first pregnancy, appear precipitous, bizarre, and alarming. When she wakes in the night terrified of the ordeal of childbirth, she needs someone to say, "When that time comes, I will stand by you."

If she does not get these things, she will survive, and it is possible that her unborn baby will survive as well. But their life will be like living without a hand.

A pregnancy care center is the result of pro-lifers thinking about how to build an artificial hand, an artificial husband. From its origins in the mid-1960s, the pregnancy care movement has tried to imagine as many kinds of support as they could, and then set about finding donors and volunteers to provide them.

Some active in this movement are men, whose fatherly impulse to provide and protect breaks over family bonds to touch the lives of strangers. They don't, as a rule, spend their volunteer hours decorating gift layette baskets with pink and blue ribbons. They are more likely to offer a Saturday-morning car clinic in a church parking lot, doing free maintenance and repairs for single moms whose cars are their lifeline to employment.

For the most part the movement is staffed and run by women. The close support that women give each other through the cycles of pregnancy, birth, and child-rearing is a tradition durable over centuries and continents. A feminist slogan of the early 1970s was "Sisterhood is Powerful!" It is hard to think of an example of powerful sisterhood more enduring and concrete than the help hundreds of thousands of female pregnancy care volunteers have given to women in need over the decades.

If a husband's first duty is to provide shelter, a pregnancy care center's help often begins with housing, either by referral to a group-shelter maternity home or housing with individual families (sometimes called "shepherding homes"). Most pregnancy care centers provide maternity clothes, birth preparation classes, and attempt to meet emotional needs with individual and group counseling. They usually offer some form of obstetric referral; a few even provide prenatal exams with a doctor or midwife on-site.

The care provided by this artificial husband goes on after the birth as well; some centers offer job training and business clothing, baby clothes and food, and postnatal housing for mother and child. Offerings are limited by the local center's resources, as well as by their fear of lawsuits (many centers, for example, no longer loan baby furniture).

The difficulty in providing an artificial husband is that the need is endless, not just a matter of getting through the initial nine-month crisis. If the mother will be raising this child alone for eighteen years, the artificial husband must either offer ongoing support throughout that time, or wean the mother to self-sufficiency. Just as her problems grow more severe after birth, the capacity of the pregnancy care center to solve the problems declines.

The problems of single parenting are so daunting and endless to both mother and child that it should never be encouraged. The familiar numbers dance: 70 percent of the juveniles in state reform institutions grew up without a parent, usually without a father. For these kids, gangs fill needs a father would supply: a locus of authority, and an assurance that the child belongs. White girls growing up fatherless are two-and-a-half times more likely to have a child out of wedlock. The chances of finishing high school drop 40 percent for a fatherless white child; for a black child, they drop 70 percent.[1]

Women benefit, too, from secure married parenting. Statistics from 1992 indicate that in cases where parents had finished high school, married, and waited until age twenty to have a child, only 8 percent of the children were living in poverty. That figure soars to 79 percent for children of parents who were unmarried, had no diploma, and gave birth before age twenty.[2] Those children don't live in poverty alone; their mothers suffer with them.

The frustrations of single-parenting can harm them both; 40 percent of reported child abuse occurs in homes headed by unmarried women.[3] Nor do men find their separated lot blissful. "Men unconnected to children and wives have enormously higher rates of violence, accidents, and criminality than husbands and fathers," says Karl Zinsmeister of the American Enterprise Institute.[4]

This is a hard word for some pregnancy care centers, which are so desperate to save unborn children from dismemberment that they will encourage any scenario the mother finds appealing. The first step in persuading a woman to choose life is helping her to visualize and love her baby; it is no wonder that, once that connection is made, many women will draw a line directly to single parenthood. Pregnancy care centers are in a poor position to counter such a choice, and 80-90 percent of their clients choose it.[5]

Single parenting has elements that are initially appealing. When actress Michelle Pfeiffer decided to become a single mom by adoption, she explained: "I thought, I don't want some guy in my life forever who's going to be driving me nuts."[6] Being free of a husband means being free to pursue a varied romantic life, free to continue the fantasy that a more perfect mate is waiting patiently around the corner. Of course, in the real world Prince Charmings prefer women who come without other men's children. A few years ago the *Washington Post* quoted a never-married black woman of twenty-two who had had children by three different men; she explained that she was playing the field for now, but someday the right guy would come along and persuade her to settle down. This is fantasy thinking on the Tooth-Fairy level, but much more poignant—and more dangerous.

A step-dad does not necessarily rescue the child from the problems of a single-parent home; he may actually make things worse. A stepfather who does not adopt his stepkids has no legal obligation to them. There may be more money in the household, but there is no guarantee that it's helping to buy the kids' shoes. "Children living with stepparents appear to be even more disadvantaged than children living in a stable single-parent family...The old stories [fairy tales about wicked stepparents] are anthropologically quiet accurate. Step families disrupt established loyalties, create new uncertainties, provoke deep anxieties, and sometimes threaten a child's physical safety as well as emotional security," says Barbara Dafoe Whitehead in her landmark essay, "Dan Quayle Was Right."[7] She cites Canadian research indicating that preschoolers with stepfamilies, compared to those living with two original parents, face forty times the risk of physical and sexual abuse.

"All too often the adult quest for freedom, independence, and choice in family relationships conflicts with a child's developmental needs for stability, constancy, harmony, and permanence in family life," Whitehead goes on. While single parenting is a prescription for poverty, loneliness, and decreasing sexual bargaining power for women, it is a certified disaster for children.

One of the marks of our failing culture is the tendency to

ignore fathers and treat them as disposable. Pregnancy workers cannot afford to perpetuate that mistake. Counseling should always carefully explore the option of marriage to the child's father, with the counselor speaking to both parents and encouraging the father to take a role in his child's life that can bring him meaning and pride. Dismissing the child's father as a cad who is bound to shirk responsibility is as self-defeating as telling adolescent girls that they will inevitably have sex.

When April told her boyfriend she was pregnant, he was angry; he threw her against the wall outside the mall and shouted at her. April, who'd earned plenty of previous scoldings at home, didn't tell her dad and stepmom. Instead, she left home one night and hitchhiked two hundred miles to her mom's apartment.

April's mom, who was unstable and often malicious, refused to take her daughter for prenatal care. At first she said she was waiting until the girl turned eighteen and would no longer be her financial burden. But on April's birthday her mother turned her out on the street, shoving all her belongings and stuffed animals into a plastic garbage bag. April spent two weeks at the county homeless shelter before they told her her time was up and she'd have to move on.

It's hard to imagine a story bleaker than this. But at this point April moved in with a Christian family who helped her gather her courage to call her dad and mend fences. He was eager to see his daughter again and to welcome her home. April took the train home a few months before the birth, patched things up with her stepmom, and found a part-time job.

One day soon after the baby's father came to visit. He felt sheepish and confused. A few days later he came back; he'd brought a quilt for the crib. The visits continued, with baby gifts appearing regularly. One day he brought a very small box. In it was a ring with a very small diamond.

A year later April returned to visit the family that had given her shelter. Her daughter was bundled against the snow in extravagant layers of pink and lace, tiny socks and shiny hard shoes at one end, a strong-willed porcelain face under blond curls at the other. April's husband was lanky and awkward and proud. He was working full time to provide a home—a small apartment—and groceries for his family. April just beamed.

Stories like this are not typical, but that is at least in part because we do not expect or encourage them. There is a presumption that "shotgun" marriages should be avoided because they are unstable and laden with problems. But single parenting is by every indicator much worse, a catastrophe damaging mother and child for decades. A marriage that eventually ends in divorce is better than a childhood with no dad at all. What's more, despite our worst expectations, the marriage just might succeed.

In their book, *More Than Kindness*, Susan and Marvin Olasky present an array of small studies yielding encouraging evidence. Teenage marriages prompted by pregnancy show surprising durability: half of black couples were still together after ten years, as were three-quarters of whites. Compared to a national divorce rate of 50 percent, these kids do well indeed. Even without marriage, young fathers who lived with their children in 1980 were still in the home in 1983 in 65-75 percent of cases. The Olaskys point out that "This rate of success for some young fathers comes despite few programs designed to assist them in their newly acquired role and a great deal of hostility toward their involvement."[8]

In these studies, the majority of men continued to date the women during the pregnancy, providing money, gifts and transportation. Majorities stayed with the mother during labor, and were involved and giving financial support over a year later. The outcome for involved dads themselves was better, too, as they were more likely to be steadily employed and less likely to be in trouble with the law.[9]

Pregnancy care workers may be infected with an attitude toward men that runs through our culture: that men cannot control themselves sexually, that they are incapable of commitment, that women are better off on their own. As we saw in Chapter 3, even men living chaste, responsible lives will vigorously trash men as a class, ignoring the evidence of their own lives, and the lives of hundreds of men they see regularly in their churches and organizations. The world is full of men who are striving to be good, responsible, and faithful. We have just trained ourselves not to see them.

The first step in solving the problems in an unexpected pregnancy is to look to the father of the child and explore whether he is capable of taking on, or growing into, the role that is naturally his. Sparks of pride in protecting and providing should be fanned into flame. Our high expectations can help him succeed in this role. Yet, as the statistics above show, even when he is heaped with rejection and disparagement his desire to succeed sometimes remains, a code of honor written in his blood.

In some situations marriage is not the answer. The father may be actively pushing for abortion. He may claim not to be the father of the child. The pregnancy may have been begun in a fleeting relationship that offers no foundation for a life together. To say that the woman should seriously consider marriage is not to say that she should never turn to other options. Where marriage is inadvisable, the woman should be encouraged to consider adoption; this option will be considered in greater depth in Chapter 9. If, however, the woman is determined to have the child and raise it by herself, she is entitled to the father's financial support.

There has been a great deal of frustration around the issue of enforcement of child support payments. According to Census Bureau estimates, 9.4 million mothers were eligible for child support payments in 1987; of those, only 59 percent had a judicial order entitling them to such aid. Only half of those women with a court order were actually receiving full payment; a quarter received partial payment, and a quarter received nothing at all.[10]

Pregnant women can plan for child support by establishing legal paternity. Here again even a brief marriage makes a difference: 64 percent of divorced and separated mothers receive child support payments, while only 20 percent of unwed mothers do.[11] A young woman may feel that it's pointless to look to the baby's father for financial help—he may be as young and penniless as she is. But, according to the Association for Children for Enforcement of Support, "studies show...that these same fathers had incomes of $15,000 a year or more within the next five years."[12] The possibility that her lover's income may rocket into the five digits over the next five years may not put stars in a girl's eyes, but every penny counts. Those pennies are harder to count if she has lost touch with the baby's father without legally establishing paternity.

New ideas for separating "deadbeat dads" from their loot regularly appear. In 1984 and again in 1988 Congress passed laws mandating techniques such as garnishment of the dad's wages and attachment of his tax refund checks. While these tactics improve collection, variations in state laws slow it, and a dad determined to avoid payments can improve his chances by keeping on the move. In 1992 child support collections were up 16 percent over the previous year, with $7.9 billion collected (at an administrative cost of $1.9 billion). However, even this collection figure represents only a fourth of the amount owed.[13]

The image of abandoned women raising children in poverty is deeply moving, and can lead to initiatives to put federal money more directly into needy pockets. A flurry of such proposals in 1992 saw pro-life Congressman Henry Hyde and Family Research Council president Gary Bauer taking opposite sides.

Bauer criticized the Downey/Hyde Child Support Enforcement and Assurance Plan for offering taxpayer-guaranteed child support payments to single moms even if they don't have support orders. The double-bind dilemma of nearly every welfare system is evident here: women without support orders are the ones in greatest need, but when the system is bypassed to meet her need, the incentive for her to pursue paternal support is eliminated.

Bauer points out that any taxpayer-guaranteed system trans-fers funds from married-couple families—ineligible for the aid—to single-parent families. Instead of taxing the married to pay the unmarried, Bauer recommends that all parents of every marital status be granted a $1000 per child tax credit.[14]

Congressman Hyde has continued to work on other aspects of child support enforcement. His proposal to make interstate flight to avoid child support payment a federal crime was signed into law in October 1992. At this writing he is pursuing legisla-tion to authorize the Internal Revenue Service to take over from the states the duty of collecting child support.

Why must some men be coerced to pay? "Many delinquent fathers are themselves living on the edge of poverty."[15] In addition, the loss of low-skill, high-paying jobs and the entry of women into the workforce mean that the dad-provider role is no longer clear or readily achievable. Nature will guide a mother in her role whether she lives in an igloo or a condo, but a father's role must be largely defined and supported by his culture. When the role becomes vague and his worth seems uncertain, reasons to go can seem stronger than reasons to stay. This is especially true when welfare payments make Uncle Sam an unbeatable rival, a suitor with deep pockets who makes no demands and doesn't leave his dirty socks under the coffee table.

What's more, as marriage has come to be seen more as an institution for the fulfillment of adults and less as a place to pro-tect children, parents' commitment to each other shifts to the flimsier foundation of self-interest. "Fatherhood has always worked best as part of a package deal that involves both marriage and child-rearing," says Frank F. Furstenburg, a sociologist at the University of Pennsylvania. "It's hard to imagine a system where the father remains strongly involved with his kids but has no rela-tionship with their mother."[16] In *Mrs. Doubtfire*, Robin Williams regularly proclaimed with trembling lip his desperate love for his children; the script ignored the probability that profession of the same caliber love for their mother might have had Williams back in the family home faster than you can say "high concept."

There are several guesses as to why men don't pay; the most popular is that men are louses. Then-candidate Bill Clinton won cheers in his Democratic convention acceptance speech for threatening to give "deadbeat dads" a financial punch in the nose. These ne'er-do-wells are a popular target.

But the reason cited for non-payment most plaintively and consistently by the men themselves is that they aren't allowed to see their kids. Over sixty bills currently before Congress seek to step up child-support collections, but few of these mandate enforcement of visitation rights. "My ex-girlfriend has never let me spend a day with my daughter, so I say the hell with it," says Norm Partica from a New Jersey holding cell, following his arrest for support non-payment. "She's not getting a dime from me until I can see my baby."[17]

David Levy, president of a non-custodial parents organization, says "We don't have absent parents so much as we have forced-away parents.... One parent gets custody and the other is reduced to an absentee cash register."[18] Warren Farrell writes in *The Myth of Male Power*, "A man who has seen his marriage become alimony payments, his home become his wife's home, and his children become child-support payments for those who have been turned against him psychologically feels he is spending his life working for people who hate him."[19]

When Dick Woods, president of the National Congress for Men, spoke before a 1991 meeting of the National Commission on Interstate Child Support, he suggested that child support payments drop in situations where the mother pushes the father out of his children's lives. Woods pointed out that in over 40 percent of divorces, the custodial parent denies the non-custodial parent access to the children.

This argument routinely provokes snorts of derisive laughter. In Woods' case, Pennsylvania lawyer Lynne Gold-Bikin retorted that it was "pure bovine scatology."[20] Ridicule is usually considered sufficient to refute the argument and to maintain the party line that the law must strictly separate payment and visitation issues. However, men keep insisting that payment feels less justified when their children are being kept strangers or, worse, being taught to hate them by a bitter ex-wife. Their sentiments are not hard to understand.

The idea of abortion as "the woman's choice" brings another conundrum into the child-support scenario. Contraception and abortion seem to promise men that sex has no consequences. But there's a catch—if a pregnancy occurs, and the woman decides to continue it, he'll pay for eighteen years. It's her choice.

Warren Farrell calls this "birth control rape." "If a man is considered a date rapist by a woman who consents at night but feels raped in the morning, then a man can feel raped by a woman who says she is on birth control at night and says she feels pregnant the next week. And if she says, 'I'm going to have the child, like it or not,' this rape of him imprisons him for a lifetime."[21]

The former president of the National Organization for Women, Karen DeCrow, sympathizes. She has stated that "Men should not automatically have to pay for a child they don't want. It's the only logical feminist position to take." In a letter to the *New York Times Magazine* a decade ago she wrote, "Justice declares that if a woman makes a unilateral decision to bring pregnancy to term, and the biological father does not, and cannot, share in this decision, he should not be liable for 21 years of support."

Once again, connectedness makes people responsible. Noncustodial dads say that seeing their children, hugging them, and playing with them makes them more eager to pay child support. On the other hand, when contraception and abortion cleave sex from procreation, and woman from man and child, it also cuts a footloose dad free. It's the "only logical feminist position to take."

Perhaps some elements in men want to "do it and run." Some slumbering elements, unsupported in our culture, want to do the right thing and care for mother and child. It's obvious which is healthier for all concerned, and which anyone working in the pregnancy care field must do everything possible to encourage.

Seventy thousand people filed down Constitution Avenue on a cold day in January, marking the anniversary of the *Roe v. Wade* decision. In the midst of the crowd came a man walking alone. He held his sizable posterboard sign with two hands above his head, and walked with his eyes fixed on the sidewalk, like a penitent in a medieval procession. As he drew nearer, the hand-lettered sign gradually became legible:

If I were more of
A MAN
My wife would not be trying
To kill our baby

1. Karl Zinsmeister, "The Murphy Brown Question," *Crisis* Magazine, October 1992, 23.
2. "Kids Count," a report of the Annie E. Casey Foundation, quoted in Susan Reimer, "Painfully Concluding that Having Babies Out of Wedlock is Wrong," *Baltimore Sun,* April 7, 1994.
3. Susan and Marvin Olasky, *More Than Kindness* (Wheaton, Ill.: Crossway Books, 1990), 56.
4. Zinsmeister, "Murphy Brown," 23.
5. Interviews with Denise Cocciolone (National Life Center), Peggy Hartshorn (Heartbeat), and Cheryl Jakubowski (Care Net), May 24-25, 1994. This is an educated guess, not a scientifically precise figure.
6. *Newsweek,* August 23, 1994.
7. Barbara Dafoe Whitehead, "Dan Quayle Was Right," *Atlantic Monthly,* April 1993.
8. Olasky, *More Than Kindness,* 139.
9. Ibid., 140ff.

10. "Child Support System Called 'Abysmal,'" *Washington Post,* March 3, 1991.

11. Ibid.

12. Geraldine Jensen with Katina Z. Jones, *How to Collect Child Support* (Stamford, Conn.: Longmeadow Press, 1991), 36.

13. "Child Support Money is Up, but Far Short," *New York Times,* January 7, 1994.

14. Testimony of Gary L. Bauer before the Human Resources Subcommittee of the Committee on Ways and Means, July 1, 1992.

15. Paul Taylor, "Delinquent Dads," *Washington Post,* December 16, 1990.

16. Ibid.

17. Ibid.

18. Ibid.

19. Warren Farrell, *The Myth of Male Power* (New York: Simon & Schuster, 1993), 27.

20. "Child Support," ibid.

21. Farrell, *Male Power,* 335.

Listening in Chicago

oming to Chicago means I can spend some time with Jeannie French. Jeannie founded the National Women's Coalition for Life in the spring of 1992, when she persuaded pro-life women's organizations to form a network that would boast a combined membership of over a million. During an NWCL leadership conference call a few months later, Jeannie broached her next idea: a national research project to study the reasons women have abortions.

Jeannie looks different than the last time I saw her, mostly because she's seven months pregnant with twins. Still, her energy leaves me behind as we hold a press conference, rush to a radio show, have lunch with a journalist, attend a reception, and walk block after block across downtown Chicago. I keep reminding her that the pregnancy is stressing her heart and her doctor ordered her to bed rest; she keeps correcting me that the only promise she made him was to stop going to the office. She pumps ahead of me down Chicago's crowded sidewalks, blond hair flying over the shoulders of her gray coat, beaming in love with city life.

On Thursday evening we pull up at a pregnancy care center

in the suburb of Palatine, one with the bulky name of Society for the Preservation of Human Dignity. The name belies its age; PHD was founded in 1970, in the first blush of pro-life sentiment when the accent was on rights and justice. Today the focus has shifted to compassion and support; a modern pregnancy care center would be named "Womankind" or "Loving & Caring" or "Heartbeat." (PHD is now used to signify "Pregnancy Help with Dignity.")

I have visited countless pregnancy care centers, from a trailer on a gravel lot just outside Watts, to a swanky office high in a big-city skyscraper, but PHD is the most impressive arrangement I've yet encountered. It is housed in a gracious brick structure built as a lavish turn-of-the-century home. The interior is lush with carved woodwork and doors set with panes of leaded glass. So many counseling rooms are strewn throughout the two floors that I lost count; all are decorated in teal, cream and dusty-rose, with wallpaper borders that burst with huge cabbage roses. This color scheme is familiar; nearly every pregnancy care center I see is decorated exactly the same way. I must have missed it when they passed the Pregnancy Care Center Interior Decor Act a few years ago.

The center's basement level is vast and overflowing with donations, neatly ordered room by room: baby furniture, maternity clothes, baby clothes washed, folded and neatly stacked in dozens of size-gender-season bins. Their abundance is such that much usable material gets passed along to other organizations: I count nine large green plastic bags stuffed with clothes, each marked "Salvation Army."

Another mark of PHD's success is its professionalism. Whereas most centers have only one or two paid staff (or none at all), PHD has seven, and over 150 volunteers. Anyone doing counseling must be a professional with a degree in the field. Counselor Lynn Sprehe is very protective of the post-abortion clients she has invited to meet with me tonight, and wants to give me a friendly grilling at a restaurant first. ("Should we walk or drive?" asks Lynn. "Walk!" says Jeannie.)

On our return we settle into Lynn's counseling room, and at 7:30 the participants arrive. There are hugs all around. Cindy, a young woman with a tangle of white-blond ponytail, shows off an engagement ring to ripples of congratulation. As we begin I describe the project then, under Lynn's watchful eye, invite anyone to share the story of her abortion decision.

After a long minute of silence, petite, well-dressed Sally plunges in: "In my case, it was date rape. The guy had been a friend, and it was New Year's Eve. Afterwards I was bleeding, and immediately I just knew inside that I was pregnant. I had the abortion six weeks later.

"It wasn't a hard decision, but it was a horrible decision. I felt like I had to do it to survive; I thought my parents would never talk to me again if they found out I was pregnant. I even imagined grandparents in heaven hating me. I tried to involve the guy. I was wishing he would marry me, and I could see no other way to continue the pregnancy. But he was such a jerk. He took me to the clinic, but I paid the whole thing; afterwards he took me to his house and ignored me while I lay there in pain and bleeding. Instead, he went out and bought a kid's race car set, and set it up on the living room rug, and invited his friends over to play!"

I interrupt to say that I'd heard of another case where the man's reaction to the abortion was to buy little boy's toys—to emphasize that *he*, not some usurper, was the child. Sally is amazed.

"I can't believe that I stood for that kind of disrespect. But I felt like such a slug. At the clinic they were so cold; the doctor didn't even tell me his name, but I thought 'This is what I deserve.' I just felt so boxed in, like I had no other choice. Every step I took, I took to function, to survive. So after that I shut down for ten years, except for anniversary reactions," (the tendency of post-abortion women to feel intense grief on the anniversary of the abortion, of the baby's due date, or the conception) "and I refused to hold a baby.

"That was fourteen years ago. Now I have two daughters, and I think, what can I do to help them? I think the main thing is awareness of your body and how it works. We didn't get much of that growing up—you remember, they would just give you a sanitary napkin starter kit, and that was that? And we have to teach girls about the dynamics of relationships: how to handle themselves with guys and not get into these situations. You've got to start young."

Cindy puts in, "You have to teach young girls to expect to be respected. I can't believe how I let myself be used. Girls need to be put back in power in those situations."

"I didn't get pregnant because I couldn't find contraception," says Martha, a subdued Hispanic woman in drab colors. "in fact, we used a condom. We were adults. I was in my late twenties, returning to college and living at home. The first time I slept with this guy I got pregnant. It was a catastrophe, but abortion was not an option for me.

"Scared as I was, part of me was also excited. I thought, 'If anyone will believe in me and help me pull through, it's my Mom.' In fact, on the way home from the doctor's, I stopped and bought a baby care book. I could imagine that she would be upset at first, but then would say, 'Well, this is what we have to do' and get into it.

"It was a terrible shock. When I told Mom, she looked at me and said, 'Well, you have to have an abortion.' I couldn't believe it. I was deeply disappointed in her and disillusioned. I said that I didn't want to, and she suggested I marry the guy, even for just a year, and then I could get a divorce.

"I just felt disgusted—like that sort of a charade would make everything all right. The guy didn't want to get married; when I said, 'I'm thinking about having the baby anyway,' he said, 'Oh no, I'd have to leave the university.' So I gave in. But if I'd only had someone to encourage me, someone to explore with me what I really wanted to do, and if I had a way to figure out the financial and practical problems, I never would have done it."

I describe the work of Mary Cunningham Agee with The Nurturing Network. Unlike most pregnancy care centers, which operate on a store-front, walk-in basis, TNN links volunteers across the country by phone. Many of the clients are college or professional women whose primary need is not raw poverty, but keeping their lives intact. Martha's first smile begins to appear as I describe this network and ask if this would have made a difference to her. "Yes," she says, "I would have gone into dreaming about it a bit more. It would have created new possibilities."

Libby now takes a turn. She is not old, but looks battered, thin, and worn-out. "I didn't have a good relationship with my family," she begins. "I was afraid to tell them. My mother was an alcoholic, and I never liked her. I never told her anything. I avoided my dad even more, because he hit me. There were no other close relatives.

"Paul was my first boyfriend, the only thing in my life that loved me; I was sort of addicted to him, and couldn't break away. So when I got pregnant I went to a pregnancy care center, but the woman there wasn't very nurturing. She was old, gray-haired, and I felt like I couldn't relate to her, couldn't trust her. She made me think of my mother. If it had been someone younger, more like me... I needed a sister, someone who would walk through it with me. If I could have made a plan and packed and walked out, knowing someone was with me all the way, I could have done it.

"I so much wanted to have a normal life, a normal family. I was doing well in school and dreamed of going to college. I would *definitely* have loved to move in with another family. But I don't want anybody to act too motherly. I don't have a good image of mothers.

"I had two more abortions over the next four years. After the second one I attempted suicide. For all of them I asked for just local anesthetic; I wanted to make sure I felt the pain. I didn't care if it was clean, didn't care if I died on the table. I never went to follow-ups, and the antibiotics they gave me I threw in the toilet. I was just spiraling down in so many ways. There was no religion for me. If anything, I had a 'God'll get you' attitude. After the first abortion I said to Paul, 'There is no God.' "

When I comment on how desperate she must have felt, others chime in. "There's too much happening," says Martha. "Everything becomes an unknown. The pregnancy disrupts every area of your life, down to the clothes you wear. Every day your body is changing, and the time is limited."

Sally says, "I had the idea that I could make this decision, get it over with, and never look back. People should know it's going to ruin your life! Why won't people listen to us when we say that it's a devastating, life-changing experience?"

"But I knew that," says Cindy. "I was totally pro-life, I knew abortion was horrible. But when it happened to me, I just felt so trapped..."

I bring up the analogy that a woman wants an abortion like an animal, caught in a trap, wants to gnaw off its own leg. The group nods and says that's exactly what it was like. Jeannie adds that, for trapped animals, as for the pregnant women, life as they knew it is over. Nothing can be the same again. No matter what happens, they will never return to the safety of their dens. Martha adds, "There's some element of self-punishment in having an abortion, a feeling that you're doing this to hurt yourself."

Cindy now takes up her story. She is the youngest of the group, and sits with her legs crossed up on the sofa, listening with bright eyes. All her clothes are inside-out; the fleecy sweats give her the cozy texture of a stuffed animal. "When I heard you describing The Nurturing Network, that there's someone who could provide homes and schools, I got all teary-eyed. That was what I needed," she says. "I was just eighteen, a college freshman, and I didn't like or respect myself. I've never enjoyed sex, but it made the guys like me. So the whole reason I got pregnant was that I was not believing in myself and respecting myself, but looking for love and acceptance from guys.

"I was in a serious relationship with a guy, and when I told my parents I was pregnant, they suggested we get married. Then I figured out he probably wasn't the father, it was probably another guy. I was drinking a lot in college. I was really too embarrassed to tell my parents I wasn't sure who the father was, so I just said I didn't want to get married. I lied to my parents and told them I'd had a miscarriage.

"When I think about what would have changed my decision, it was if I'd had someplace that would have accepted me and taken me in. Either a family home, or one with all girls my age and we could do it together. I didn't even know there were places like this pregnancy center."

I mention that most pregnancy centers are saying their biggest need in persuading women to continue their pregnancies is for adoption to be a better option. I ask if making an adoption plan would have made the difference for anyone.

"No!" says Cindy, emphatically.

"I think I could have," says Libby. "I never wanted kids. I never saw a family as healthy." Libby, who came in looking crushed, has been brightening during the course of the evening. She likes having a group to share in. Occasionally a weak smile appears.

The last in the circle is May, a slender and ebullient black woman in brilliant yellow and white. While the women I meet in these groups are generally subdued and wistful, May came in beaming and talkative, full of good cheer. She is an airline stewardess, but has recently taken a second job in downtown Chicago so that she can force herself over her "city phobia." Obviously May is a strong person who takes her life in hand.

Her good spirits seem even more unusual when she begins her story. "My abortion was one year ago today. I was very much in love with the baby's father, and I thought he was in love with me. I was traveling, and called him from Las Vegas with the news. It took him *four days* to call me back. It was a *big* shock. I was so filled with bitterness. I thought he loved me! I had a harder time getting over the love loss than getting over the abortion.

"So I let him talk me, *coerce* me into an abortion. It wasn't the circumstances that made me do it. I had the finances and the career and so forth. He was a forty-three-year-old man; he could have paid child support. But I just let myself be led into it. I consider myself a victim and a fool; I was old enough to know better."

May is getting wound up now, laughter over her rage. "Now I hate all men, they're animals. I will never let a man touch me *or— rape* me again. To me that's what it is. Even the thought of it— yuck! He belittled me, that fake. What a game he played!"

May's vivid energy contrasts with the other four women's subdued tone. I remember the adage that "Depression is anger turned inwards." The others have talked about how their experience led to self-hate, even self-destructiveness and suicidal thoughts. May's anger seems to be steadily beamed at one fellow who, I hope, never meets her in a dark alley.

I ask the group whether their abortion experiences changed the way they saw the child's father or men in general, as it so obviously did in May's case.

Martha says, "Yes, I was really disappointed in him. I judged the man as weak. But I stayed with him two more years. I just couldn't see myself with someone else—I thought I was a—"

May interjects, "Murderer."

Martha finishes, "Slut. I couldn't break up with him." Now Martha looks down, then goes on into something she apparently hadn't meant to share. "I had a second abortion two years later. This time I went by myself and used a false name; I wanted it done secretly and as fast as possible. I felt frantic.

"When I was on the table, the doctor said, 'The baby's too big, and I can't do it. You'll have to go somewhere else.' I just freaked out and started screaming. I just felt like I had to have it over with *now*. So the doctor went ahead and did it. I was really a mess. After the first abortion I knew I needed help, and I even went for family therapy. But after that the self-sabotage kicked in."

As we talk about how abortion can crumble your self-esteem, Jeannie brings up a sensational case which has just broken on the news, that of Lorena Bobbitt. Jeannie had heard Bobbitt in a TV

interview allege that her husband had once hounded her into having an abortion, telling her that she wasn't fit to be a mother. On
the night of the incident she went into the kitchen and saw a
knife lying on the table. Jeannie quotes Bobbitt: "'I thought
about the abortion, and I picked up the knife.'"

Smiles spread around the room, and Sally says, "What a wonderful fantasy." Bobbitt's example is one that the post-abortion
women here clearly enjoy. Perhaps it is for the best that anger is
usually turned inward.

We wrap up with several questions. Libby asks why she has
never wanted children. May asks, surprisingly, why she sometimes
has an impulse to go over to the guy's house, lie to him about
contraception, and get pregnant again on purpose. We ask Libby
and Martha about the difference in decision-making between a
first and second abortion; they emphasize that it is very different,
that the second abortion is almost a foregone conclusion. Each
remembers feeling urgently that she needed to get it over with as
soon as possible. They agree that it would have been much harder
for someone to talk them out of the second abortion than the
first.

Sally tells the story of how her healing began. She had
assumed that she was going to Hell: for Catholics, abortion is a
mortal sin. "I couldn't do any worse. It's not like, if you slip up
again, they send you to *Hell* Hell." She felt unfit to give her two
young daughters any spiritual instruction. She attended a church
retreat in order to look over the other young mothers and select a
worthy candidate to whom she could turn over her daughters'
spiritual instruction.

"When the priest invited anyone who wanted to to come up
for confession, I thought, 'Not me. What's the point?' But to my
amazement my legs just stood me up and started walking forward.
You could choose between a chair in front of the priest and one
behind him; I thought, 'I'd rather not have him looking at me,'
but somehow I went and sat in front of him.

"When I looked at him and said, 'I had an abortion,' I

thought he would be horrified. But instead he looked at me with such love. And the thing that he said that I'll never forget, the thing that really started my healing, was this: 'When you were up on that table, Jesus was right there with you.'" The tears are streaming down Sally's cheeks.

Martha says, "Yes, for me too! I made my confession at a retreat. The amazing thing was, the priest was seriously ill. In fact, they were about to take him to the hospital with a heart condition. But he stayed long enough to hear my confession. I always felt like that was a special gift from God, that God was saying, 'You are special, and no matter what the circumstances, I will make room for you to receive forgiveness.'" Martha sheds some tears too, then chuckles. "I thought, 'Maybe I'm lucky the priest was sick. If not, he might have given me heck!'"

Libby looks on enviously. "That's really wonderful that you worked through forgiveness with a priest. To me, it's still unfinished."

I finally ask the summary question: "What did you need to continue the pregnancy?" The answers are similar.

May says, "Being in love made me lose confidence in myself. If I'd stuck to what I believed, if I'd listened to myself and respected my own decision, I would have had that baby."

Martha agrees. "Give them love, support, and practical information. Just keep that hope alive."

"I did phone a pregnancy hotline," says May, "and they prayed for me, but it really wasn't enough. It would have to be someone I knew and respected, someone who would say to me, 'You can do it.' It has to be face to face, on a daily or weekly basis."

Libby adds, "Urge people to come in for counseling a few times before making the decision." "If I were counseling someone," says Martha, "I would say, 'I've already done this before, and it's just too horrible to go through.'"

The evening comes to an end, and we say good-byes as the group breaks up. Jeannie and I make our way back to her car. The night air is cool and bracing. We talk about the pattern that seems to be emerging: that pregnancy care centers say that women's greatest need is for financial help and housing, but the women themselves almost uniformly point to emotional and relational problems. We hypothesize: Perhaps the women who go to centers have already worked out their relational situations. Jeannie recalls the classic psychological theory that a "hierarchy of needs" extends from the basic necessities of survival to emotional and spiritual concerns. She says, "It's like Maslow's ladder in reverse. Once the emotional needs are met, people can think about meeting their practical needs."

Solving other people's emotional and relational problems is a tall order. As we get into the car I ask Jeannie whether, when she first envisioned the project a year ago, she thought it would be like this. "In a way, I guess," she says, as she wedges the twins behind the wheel. "But I sure thought it would be easier."

"MOM? DAD?

I need to tell you something."

Oooh, you're going to be in trou-ble!" Your best friend's eyes widen brightly with terror and something like glee. Your stomach sinks and you fall after it, down the endless hole opening beneath your feet. Anything, you can handle anything, you can fix anything. "Just don't tell my parents."

Odds are that anyone reading this book once spent some time as a teenager. Many of the wild emotions and convictions of those years now seem quaint or even incomprehensible (what was it with Ringo, anyway?) But the memory of one emotion springs up daisy-fresh—the awful fear of Getting in Trouble.

When a teen discovers she is pregnant, she fits the textbook definition of "a girl in trouble." The ordeal of telling her parents may loom larger than any other concern she has. It might not be their anger she fears; teens also conceal their mistakes because they fear disappointing, saddening, or burdening a parent, or simply because they are afraid of looking foolish at a age when being cool seems more important than breathing. One hip mom kept a cookie jar full of condoms on the kitchen counter for her teens; her daughter became pregnant and had an abortion secretly, rather than admit she'd fumbled contraception.

In the pamphlet titled "Don't Panic! How to tell your parents you're pregnant," mini-cartoon frames depict the range of a girl's fears:

(Mom fainting) "Mom...are you OK?"
(Mom and Dad crying) "Where have we failed?"
(Dad choking you) "How could you do this?"
(Mom walking away) "It figures. Why couldn't you be more like your sister?"
(Mom with phone) "We're making an appointment for an abortion now."
(Dad looking for gun) "Where's my gun? I'm going to kill that boy!"[1]

Information from post-abortion listening groups and case studies indicate that panicky pregnant girls can be very poor predictors of how their parents will react. One who was braced for violence got instead a hug and "I love you" from her saddened dad. One who expected her mom's grudging delight instead was ordered to have an abortion. More than one imagined that the news of her pregnancy would cause her parents literally life-endangering shock, although no actual health problems existed to prompt such a guilty fear. Sometimes these missed expectations are due to the girl's incomplete understanding of her parents, and sometimes the shock of the news causes parents to react in ways that surprise even themselves.

For many girls, the first impulse will be not to tell her parents. She can do this in two ways: by ignoring the pregnancy and hoping it will go away (seldom an effective strategy), or by having a secret abortion.

In the first case, the girl tries to conceal the pregnancy, perhaps even to herself. At six or seven months continuing this course usually becomes impossible. Her parents may confront her with their suspicions, and a decision must be made either to have the baby, or to have a late abortion. Late abortions—those done on viable babies—are far more dangerous to the mother than child-birth, and are grisly and harrowing to all involved, not least the child.

About ninety-six hundred abortions are done each year after twenty-one weeks of pregnancy.[2] In 1981 Dr. Willard Cates of the Centers for Disease Control estimated that four hundred to five hundred times a year babies were born alive after late abortions, making it an everyday occurrence.[3] In nearly every case the babies are left to die, or encouraged to do so by various means. These post-abortion live births now occur rarely, due to increased reliance on preventive methods that cut up the baby instead of poisoning it.

Other girls will seek to conceal the pregnancy by having an abortion without their parents' knowledge. It is a choice that most Americans oppose; teens are well-known for making even less-momentous decisions in impulsive, ill-considered, and risky ways. On a related topic, Dr. Samuel A. Nigro of Case Western Reserve University says, "What happens when you give [adolescents] a car? When you give them alcohol?... No adolescent should be allowed to obtain contraceptives from a school-based clinic or anywhere else unless they have a note from their mother that their room has been properly cleaned for an entire month."[4]

Minors are called minors for a reason. In *Planned Parenthood v. Danforth* (1976), the Supreme Court stated that abortion is "a grave decision, and a girl of tender years, under emotional stress, may be ill-equipped to make it without mature advice and emo-tional support. It seems unlikely that she will obtain adequate counsel and support from the attending physician at an abortion clinic."

A teen may not know how to shop for health care; she may pick a name at random out of the yellow pages, choosing the ad with pretty flowers, or phone around for the cheapest price. The results can be fatal. In Manhattan, thirteen-year-old Dawn

Ravenell died in a secret legal abortion. The doctor, at trial, shrugged: "I've done thirteen-year-olds before. When they're ten, maybe I'll notice."[5]

In St. Louis a fourteen-year-old leapt to her death after a secret abortion. If the mother had been notified, she could have told the clinic that the girl had been hospitalized three times for psychiatric problems.[6] Even in a case of incest, a secret abortion helps the perpetrator more than anyone else. A twelve-year-old was taken to the abortion clinic by her abusive brother; there she received an abortion appointment, a bag of condoms, and a lecture on "protecting herself"—before being sent home again with her brother.[7]

Polls show regularly that a majority of Americans, about 80 percent, approve laws requiring that parents be notified before abortion.[8] Thirty-eight states have some sort of parental involvement law, although in fifteen of those it is not enforced for various reasons. In order for the law to be constitutional, the girl must have the option of notifying someone other than her parents, usually a judge.

Some laws, however, allow the girl to notify any adult—her eighteen-year-old boyfriend, for example—or, most laughably, the abortionist. Laws like these are usually proposed by one wing of the local abortion rights movement in an effort to end-run public demand for notification laws, while another wing vigorously condemns them as restricting choice for what is usually described as "the youngest and most vulnerable."

These laws give the appearance of requiring abortion clinic personnel to inform a girl's parents, but include loopholes allowing them to forego notification if they think the girl is mature enough to decide for herself, or (even if she's obviously immature) if they think that notification is not in her best interest. This wide and beckoning loophole was garnished in Maryland state law with the addenda that the abortionist could face no penalties for not notifying, no matter what his reason, and was protected even from a parent's lawsuit. These loopholes are usually described as "safety valves", and it is obvious that they make one participant in the drama—the one who receives the cash—feel markedly safer.

But the "safety" is purported to be for a girl who, if she knows her parents will be notified about a legal abortion, will instead seek out an illegal one. We are invited to imagine a girl who will be physically abused if her parents learn of her pregnancy. As with the case of the incest victim cited above, the assumption is that it is all right for her to continue living in a generally abusive situation, so long as she escapes abuse for this specific cause. Proponents of these laws do not also ask that teens be able to conceal report cards, speeding tickets, arrests for underage drinking or vandalism, or other likely producers of parental anger. Nor do they require the abortion clinic to report abusive parents to authorities who could protect the girl. The point of giving her a secret abortion seems to be to enable her to go on living with abuse.

Although parental notification laws have been in effect to varying extents for many years, examples of girls having illegal abortions as a result are scarce. The story of Becky Bell is often produced: this seventeen-year-old girl died in Indianapolis of a raging lung infection. Her parents claim that she had someone induce an illegal abortion, in order to conceal her pregnancy and avoid notification.[9]

The story has many problems, however. Bell's autopsy showed infection in the lungs, but none in the reproductive tracts, nor was there any scratching or damage from coathangers or other instruments.[10] A reporter was unable to find anyone—clinic personnel, emergency room workers, school counselors, police—who had heard of an illegal abortionist in town.[11] And the night Becky died the doctor told her mother that he wasn't sure he could save the baby;[12] it was apparently still unaborted at that point. It appears that Becky died, tragically, of the same sort of overwhelming pneumonia that killed Jim Henson.

The sad story of Becky Bell is the only one that opponents of parental involvement laws have been able to muster, and falls far short of proving their case. The Bells, once ubiquitous wherever these laws were being considered, have nearly dropped out of sight in the last two years. Varying packages of parental involvement laws continue to roll through state after state, with high public approval.

One unexpected outcome of these laws indicates that, when necessary, teens can exercise more foresight and responsibility than anticipated. A notification law was in force in Minnesota for six years, during which time the teen abortion rate fell by a quarter, a not-unexpected occurrence. What was unexpected was that the birth rate fell as well. Overall, the pregnancy rate for ten- to seventeen-year-olds decreased 20 percent, while the rate for eighteen- and nineteen-year-olds went down 25.4 percent.[13] Knowing that their parents would find out about a pregnancy one way or the other was too high a price for teens to pay. As Jacqueline Kasun wrote, regarding a similar drop in pregnancies after the passage of the Hyde amendment restricted public funding of abortion, "Faced with a price for a formerly 'free good,' such as an abortion, consumers turn to a less costly substitute—in this case, apparently to the prevention of pregnancy."[14]

Those who counsel pregnant teens need to be aware of the kinds of fears these girls may have, and encourage them to inform their parents as soon as possible. The image of a face-to-face confrontation may be overwhelming; it might be easier for her to write a letter or card, or to phone a parent from a friend's house. Some centers, like the Pregnancy Aid Center in College Park, Maryland, will go with the girl and help her break the news, either at her home or neutral ground such as the local McDonald's.

The biggest surprise in the post-abortion stories heard in Real Choices' listening groups was the frequency with which women said their mothers pressured them to have the abortion. This disrupts expected archetypes and can throw a lasting chill over mother-daughter relationships. Even if the rest of the world and common sense is telling the girl that continuing the pregnancy will be too hard, she has a deep-seated expectation that her mom will somehow favor it.

The mother archetype represents the welcoming of babies, birth, and life. Mom also fills the indispensable role of champion encourager when her daughter enters the childbearing cycle herself. It is wisdom passed down "from mother to daughter" about pregnancy, labor, nursing, and child-rearing that turns the wheel of life one more time. When mom refuses this role and tells her daughter that she is not competent to handle the challenges of pregnancy, it's a serious blow.

But moms push for abortion because they are moms, tigresses defending their young, even against their own grandchildren. When, just a few hours before Becky Bell's death, the doctor told her mother that Becky was pregnant, he added "I'm not sure we're going to be able to save the baby." "I don't care about that baby," retorted Karen Bell. "Save *my* baby."[15]

Not all motives are pure; sometimes parental opposition to abortion is discouragingly self-serving.

Bill was a cheerful man, a middle-aged clergyman who tended toward a conservative stand on "family values;" if asked, he'd say he was against abortion. His son and daughter were in their teens when Mary unexpectedly got pregnant again. There was plenty of good-natured joshing at church about their being too old for such carrying-on. When the baby was born, Bill showed off his new baby daughter with blushing pride.

Pride has two sides. Just months after her baby sister was born, sixteen-year-old Sue told Mary she was pregnant, the result of a fleeting liaison at a party. The two shed some tears and shared some worries. Both felt deeply ambivalent about which course Sue should take. Mary wanted her daughter to improve her academic performance, graduate, and even attend a college; having a baby would diminish those hopes. But Mary also knew that a surprise baby could be a dazzling joy. She could not urge abortion.

They decided to tell Bill. The jovial smile vanished as he descended into glowering silence. At last he spoke. "The most humiliating thing that can happen to a man," he brought out slowly, "is for people to know his wife is cheating on him. The second most embarrassing thing is for his daughter to get knocked up. I can't allow this. You have to have an abortion."

When Sue confided in a friend about this, her face still wore a look of dazed sorrow. "How could he have said that?" she asked forlornly. "He never said anything about what this meant to me, or asked about what I wanted. It was only him. I never knew he would act that way when I was in trouble and needed him. If I can't turn to my dad, who can I turn to?"

She was genuinely undecided about what to do. "I know I can't handle raising a baby. I'm having enough trouble already, just making Cs. But I keep thinking about this girl in my class. She has a real bad reputation; she's pregnant and she doesn't even know who the father is. But she's keeping that baby. She comes to school as pregnant as can be, and if anybody says anything she just stares them down. Really, everybody is starting to say how much they respect her. They know she's going through all this to save her baby's life."

Mary was misty-eyed and uncertain, aching for her daughter. Sue was bewildered. Bill was determined. From the first day he never wavered in his insistence that Sue have an abortion. A friend who had been taken into the family's confidence gently urged Bill to consider his own new baby, and reconsider his grandchild's life. Bill's grin changed instantly to a snarl: "Mind your own damn business."

Sue had an abortion. In a year she graduated and went to junior college in her grandparent's town, eight hundred miles away.

When teens face such parental opposition, what do they need to continue a pregnancy? Many in the listening groups stressed the need for someone to stand by them. If the parents and the baby's father turn away from her, another loving person can step in and give her the reassurance that she can do it and she's not alone.

When the conflict is between a teen and her parents, the most urgent practical need may be for housing. Even if parents are not pushing for abortion, tension levels may be such that time spent apart from each other is best for the relationship.

Maternity homes—institutions where unmarried pregnant women can live together and prepare for motherhood—have dotted the American landscape for over a century. The Florence Crittendom Mission homes first opened 1883, established by a grieving dad in memory of his young daughter. These homes initially embraced a wide range of women in trouble: pregnant women, prostitutes, single mothers, seduced and abandoned girls, and women in danger of falling into one of those categories. The chain of Crittendom homes served over 500,000 women in fifty years.[16]

A modern, exemplary maternity home is the LIGHT House (the acronym stands for "Life Is Given Hope for Tomorrow") in Kansas City, Missouri. When Kansas City Youth for Christ felt a challenge to do something for pregnant women in their community, they responded with brisk efficiency. They put in a lowball bid for a former convent on six acres of land. (Stories are told of LIGHT House's founder, Marilyn Lewis, scooting down the halls of the vast, empty building on roller skates). The organization then raised $1.2 million in two months via a walkathon and a telethon, and paid cash at settlement. The first baby was born to a resident six months later.

"The girls who come here often have no support system at all—their parents, friends, and society in general are all negative," says Donald E. Philgreen, LIGHT House's Medical Director.[17] Being in a group-setting home can give women the feeling of peer support and encouragement they need most. The average age of a resident is eighteen, and parents are usually glad to have the girl go.

"Our experience is that, if she can get to a place where she will have food and shelter for the next six months, it's rare for a parent to disagree. In fact, they tell us to 'Straighten her out,'" Philgreen chuckles. All services are free to the girls. While insurance or Medicare may cover some of the residents' medical costs, over 70 percent of funds come from donations.

Another popular approach is to house girls with individual families, a system usually known as "shepherding homes." Most pregnancy care centers will have a list—usually shorter than they'd like—of families who'll welcome a guest for the duration of her pregnancy. It is a demanding ministry, dealing with adolescents who come with more than their share of worries, and takes a couple that has both big hearts and hard heads.

The Nurturing Network has thoroughly developed the home-shelter concept. Focusing on the needs of those most likely to have an abortion—middle-class, educated women in their early twenties—TNN links resources by phone across the nation, offering medical care, legal aid, assistance with employment and college enrollment, as well as housing.[18]

Couples who wish to provide housing fill out a lengthy, detailed form; girls will be matched as closely as possible with families similar to their own. Many women need the comforting, personal experience they receive in a shepherding home more than the peer support of a group maternity home. TNN lists about seven hundred Nurturing Homes nationwide.

A verse of Scripture often used in pro-life meditations is the poignant line from Psalm 27, "For my mother and my father have forsaken me, but the LORD will take me up." Pro-lifers regularly apply this to the unborn child, whom we are called to defend even when rejected by her parents. But it is just as true of the teenage girl rejected by her parents, and our call to help her is just as urgent.

1. "Don't Panic," the Repair Shop, PO Box 6835, Burbank CA 91510. Many other titles, all well-written and attractively illustrated.

2. .06% of 1,600,000. AGI (Alan Guttmacher Institute) Facts in Brief, March 1993.

3. Liz Jeffries and Rick Edmonds, "Abortion: The Dreaded Complication", *The Philadelphia Inquirer*, August 2, 1981.

4. "Tidbits", *Sisterlife*, Fall 1992.

5. Ray Kerrison, "Horror Tale of Abortion," *New York Post*, January 7, 1991

6. Andre Jackson, "Deliberations Set Today in Abortion-Suicide Suit," *St. Louis Post-Dispatch*, March 1, 1991

7. Mary Jean Doe, "Abortion Makes it Easier for Abuse to Continue," *Baltimore Sun*, March 1, 1994.

8. Teen under 18 should notify a parent: 80% (*Washington Post* poll, 1992); Mostly favor parental consent for girls under 18: 69.4% (Gallup, 1992); Favor one-parent notification for girls under 18: 80% (Wirthlin, 1992). Note that consent is stronger than notification; the two are bracketed by the term "parental involvement."

9. Rochelle Sharpe, "Abortion Law: Fatal Effect?" Gannett News Service, December 1, 1989.

10. Indiana University School of Medicine, Department of Pathology, Autopsy Report #88-0880, Rebecca Suzanne Bell, September 17, 1988.

11. Joe Frolik, "Abortion Debate Shifting," Cleveland *Plain Dealer*, Reiterated in conversation with author, September 7, 1993.

12. Sue Halpern, "Death by 'Criminal Abortion,'" Louisville *Courier Journal*, August 6, 1990.

13. J.L. Rogers et al., "Impact of the Minnesota Parental Notification Law on Abortion and Birth," *American Journal of Public Health*, March 1991.

14. Jacqueline Kasun, "Cutoff of Abortion Funds Doesn't Deliver Welfare Babies," *The Wall Street Journal*, December 30, 1986.

15. Halpern, "Death by 'Criminal Abortion.'"

16. Marvin Olasky, *Abortion Rites* (Wheaton, Ill.: Crossway Books, 1992), 200.

17. Donald E. Philgreen, personal interview with author, May 5, 1994. Philgreen urges prospective residents to phone 816-361-2233 and ask for Hope.

18. The Nurturing Network's phone number is 1-800-TNN-4-MOM.

Listening in Washington, D.C.

he night is black, but light glitters along Wisconsin Avenue, ricocheting off the shiny cars and glass-fronted buildings. The street is ablaze with white light, while pedestrians dart through the maze of lanes and tangled cross-streets. I have been circling the area for a quarter hour trying to find the church where the hearing is to be held. After getting (wrong) directions I finally stumble on it: an extensive pile of red brick, extending far into the block, and utterly dark. In comparison, the McDonald's across the street looks inviting and festive. Fast food seems like a more certain source of life and joy than the hidden, brooding church.

Susan, the local coordinator, has worked untiringly to set up the evening. In the beige meeting room she has set chairs around a central table, with refreshments arranged in the center. Each attendee received materials about the project ahead of time, so after brief preliminaries we can begin.

Elizabeth, a brunette with alert, dark eyes, takes the lead. She has had two abortions; the first, when she was sixteen, took place in 1968. She was in a casual relationship with a boy, and got pregnant the second time she had sex. "I hardly even knew how babies were made," she says, "and the guy was even more immature than me, which is hard to believe. We were both lost people, struggling. I didn't know there was such a thing as abortion; it was my mother who talked to the doctor and set it up.

"I fought her on it, but she was adamant. She had seen other girls have their lives destroyed by gossip as the community turned away from them; they would live up to that image of being a slut—you know, 'I've got the name, I may as well play the game.' My mom said, 'That's not going to happen to you.'"

I ask if she was ambivalent about this course—did some part of her fantasize about having the baby and starting her own family? Elizabeth responds, "Yes, in fact I had a husband all picked out— a former boyfriend." The other participants smile at this. "Of course, he wanted no part of that. He took off running, and I don't think he's been seen since."

Chuckles spread across the group. I realize there's a different tone here than in previous gatherings. These women seem relaxed and confident, and even with such difficult discussion material at hand they laugh comfortably. Four of them, that is. Sandi came in looking pale and subdued; she wears a navy sweatshirt and no makeup. Her smiles come a few seconds late, socially correct but fleeting. Sometimes she lowers her head into her hands. Tonight she will be the last to tell her story.

"The thing I was fighting most was a sense of shame, the image of people shaking their fingers at me—and some people did! If I was going to continue the pregnancy, I would have had to have a support system: someone to tell me that I was a decent, good person, and that I would be taken care of. The Nurturing Network has a whole wonderful program now, and I think if there had been something like that then, I would not have had the abortion.

"But at the time the prospects were pretty grim. You went to St. Anne's Maternity Home, where, according to the scuttlebutt, the nuns kept you in seclusion in sackcloth and ashes for the next eight months. It was a horrible prospect to imagine. If I had had a family situation, away from my own family and school, it might have worked out—if I could have avoided the shame and the stigma of being called a slut."

I ask about the circumstances of her later abortion, at age twenty-four. "The situation was equally dysfunctional; I was in a relationship for three years with a married man who was living with *another* woman. When he said, 'No, I won't stand by you,' I told him good-bye. All my emotions had been bound up in this man. I was so traumatized that I don't know how I could have avoided abortion at that point. I had no spiritual resources. I walked away from the church after my first abortion; I figured God had written me off, since I couldn't live up to the ideal of what a good Catholic girl should be."

We discuss that in some ways it's easier for a teenager to continue a pregnancy than for an adult; a twenty-four-year-old can't tell her boss that she's going to visit a relative in Kansas for a few months. "In fact, at the time of the second abortion I was living with my mother, and I didn't want her to know," says Elizabeth. "That would have made it a *little* awkward."

"With the first one, my mother's attitude was, 'I can't let this happen to you, you're my baby,'" Elizabeth goes on. "How can you fight against that? If she had said, 'Get out of my house,' I could have said, 'OK.' But 'I can't let this happen to you'—how can you fight against that?"

Talk of parents prompts Kelly to begin her story. "I was twenty-two when I got pregnant. I always had before me the example of my older sister, who had a baby out of wedlock. I remembered how terribly hurt and shamed my parents were, so I thought, 'OK, I'll be your best and brightest.'

"I was nineteen weeks pregnant before I realized it; I rationalized that I always had irregular periods, and didn't really admit what was going on. When I did, I was mostly worried that if I told my dad, he would die of a heart attack—not that it would break his heart, but that he would literally die."

I ask if her father is in poor health. "Not really, but he was always a great worrier. He was very kind and loving, but I was afraid this would destroy him. Not so much my mother. To this day they don't know. I often think I could tell my mother, but I don't think she could keep it from my father—and I just couldn't hurt him that way.

"I had been dating the boy for four years, but he was terrified. He didn't want to admit that it was his child." A chorus of "Oh!s"—that really is a painful, and humiliating, rejection. "For my part, I was on that college-career track and didn't think I could handle beginning a family.

"I did go to a pregnancy care center for my pregnancy test. While I was waiting for the results, they showed me photos of aborted fetuses. I guess this was supposed to make me realize what I was doing, but it had the opposite effect—it made me angry, just shut me off like that." She snaps her fingers. "In a way those pictures become a self-fulfilling prophecy."

Picking up on this last phrase, I comment that sometimes the grisly photos coincide with the woman's plummeting self-esteem in a thought like, "Yes, I'm just the sort of person who would do something that terrible."

Elizabeth adds, "And they hadn't even told you about any alternatives yet." She goes on, with exaggerated emphasis, "You're thinking 'I don't have any *choice*, and now you have to tell me that I'm a *murderer* on top of the fact that I'm a *slut* and I have no *choice*." As the group begins to giggle, someone sings out, "And have a nice day." More laughter. "Thank you for sharing that with me," Elizabeth concludes archly, while Bette chimes in, "And I'm probably going to hell, on top of it." Elizabeth finishes, with dignity, "This is, in fact, *not* one of my better days." The tumbling giggles remind me that this is *not* one of my typical groups.

As the laughter subsides I ask if Kelly broke up with the boy after the abortion; she says that the relationship lasted a couple more years, then she went into "a lot of typical post-abortion things, for example promiscuity.

"But I do remember a frantic week—they had told me, 'We

have only one week to do this', because I was so far along. I remember thinking that, if I'm five months along, there's only four months to go, maybe I should stick it out. I was making phone calls to different colleges, trying to find an internship or something so I could finish the pregnancy. It didn't click, and all of a sudden it was like, 'This is the last day, and if we don't do it now, we can't do it at all.'"

The larger the baby, the more difficult the task of getting it out before birth, and the more dangerous to the mother. In the first three months, the fetal child can be pulled to pieces and vacuumed out of the womb with a narrow-gauge plastic tube. (Before the suction aspiration machine became available in the early 1970s, the usual method of cleaning out the uterus was by scraping with a metal blade called a curette; this was Dilation and Curettage, or D & C, far more risky than the newer suction method.)

After the first trimester, the fetus can be killed by injecting a poisonously concentrated salt solution into the womb, after which natural labor will set in to expel the dead child. This lengthy procedure—sometimes lasting twenty-four hours—is hard on the woman, who feels the child thrashing in its chemical-burn bath for an hour or so until it dies, and who may be alone when the napalm-red body of her son or daughter is born. No woman who sees this ever forgets.

A late-pregnancy method that is easier for the woman—but harder for the doctor—is the procedure known as Dilation and Evacuation, or D & E. The woman visits the doctor a couple of days before the procedure to have natural-fiber rods (called laminaria) inserted in the mouth of the womb to slowly open it. When she returns for the procedure she is usually placed under general anesthesia. The doctor then reaches into the womb with forceps and by brute force pries off pieces of the child—a leg, an arm—and reassembles them on a table nearby. When the bloody jigsaw puzzle is complete the procedure is over. Most clinic staff find this process emotionally grueling; at one clinic specializing in

D & E abortion, eight of fifteen staff members reported emotional problems, experiencing the procedure as "destructive and violent."[1]

The risk to the woman is greater, too, as during the process jagged pieces of the fetus can damage the interior of the uterus. More recently a procedure has been developed to avoid such uterine damage. In Dilation and Extraction (D & X) the living fetus's limbs and torso are delivered feet first, up to the head; a tube is inserted into the base of the skull and the brains are suctioned out, killing the child. The doctor who presented this technique at an abortionists' convention said that he had done over seven hundred of these and was pleased with the results; a colleague was using the technique through the ninth month of pregnancy.[2] It is not yet known whether D & X will replace D & E as the late-pregnancy method of choice.

Kelly tells us that her abortion was a D & E. "I didn't have general anesthesia—they did it under local. They dilate your cervix for two days and the third day you have the procedure. So the first two days I was basically in from 8:30 A.M. until 6:00 P.M., as they inserted laminaria, had me wait, brought me back to check that everything was placed properly, and so forth."

"And I thought I went through hell," comments Elizabeth.

"Yes, it was pretty traumatic," Kelly sighs. "They tell you 'Once we start, we can't stop.' And you're thinking—and it's obviously very sick, you're nauseous..." she trails off. I ask Elizabeth if her first abortion was the old-fashioned D & C.

"No, it was the middle of the second trimester, a saline abortion. So I literally went through labor. But I didn't go through," she gestures to Kelly, "what you went through."

"Well, there's no nice way," says Kelly. "We've all heard the graphic details. But if I'd had a saline abortion I think I would have ended my life right then. In my case you're seeing what you're trying to tell yourself you aren't seeing, but you obviously are..."

"I had a really active denial process going there," says

Elizabeth. "It helped that I didn't know what was going to happen. The doctor said, 'We're going to give you an injection of saline.' He didn't say, 'You're going to go into labor and give birth to a dead fetus.' So ignorance was a big help there, as well as denial."

Kelly agrees. "The procedure destroys the things you make up to make it easier on yourself. I actually had this conversation with God, where I said, 'I'm going to send this one back to you, and then when I'm ready to get married, *this same baby's* going to come back.' I really believed that.

"The counselors at the clinic told me, 'Be careful because you're Roman Catholic, and they'll come after you with the Catholic guilt, if not now, five years from now; they're going to try to make you believe that what you've done is wrong, but be strong and rise above it.' The first two years after my abortion, I was probably the strongest pro-choice supporter you could find. It was my way of making sure that what I had done was right. I often wonder about some of the louder pro-choice voices out there, because I remember feeling like that. You have to keep telling everybody that you did the right thing."

"I was a big contributor to Planned Parenthood and NARAL," says Elizabeth. "It was like: this must be the right position, because I have to be okay; if not...I'd have to look at what I've done."

"I went the opposite way," says Bette. "But to start at the beginning, I was nineteen, and I was having problems even admitting that I was having premarital sex. I was having a lot of guilt, and I rationalized it by saying, 'We do love each other; at least I'm not a—slut.'"

Bette gestures unconsciously toward Elizabeth as she says this, who responds by leading the group in an eruption of laughter. "Like Exhibit A over here," Bette continues, provoking more mirth. It takes a minute or so for order to resume.

"I didn't mean it to sound like that, of course," says Bette, wiping the laughter-tears from the corners of her eyes. "I meant that it was a relationship with someone I loved. We stayed together three years after the abortion. In fact, as sick as it sounds, I stayed with him partly because I felt we had a special bond: he was the father of my dead child.

"I also thought, how could anyone else ever love me? If I met another guy and one day had to reveal this secret, he might say 'You did what? You're out the door.' But this guy knows it all and still says he loves me.

"I had very regular periods, right to the day, so when I was late I knew something was up. I panicked; I started telling God, 'I'll do anything, I'll never have sex again, I'll become a nun, I'll give a pint of blood a day, whatever you want.' I took a pregnancy test and when it came back positive I was saying, 'How accurate can those things be? They're only $12.' I just kept clinging to hope.

"My boyfriend and I had decided that we weren't ready to get married. Since I was adopted, I said, 'I think adoption is the way to go.' He said 'I can't live my life knowing my flesh and blood is out there being raised by someone else.' We had a huge fight. I kept saying, 'But I was adopted, I turned out okay; you supposedly love me.' I was really hurt.

"I ended up sitting on my sofa with him and my friend Carrie, while she told me that she had had an abortion, that it wasn't so bad, it didn't hurt, it's over quickly, and so forth. I kept thinking, 'I can't believe this is happening to me; this isn't what I want.' When I went to answer the door, I could hear my boyfriend saying to her, 'Carrie, you've got to talk her into this.' I was furious to think my friends were plotting against me.

"But I was worried about how I could tell my parents. If I had had someone to go with me, just to verbalize the fact that I was pregnant, it would have helped a lot. I know they would have supported me in continuing the pregnancy. But I couldn't bear to tell them I was having sex. I was so embarrassed, and I felt panicky about solving the problem quickly.

"Carrie gave me the number of the doctor who did her abortion, and I called to make an appointment; they told me I was too early, and would have to wait a week. I decided to have a pelvic exam at the University medical clinic to confirm the pregnancy, and the young doctor there really seemed to want to help me. He told me that I'd have to call back next week for the results, then he sat down to talk with me. He gave me brochures about pregnancy and adoption and seemed very kind. But I sat there with my head down, embarrassed and humiliated, thinking, 'I *am* pregnant, I *am* pregnant; he says I need to call next week, but if I'm not pregnant why's he talking to me like this?' As I look back, it seems like he was the only person who really was reaching out to help me. But I just couldn't accept it from him—I felt so embarrassed.

"A week later my boyfriend and I were on our way to the abortion, an hour-long drive to the next city. On the way I actually made my boyfriend stop the car so I could go to a pay phone; I had this urge to call that young doctor and talk to him one more time. I asked for the results; he said, 'Well, it's confidential, you really need to come in.' I think he was just buying time, hoping to talk to me once more. I had to get on with it at this point. I hung up on him and we drove on.

"When I arrived for the abortion I was prepared for nothing. The only counseling I got was that, while the nurse took my blood pressure, she asked, 'Are you sure you want to do this?' and I said 'Yes.' When I first saw the doctor I was already in stirrups; she talked the whole time, saying 'You'll feel some cramping, this'll take a few minutes, are you doing OK,' and I kept thinking, 'I can't believe I'm doing this.'

"As soon as it was over I fell into a very deep depression for several days. I was a total basket case. All I could do was lie on the sofa; I wasn't going to classes or anything, and told my friends I was sick. Then I decided I just had to push it down and get on with my life, so that's when I moved on into repression and denial. But I thought, 'I'm never going to forget I've done this terrible thing. I'll never be who I was before—never be who I thought I was.' I told my boyfriend, 'This goes against everything that I believe,' and my boyfriend said, 'Me too.'

"If just one of those people, my boyfriend or another friend, had said, 'We can get through this, I'll be there for you,' I could have made it. But I feel like they were saying, 'I'll be there for you...if you have the abortion.' No one was extending themselves to be there if I didn't do what they wanted. I became very dependent, too; I wanted someone to take care of me, I wanted someone to make my decisions."

"People say to you, 'You're not ready to have a baby,' and you think, 'They sound so sure—I guess I'm not,'" adds Kelly.

"I knew there was a baby," says Bette. "I told my boyfriend, 'You know this is a baby,' because I was angry at him for pressuring me to do something I didn't want to do. But I never thought about how I could raise it or support it. I just thought, 'I'm pregnant, and this is a baby, and I'm going to kill it.'" She laughs at this brutal summary. "My reasons didn't even touch upon 'How am I going to support the child?' It was more or less 'I'm pregnant, I don't want to be...'

"I hear people say that women abort for convenience," Bette goes on. "It wasn't that, as if the practical worries made pregnancy too inconvenient. It was more a feeling that this is simply not the way life works. I'm single, I'm too young to be married, too young to have children, I have to finish college. Pregnancy is not part of it."

Kelly agrees. "It wasn't so much, 'I don't have the money for a baby.' I was smart enough to know that there were resources out there to help me, financial help or adoption. It was more like, 'I'm just not supposed to be pregnant now.'"

Elizabeth brings up another pressure: the need for secrecy. "Of course with me, it was a married man, living with another woman, and having an affair with me, and probably twelve other women too, for all I know! How could I be pregnant and not tell people who the father is? Someone would find out. We worked in the same place. This had to be a very secret affair."

"All that secrecy. I lived with that," Bette adds. "I thought of it as my skeleton in the closet; I was going to go to the grave with only three people in the whole world knowing—my boyfriend and my two friends. Now practically the whole world knows!" I recall Bette in her role as pro-life organizer, standing at the microphone to tell her story at a vigil for women who died of injuries from legal abortion.

"I felt like no one could know the secret," Bette explains, "because I was so devastated and so ashamed. I felt a conflict because my behavior was totally different from my beliefs. If I had been in better spiritual shape, if I'd felt like I wasn't totally alone and God was up there helping me out, I wouldn't have done it."

I point out that there's a double bind in this situation for people like Bette with strong moral beliefs: if you're noble and good and strong, you certainly don't kill your baby. But if you follow that through and continue the pregnancy, you fear that people will point a finger at you and think you're a slut—not someone noble, good, and strong.

Bette agrees. "So by choosing abortion I could make sure I was the only one who knew that I wasn't noble and good and strong."

Elizabeth adds, "And maybe I can get through my life without anyone else figuring it out."

I ask Sandi and Barbet if they want to say anything about their experiences, and Barbet volunteers right away. "I know I've repressed a lot of this. I was twenty and dating a guy from Germany. I knew I was pregnant even at the moment of conception, and by the time I was two days late I was sure. He'd had a girlfriend in Germany who had had an abortion, so he told me, 'Don't worry, there's nothing to it, just do it as early as you can. It's quick, it's easy, it's over.'

"We came up with every rationalization in the world." Barbet begins a sing-song recital: "Too many people on the planet, we're going to die of starvation. Don't bring an unwanted, unloved child into the world. You can't possibly carry a child for nine months and put it up for adoption. People at pregnancy care centers are religious fanatics. And you don't want to get *fat.*

"To me at that time, having an abortion didn't seem like a big deal," Barbet goes on. "I was hanging around a very liberal college crowd, and all my friends were pro-choice. I was told that it was just a bunch of cells, with less development than some primitive stage of fish. So I made an appointment for two days after Thanksgiving—that's the anniversary. I went without my boyfriend, because he didn't want to miss his flying lesson." She rolls her eyes.

"There was very little pre-abortion counseling. Before I knew it I was on the table. They gave me no sympathy, other than somebody holding my hand, then this loud machine—horrible—then it was over." She ponders this, as if still finding it hard to believe. "We went into the recovery room and some women were vomiting and fainting. I didn't feel so hot either—I was seeing spots in front of my eyes. I went home that night, and my boyfriend had invited friends over for tea and cake! Hours later, after they left, I told him I wouldn't ever, ever, *ever* do that again."

I turn toward the still-silent Sandi, who has ridden out all our lively talk and laughter with a wan smile. "Sandi, do you feel like talking? You don't have to if you don't want to," I offer quietly.

"Yeah, I just, yeah," she says, collecting herself. "It's interesting to listen to other people. I've thought about my abortion a lot. It was when I was a sophomore in college, back in 1982."

As Sandi begins her story, the earlier suggestion of depression and lassitude fades. She appears on the contrary to harbor a calm intelligence and a deliberate quality. Her quietness seems rooted in self-possession.

"I had been raised Catholic, but my father was an atheist. I was the youngest of five girls, and when my sister got pregnant, my dad forced her to have an abortion. This was completely against my mother's beliefs, but she was helpless to fight it. Then another sister got pregnant; this one was pretty strong-willed and she refused to have an abortion, and ended up having the baby.

My dad threw her out of the house, but eventually he came to accept it and they were reconciled.

"I learned from my sisters' mistakes, and was determined to be the one who never did wrong. I had a close relationship with God in high school, but as the years passed I wanted to make decisions in my life without him. I got involved with a guy who I knew wasn't good for me—I got raped, in my opinion—and that threw me into a lot of confusion. One day I decided to start drinking. Pretty soon I was involved with alcohol and guys and thought that was the way to begin a relationship—this is what guys want, this is normal, this is what I'll do.

"So when I was a sophomore in college I visited a friend who was graduating. I had already told him that sex was out of the question, but we went to a party and I got drunk, then somebody gave me something to smoke. After that I don't remember much, but I'm pretty sure that that's when I got pregnant.

"When I found out I was pregnant, I wouldn't consider abortion. But when I told the guy that I planned to go the adoption route, he said, 'How could you even consider it?' He wouldn't be supportive of the pregnancy, but he offered to pay half the cost of the abortion.

"When I think about the decision to have the abortion, I remember several things. One factor, although it wasn't conscious, is that I wanted to do anything I could to hang onto this relationship. Two, I wanted to keep my scholarships and not interrupt my education. Three, my dad had died just a year before in heart surgery. The guy told me, 'If you tell your mom, it could be the last straw.'"

"What a prince!" someone says.

"Another part of my decision was the rationalization that I considered this life we're living to be not all that great. I was thinking that life is pretty tough, and I didn't ask to be put here. So what if this kid skips over this life and goes straight to heaven? That was my thinking, like I was doing it a favor in a way.

"When I went in the recovery room everyone was just bawling their eyes out, but I felt very closed. The next day I was home alone and resting, and I felt like God spoke to me. What I felt he said was that I didn't have the right to make that choice. I did not have the authority to decide to take my child's life. This meant a lot to me at the time, but it didn't change my life. I still was getting into bad relationships with men and drinking. All that changed over time, as God led me on.

"In the last year or so God has been showing me that every single part of my decision has dramatically affected my life since then. The fact that I didn't want my mother to find out has affected my relationship with her and even her relationship with my sisters; she compares them with me and thinks that I'm the daughter who never let her down. She reacts to my other sisters as if she's always disappointed in them, and I've allowed this unrealistic view to continue."

The group listens attentively to Sandi. The woman who initially appeared most damaged, most fragile, is turning out to be a surprising source of stability and insight.

"Another area is with my career. The fact that I didn't want to interrupt my education led to a compulsive need to advance in my work, and I became a nervous wreck about it. I wasn't able to relax until I realized that God was taking care of me.

"The abortion decision also impacted my view of children. I have thirteen nieces and nephews, and I was always very critical of them, always saying, 'Keep them quiet,' 'You're in the way.' Then God said to me, 'You don't have to keep on making that choice.' It was as if I had to keep proving to myself that I had done the right thing in clearing the baby out of my way." This insight is so striking that it causes a hubbub of discussion.

Then Sandi continues her carefully thought out presentation. "The most valuable thing, one that has taken years and years for me to come to realize, has to do with my decision that it was okay to let this kid die, because this life isn't so great anyway.

"I've come to realize that there is tremendous value in this life, that it really is a gift. Coming to that was the toughest part for me, because then I had to admit that I took this great gift away from my child. But I also realized that, even though I did this terrible thing, God loves me; he loved me even before I said, 'I'm sorry, it was wrong.' I'm coming to the realization that I have individual value in God's eyes, that he loves me as a person, and there is a reason he created me."

A few eyes are glistening as Sandi goes on quietly, "There's a lot of other things. One day when I was getting ready for work, God said to me, 'You know, you're a mother.' That was a real healing for me, to get to the point where I could say, 'I can mourn for this child.' Women after abortion don't have anywhere to go to mourn the death. Everything's supposed to be okay, it's supposed to be fine because it's what you needed to do, and there was nothing there in the womb anyway. But God says: 'You're a mother.'

"And after so many years of having wrong relationships with men, I just was unsure about whether I could have a right understanding and the right motives. God said, 'You don't ever have to give yourself to anyone outside my will again.' I still was afraid of attracting men in the same old ways, and God said, 'I am going to give you back your femininity.' I could learn to be a woman all over again, in a healthy way.

"It's also really important to me now to tell my mother about the abortion. It will correct our relationship for her to know that I did let her down. It will do a great deal of good, both between us and in her relationships with her other daughters."

This leads the women to reflect on the people in their own lives who know, or don't know, about the abortion. Should they tell?

Barbet says, in a shaky voice, that she has a daughter who is just 19 months old. "Sometimes I ask myself, am I going to tell her? What if she thinks that I would throw her away too?" As she breaks into real tears, she looks down, saying, "I didn't mean to cry."

"Premarital sex is a secret," says Bette. "The abortion is a secret. You mourn in secret. It's all a big dark secret, and that's not a healthy way to deal with it. When I finally told my parents, they actually took it much better than I expected. But we decided not to tell my grandmothers; it would be too much for them."

Elizabeth adds, "My mother suffered a great deal from my first abortion, and she blames herself for everything that went wrong in my adolescence. If I told her about the second abortion, it would only make her miserable."

"My big fear was in telling my pro-life friends," says Bette. "It seemed like I would be telling them, 'I did what you despise.' But I was surprised at the way people accepted me. They were able to recognize and validate my pain. The pro-choice side can't do that—they have too much need to pretend that it isn't there."

The pressure of time forces us to break up the meeting. Chairs scoot back across the linoleum, and the remains of the snacks go into a bag. The group is in a more reflective mood now, compared with the earlier jocularity. Outside on the sidewalk the dim church looms once more overhead, while the noises of traffic reach us from the busy street one block away. In the vast and vacant parking lot we say our good-byes, hug, and lock ourselves into our metal capsules to follow our solitary paths home.

1. Dr. Warren Hern and Billie Corrigan, of the Boulder, Colorado, Abortion Clinic, in a paper presented to the 1978 Planned Parenthood convention; cited in Liz Jeffries and Rick Edmonds, "Abortion, the Dreaded Complication," *The Philadelphia Inquirer*, August 2, 1981.
2. Diane Gianelli, "Shock-tactic ads target late-term abortion procedure," *American Medical News*, July 5, 1993.

Adoption: Grief and Grace

I n the summer of 1993, Real Choices sent a survey to almost two thousand pregnancy care center directors, asking them to rank-order a list of possible problems a client might report. Respondents were asked to rate each item twice, indicating both how frequently it occurred and how difficult it was to solve.

Surprisingly, the same item rose to the top of both lists: adoption. The problem most frequently encountered when a woman was having difficulty continuing a pregnancy, the center directors said, was that "Adoption appears too difficult (practically or emotionally)." The same entry was rated the hardest problem to solve.

In a sense, of course, the difficulty of adoption is less a problem for the woman than it is for those who are trying to help her. Adoption can resolve many of the problems of unplanned pregnancy positively, permitting the woman to go on with her life plans while bringing the child into a safe and loving harbor. The difficulty lies in helping the woman to consider the possibility, getting past the emotional hurdles and practical worries involved, without leading her to feel that the counselors are only using her to get to her child.

It is no surprise to learn that adopted children enjoy many advantages over single-parented children. They grow up in homes which enjoy a much higher level of income, and their adoptive moms are, on the average, older and better educated. But the birth mothers who choose adoption win, too. Compared to a single mom, a birthmom who relinquishes her child is more likely to get a good education, get a job, and get married. Their salaries on the job are higher, as well. Single moms get the fuzzy end of the lollipop in every way: they are more likely to go on welfare, less likely to ever marry, and more likely to have another unwed pregnancy. When they do, they are more likely to have an abortion[1]— one more reason for pro-lifers to look for ways to help her make a positive choice this time around.

The arguments in favor of adoption are plentiful, and, as a solution to unplanned pregnancies, adoption finds enthusiastic public support. In a 1991 Gallup poll, 82 percent of respondents favored adoption over abortion.[2] An unreleased poll asking similar questions found that pro-adoption responses topped 90 percent, with many respondents spontaneously expressing relief, almost gratitude, to the pollster.

All this goodwill is not necessarily good news for the defenders of abortion. Their case is a difficult sell to begin with, as abortion is not intrinsically appealing. The procedure does not have an upbeat side, and no abortion slogan can be printed on a bumpersticker next to a smiley face. Nora Johnson expressed this problem more frankly than most: "Perhaps *the* major problem of pro-choice public relations is that the image of this procedure we so believe in—of someone scraping or vacuuming out a woman's insides, digging between her legs into her tender sexual passage, blood, gooey tissue, injured fetus all falling out—is esthetically a disaster. Are we really pro *that?*"[3] Ms. Johnson is, in fact, pro that, but she recognizes the P.R. problems.

Read that passage, then picture the children in the DeMoss Foundation's "Life. What a Beautiful Choice" ad campaign, and you see what abortion defenders are up against. This may be why the DeMoss ad series provoked such immediate cries of outrage. "I probably hopped out of the chair and started screaming and pacing. I was very, very angry," was how Debbie McKenny, chair of Pittsburgh NARAL, reacted to the serene and rosy children in the ads.[4]

An interesting element in the cascade of anger directed at the ads was the persistent assumption that they were promoting adoption. Both *Newsweek* and *Glamour* described the ads as pro-adoption, although it was the topic of only one of the series' first flite of three ads. "This confusion between anti-abortion and pro-adoption messages leads one to suspect that the two are inextricably linked in the media's mind as dangerous to those who claim to be 'pro-choice,'" writes Maria McFadden Maffucci.[5]

Some believe that there is a concerted effort afoot in the pro-choice camp to discredit adoption. An article by Marvin Olasky in *National Review* was frankly titled, "The War on Adoption;" in it he cites magazine articles and short stories, TV shows and books that present adoption as dangerous either to the adoptive parents or to the child, and as exploiting the biological mother. In a study of thirty-nine TV programs dealing with adoption, half concerned legal difficulties with the process, with almost a third of the plots featuring an underhanded agency trying to work a "shady deal."[6]

Of course, storytelling depends on conflict, whether in journalism or fiction, and a placid, uneventful adoption story would be as brief as a Hallmark card. Adoption problems were a staple of storytelling long before the abortion wars. Wicked adoptive stepparents have made children miserable from Cinderella to David Copperfield; Miss Hannigan attempted to work an extremely "shady deal" on Little Orphan Annie and Daddy Warbucks. The popular 1956 thriller, *The Bad Seed*, delivered one of the most insidious anti-adoption messages imaginable: that adopted children carry their biological parents' evil traits ineradicably in their genes. Even modern adoption opponents haven't gone that far.

That quibble aside, Olasky builds a stronger case with quotes from pro-choice sources that stress relentlessly the undesirability, unfairness, and unending pain of adoption. Olasky believes that "three strategic needs of the pro-abortion mindset underlie the War on Adoption." The first is the need to paint the child as the property of its mother, so that in disposing of it her emotional needs come first. Second, the superiority of two-parent families must be denied, so secure adoptive couples are presented as exploiters of helpless pregnant women. Third, happy adoption stories are a piercing reminder to a post-abortion woman struggling to stay content with her choice. Unhappy adoption stories, on the other hand, can give her the kind of company that misery loves most.

Olasky's theory gets support from some unlikely quarters. Harvard Law professor Elizabeth Bartholet, a pro-choice single mom by adoption, agrees that "in today's world many who see themselves as progressive attack adoption as an exploitative institution."[7] Adoption is presented as dangerous to children and other living things. Bartholet quotes an article in the *International Journal of Psychoanalysis* which conjures an "'adopted child' pathology, which can flower into narcissistic character disorder, psychotic episodes, delinquency, homosexuality, fantasied or attempted suicide, incest, homicide, fratricide, murder of one or both adoptive parents, and to patricide or matricide."[8] Discovering a pathology this complete is the equivalent, in the psychology biz, of winning the Grand Prix; at conferences, the authors of such articles are hoisted up on their colleagues' shoulders and paraded around the room to toasts of champagne.

Anti-adoption media angles had the increasingly-liberal *New Yorker* thinking as well. A lengthy story on the tragic Jessica DeBoer case in those pages included an examination of "the anti-adoption movement," particularly a "secretive radical organization" called Concerned United Birthparents. CUB wants to see all adoption abolished; adoptive parents would instead become the child's maybe-temporary guardians.[9] A subsequent editorial in the

New Yorker examined media attacks on adoption generally and observed stoutly that "an honorable institution is under attack and deserves better." The editorial concluded with a surprising burst of patriotic fireworks: The U.S. should particularly defend adoption, as we are figuratively a nation of adoptees. "The vast migrations that populated this continent, the uprootings and replantings and recombinings of people and peoples (sometimes in sorrow, sometimes in hope) can be seen as a historical experiment in mass geographical adoption...the power that the heart has over the blood."[10]

The battle over public opinion is to some extent irrelevant within the walls of the pregnancy care center. Ninety per cent of Americans may wish the client would choose adoption, but the number who actually do so is infinitesimal—about 1 percent. The most common reason given for this reluctance is visceral: "I could never give my baby away!" Whereas adoption was once about what is best for baby, it now is about what will meet the birth-mother's immediate emotional needs. When she looks into her quailing heart, adoption just seems too hard.

By the frustrating illogic of that heart, abortion may appear more appealing. The woman seems to face two impossible alternatives: I can't raise this child and I can't stand letting it go—so I'll just erase it. Denial is an attractive response to many difficult situations in life, and abortion serves denial better than adoption or childrearing would. "I couldn't stand not knowing where my baby is," is the way this rationale is sometimes expressed.

Considered literally, this is chilling. The baby does not, in fact, disappear; it is *somewhere*. The woman who fears wondering "where it is" can imagine worse things than another woman's hands braiding her daughter's hair on the first day of kindergarten. One drizzly April day I stood on a gravel roadside in Montgomery County, Maryland, and gazed across fields at an unnaturally-shaped green hill lowering in the distance. My companion, a longtime pro-life activist, said, "I estimate that there are five thousand aborted babies in that landfill."

Sometimes the woman has a more poignant reason for being reluctant to consider adoption: "Nobody would want my baby." When a minority woman says this it has undertones, at least, of "Nobody wants me." One woman, carrying a mixed-race child, was reportedly discouraged from adoption by her abortion clinic counselor: "Face it. Nobody wants a zebra."

This is inaccurate, fortunately. While it is well known that healthy white infants are in great demand, black and mixed-race babies are also adopted with little delay. Popular imagination, which supposes that minority children are unadoptable, is confusing babies with older children in foster care, who can face adoption delays for various reasons. Babies go fairly quickly, though the situation varies around the country, and in some places there may be a wait of a few months. More black adoptive couples, and white couples willing to adopt transracially, are always needed.

Since we are concerned here with helping women in unexpected pregnancies, it is the adoption of babies that concerns us most, and, as mentioned above, babies of all races go fairly quickly. Pregnancy center clients should not fear their babies being rejected. The children who wait for adoption are older kids who for the most part did not enter the system as babies, but fell into it when their biological families came apart due to drugs, incarceration, family violence, or other causes. While it's commonly thought that older kids and special-needs kids "never get adopted," half of all adoptions each year fit those categories.

It is true that 90 percent of the children in foster care will never be adopted. This is because 90 percent of the children in foster care are not *available* to be adopted; the biological parents have not relinquished their parental rights. Foster care is not a baby store where couples can go to pick out the child they like best. For these 90 percent of the kids in the public welfare system, caseworkers are still hoping to reconstitute the biological family, a goal called "family preservation." The reluctance to terminate the rights of even abusive parents can "turn adoptable two-year-olds into ravaged and virtually unadoptable seven-year-olds," says Olasky.[11]

That minority children wait at all is partly due to official resistance to allowing them to be placed in white families. "Racial matching policies," says Bartholet, "represent a coming together of powerful and related ideologies—old-fashioned white racism, modern-day black nationalism, and...'biologism,'" the assumption that adoptive families should be crafted to look like biological families.[12]

The second of those items may be the most powerful. For twenty years, the National Association of Black Social Workers has insisted that "Black children should be placed only with Black families...[we will] work to end this particular form of genocide."[13] In fact, black children raised by white parents have been shown to be well-adjusted, proud of their racial heritage, and comfortable with both whites and blacks generally.[14]

There are roughly 400,000 children in foster care nationwide, with about 38,000 available for adoption. These children wait an average of two and two-thirds years to be adopted; the reasons vary. One is the lack of black adoptive couples: although only 14 percent of all children are black, they make up 38 percent of all children in foster care awaiting adoption. Some social workers will delay these children's adoptions for years, searching for a black couple and turning away whites. Black children in foster homes, bonding with white foster parents, may be taken away if it is suspected that the parents will apply to adopt. The child will be moved to a black foster family, though it may have no interest in adopting.[15] In a notorious 1989 case in Cincinnati, a black child was removed from a white family that offered to adopt him and hastily placed with a black family in upstate New York. There the boy was abused and ultimately killed.[16] This incident spurred Sen. Howard Metzenbaum to sponsor the Multiethnic Adoption Act, which forbids discrimination in adoption placement.

Race is just one item slowing adoption; "special needs"—physical or mental disability, emotional problems, or preservation of a sibling group, for example—is another. Here, again, babies move quickly. The National Down Syndrome Adoption Exchange waiting list averages 100 to 150 couples at any time, all hoping to bring a child with Down Syndrome into their family. There is a similar waiting list for spina bifida babies, and adoptive parents are waiting for terminally ill babies as well, including those with AIDS. Adoption of special-needs children can frequently be assisted by federal and state subsidy programs.

Adoption of special needs babies does not immediately bring to mind the words "Operation Rescue." Yet Operation Rescue National has over the last few years taken on the cause of special needs children with characteristic verve and tenacity. ORN's "National Adoption Project" has produced brochures and a video urging special-needs adoption, and has received phone calls from almost a thousand interested people.

Just over half of all adoptable older children have special needs. When the neediness manifests as emotional problems, perhaps caused by the insecurity and shattered trust of being shuttled through a succession of foster homes, the child may be too emotionally fragile to be adopted. The intimacy of a family home may be too intense for him to bear; he may be unable to relate to others outside a narrow range of fear and aggression. This child may respond best to the firmness and security of a campus situation, living with other same-sex children under the direction of a houseparent, as he learns to trust again.

The hottest debate in the adoption field currently is over so-called "open adoption." Proponents contrast it with the older system, in which a figurative wall stood between biological and adoptive parents. The birth mother would have no knowledge of where or to whom her baby was going; it might even be whisked away from her before she woke up from anesthesia, so that she could not know its gender.

Though it now strikes many as cruel, closed adoption was actually intended to protect the best interest of all parties, including the birthmother. It was assumed that giving up a baby was terribly hard, and the brisker the separation the better: the less she had to remember, the less she would feel haunted.

This was a previous generation's preferred way of resolving separation dilemmas, and not only in the arena of adoption. A fast-forward tour of black-and-white movies shows hundreds of people bravely withholding information in the interest of protecting someone else. A scarlet woman on her deathbed does not reveal to the young man attending her that she is actually his mother; a convalescent wife, noting the creeping blindness that signals her imminent death, bravely waves good-bye to her husband as he leaves on a trip. It was the way they did things then, and the nobility of it all dampened a lot of hankies.

Theories of grief management changed, and so did adoption. Now it is assumed that giving up a baby is terribly hard, and the more gradual the separation the better. The more the biological mother has to remember, the more she will feel reassured.

Open adoption can take many forms. At its minimal end, the birthmother has some say in selecting the adoptive couple, and may even meet them before the birth, though identifying information is withheld. At the other extreme, birthmother and adoptive parents become kitchen-table buddies. In one case, an adoptive mother of three extended her natural ebullience and capacity for nurturing to the children's biological mothers. Two of these birthmoms responded warmly, and came to feel close enough to the adoptive parents to send the dad cards on Father's Day. Sometimes these birthmoms were invited along on family vacations.

Between those two poles lie a range of options. Pregnancy center volunteers are generally grateful for open adoption alternatives; when a client is fearful of "giving up" her baby and "not knowing where it is," openness makes those losses less absolute. Simple reality, too, is that the enormous demand for adoptable babies (forty infertile couples for each one), has created a "sellers' market that puts the pregnant woman in the catbird seat," says Anthony Carsola, a Beverly Hills lawyer who has been involved in over three thousand adoptions. Carsola believes that, given the choice, most birthmothers prefer open adoption.[17]

A brochure from the Southwest Maternity Center/Methodist Mission Home demonstrates this dynamic. It promises birthmothers that "Open adoption means you control the decisions..." while putting in the mouths of adoptive parents, "We want an open adoption because we desperately want a child to love." One party is in control and the other is desperate, a fairly accurate snapshot of the locus of power on the adoption scene today.

Another brochure from the same organization shows a triangle on its cover; the apex is labeled "Birthparents," while "Adoptive Parents" and "Adopted Children" lie along the base. The text describes these as the members of an "Adoption Triad," with particular focus on the adult members of the team. They have a "long-term commitment" to each other and, whether they become close friends or communicate only occasionally ("the closeness of the relationship varies just as our relationships with other members of our families"), it will "always remain an important relationship."

When the brochure defends open adoption on the grounds that "the adoption process will have the greatest impact on the lives of the adopting parents and birthparents," even advocates of the process should feel some hesitation. Aren't we forgetting someone here? Isn't it, in fact, the child who will sustain the greatest life-impact? The flaw in these presentations of open adoption lie in keeping the issue framed as one of adult needs, particularly the emotional needs of the birthmother. Gazing into that mirror, she may well conclude that abortion meets her emotional needs better. This flaw can be fatal.

But, the brochure goes on, open adoption is good for kids, too, because "Adopted children want to know." The standard defense of openness in terms of the child's welfare is that, without this information, adopted children suffer from "genealogical bewilderment."[18] They are "amputees" who will spend their lives searching for the missing part, according to Concerned United Birthparents.[19] (A sub-controversy here is the CUB insistence that biological ties eternally supersede all others, part of the "biologism" that Bartholet sees driving the futile, costly fad for infertility technology—and also undergirding the prejudice in favor of the traditional nuclear family, which she deplores.) The Southwest Maternity Center brochure warns that children of closed adoption carry the "strong suspicion" that "the people who brought them into the world were criminals, or insane."

The genealogically bewildered don't show as much interest in resolving their confusion as their analyzers expect; only 1-2 percent of adult adoptees search for their birthparents.[20] Those who do may discover that their "strong suspicions" are uncomfortably confirmed. "Sacramento Parent" wrote to Ann Landers that she adopted a four-year-old who was a victim of her birthparents' sexual abuse and severe neglect. "Should I tell her that her parents lost three other children to the courts and never bothered to try to get them back?... What is my child going to find if she begins a search for her birthparents? They could be dead from a drug overdose or in jail." Landers counseled Sacramento Parent to tell her daughter everything when the time was right; "the naked truth is always better than the best-dressed lie,"[21] a notion that would have philosophically bewildered our grandparents.

Mary Beth Seader and Bill Pierce of the National Committee for Adoption are often the lone voices arrayed against open adoption. Seader and Pierce acknowledge the grief that birthmothers can feel, but point out that loss is a normal human experience, worked through in stages.[22] When grief is unnaturally protracted and severe, the woman has gotten "stuck" in the process. She may be caught in the "anger phase," furious with herself and others, swept with longing to contact the baby again.

Common sense tells us, Seader and Pierce say, that satisfying that urge will not help her move on in her grief. For all concerned, continued contact keeps the edges of the loss fuzzy and undefined, and the separation process is arrested. Even Carol Anderson, the president of Concerned United Birthparents, acknowledges that open adoption isn't solving the birthmother's problems: "suffering from more ambiguous losses..., these birthparents seem to remain in a frozen, childlike state." Indeed, a 1990 University of Texas study found that birthmothers who made confidential adoption plans resolved their grief more easily than those with open plans.[23] Seader draws an analogy to the effect of receiving a photo every Christmas from the boyfriend who dumped you in high school.

Open adoption doesn't clearly benefit the child, either. Children are the ultra-conservatives of the world, demanding rigid consistency in the way laces are tied and sandwiches are cut. Their need for security is not met by shifting, intermittent relationships of emotional intensity, as we have seen in the day-care and step-parenting dilemmas. A book on the positive effects of open adoption cites the story of Jennifer who, at four and a half, began to vehemently deny to her adoptive mother that she had grown in the womb of her birthmother. The book is "full of stories like Jennifer's" say Seader and Pierce, who wonder what effect it has on children to be constantly reminded of the existence of multiple parents.

Elizabeth Bartholet sees a mixed blessing in the child's sense that her family, with its extra parents, is different. "*Most* children today grow up with a changing cast of characters" due to single parenting, divorce, and remarriage. She goes on, "Freeing ourselves from the traditional model [of the nuclear family] forces us to think about what should be central to the concept of family."[24]

Bartholet argues relatively conservatively that adoptive families are inevitably different from biologic ones and there should be some measure of information sharing, though not of control. Others will broaden the insight to argue adoption rights for singles and gays, just as child custody has been argued, on the grounds of rethinking "the concept of family."

While the pro-life community remains divided on the question of open adoption, it is rapidly uniting on the need to find ways to talk to clients about the adoption alternative. June Ring of the Pro-Life Adoption Network cites a study indicating that in 40 percent of counseling situations adoption is not even mentioned to clients. It may be that the primary question of choosing between life and abortion eclipses the possibility; it may be that counselors are afraid of giving the appearance of grabbing the baby away from the mother. They may also have a murky idea that, if the woman makes an adoption plan and then regrets it, she will come back and sue.

One way to create time to discuss the issue is to schedule a second appointment with the client. Eight out of ten pregnancy center clients don't come back for a follow-up visit. This situation can be markedly improved by asking her, at the end of the first visit, when she would like to come for her next appointment.

A second problem is the counselor's discomfort concerning the extent to which she should be directive. Mary Beth Seader acknowledges that counselors are "in a very difficult position," but reminds them that they would not accept a mere values-clarifying, whatever-you-want-to-do-dear role when the client is leaning toward abortion. Counselors are there to combine "unconditional love" for the client with a "challenge to make appropriate decisions that will help them too."[25]

Seader suggests that counselors examine their own attitudes toward adoption and clear out myths; that they not try to be "adoption counselors," but refer the woman to professionals; and that they look for appropriate opportunities to discuss adoption with every client.

But how to break that ice? June Ring of the Pro-Life Adoption Network has developed a comprehensive seminar and training manual to help pregnancy centers present the adoption option. She advises counselors to beware of overemphasizing the numbers of eager infertile couples; "Adoption is first and foremost for the child, not the infertile couple," says Ring. She also suggests helping the client think objectively, not emotionally, by posing questions in the third person: "Why would someone plan an adoption? Why would someone single parent?"

A set of concise, direct materials to aid counselors has been developed by Marlena Moore and Jackie Stippich of Bethany Christian Services of Maryland. Moore herself is a veteran of two crisis pregnancies—one ending in abortion, one in adoption. "My abortion left me hurt, guilty, and ashamed. My adoption experience was a choice of love, sacrifice, courage, and peace," says Moore.[26]

Too often counselors are silenced by clients' statements that they don't want to consider adoption, and the specific reasons for that reluctance go unexplored. Stippich's "Sample Lead-In Questions" simply call for persistence:

> Client: I'm not interested in adoption.
> Counselor: May I ask, what is it about adoption that makes it seem uninteresting to you?
> Client: I just can't imagine giving a child of mine away.
> Counselor: What part of adoption is hard for you to imagine? (...until you hear it, you will not be able to identify misconceptions/fears of the client, nor will you be able to deal directly with them.)
> Client: I'd rather have an abortion than carry this baby 9 months and give it away.
> Counselor: What is it about adoption that you find unacceptable? Is it the carrying of life for 9 months, or the giving it away?

Moore also criticizes the "Adoption, not Abortion" slogan for seeming to assert the child's interest without explaining that adoption also serves the mother best. "Until we can defend an adoption over abortion for the benefit of the mother as well, our slogan will continue to fall on deaf ears." She advocates explaining to the pregnant woman that adoption will enable her to love her baby as well as take care of herself and follow her own life plan.

Simple persistence pays off. The National Council For Adoption Factsheet cites a 1991 study which showed programs that included discussion of adoption with every client, compared to programs that did not, were seven times more likely to have teens make an adoption plan. When the teen's parents were involved, they were six times more likely to choose adoption. Teens asked to compare adoption with parenting were also six times more likely to choose adoption. (Take heed, however: programs to introduce clients to teen parents made them four times *less* likely to choose adoption.) Resistance to adoption does not run as deep as pregnancy counselors fear. Sometimes all you have to do is ask.

Flannery O'Connor once said that her harrowing short stories were all about the same thing: the action of grace upon a person who is not very well able to bear it. The conundrum here is that sometimes grace is hard, almost unbearable; sometimes it is twined with grief. The points at which God's grace is hard to bear are the points at which receiving that grace requires denying ourselves, dying to self, and taking up a cross. Sheldon Vanauken expressed something like the same idea when he titled his autobiographical account of marriage and widowerhood *A Severe Mercy*.

Opportunities to confront God's severe mercy, his unbearable grace, confront us again and again in the arena of unplanned pregnancy, and the constellation of lives it touches. Adoption brings in another ring of lives, spreading the grief and the grace out further.

An adolescent girl, confronted with pregnancy and planning adoption, faces challenges beyond her years: love and loss, birth pangs and grief pangs, passage from childlessness to pregnancy to childlessness, returned to a life "just like it was before"—except it never will be. It is too much to expect her to bear. Yet she does, and comes through a changed person, if she will permit it, one who knows in her depths the grace that comes with pain.

The woman who counsels her, who pictures her own small daughters sitting in that chair someday, may feel an overwhelming yearning to lift the burden from those narrow, trembling shoulders. There is no way to do so; whatever portion we can help carry, she must bear the greatest weight alone. The hard experience stretches her, and our inability to fix it stretches us, like an arm stretched out on a cross. Walking together through these periods of grief, we learn to bear the scars of grace.

1. National Council For Adoption, *Factsheet on Adoption*, 1993.
2. "Abortion and Moral Beliefs," commissioned by Americans United for Life, released February 28, 1991.
3. Nora Johnson, "Whose Life Is It?", "Hers" column, *The New York Times Magazine*, January 23, 1994.
4. Marvin Olasky, "The War on Adoption," *National Review*, June 7, 1993.
5. Maria McFadden, "The Choice That Pro-Choicers Aren't Pro," *National Review*, June 7, 1993.
6. Olasky, "War on Adoption."
7. Elizabeth Bartholet, *Family Bonds* (Boston: Houghton Mifflin, 1993), xxi.
8. Bartholet, *Family Bonds*, 175.
9. Lucinda Franks, "The War for Baby Clausen," *New Yorker*, March 22, 1993.
10. "Adoption Country," *New Yorker*, May 10, 1993.
11. Olasky, "War on Adoption."
12. Bartholet, *Family Bond*, 93.
13. Ibid., 95.
14. Mona Charen, "Racial Identity Casualties," *Washington Times*, February 22, 1994; Zoe Maxwell, "Walking the Talk," *World*, April 2, 1994.
15. Bartholet, *Family Bonds*, 98.
16. Maxwell, "Walking the Talk."

17. Interview with author, March 5, 1994.
18. Mary Beth Seader and William L. Pierce, "Parent Access After Adoption," *Children and Family Issues*; the popular term was coined in 1952.
19. Lucinda Franks, "Baby Clausen."
20. NCFA *Factsheet*.
21. Ann Landers, "Truth is Best for the Adopted Child," *Los Angeles Times*, November 6, 1991.
22. Seader and Pierce, "Parent Access."
23. Candace Mueller, Mary Beth Seader, and Brenda Destro, "The Adoption Option: a Training Manual for Pregnancy Counselors," submitted to the US Department of Health and Human Services, Office of Adolescent Pregnancy Programs, October 1992.
24. Bartholet, *Family Bonds*, 59, 60.
25. Mary Beth Seader, "A Supportive Environment for Adoption," publication of the National Committee For Adoption.
26. Letter to author, March 31, 1994.

## CHAPTER TEN

Listening in Phoenix

B y December, residents of Phoenix, Arizona, are getting warmed to the local hobby: gloating about their weather to visitors from the North. "So you came from Baltimore, eh?" they ask, with barely suppressed glee. "Bet you already have snow on the ground. Bet you wish you lived here."

At home it is sodden and gray, not yet blanketed by the white-out of snow that covers a multitude of sins. Here the skies are pale blue, the temperature temperate, and light breezes tease the treetops.

That is, whenever they can locate a tree. Viewed from an airplane, the limitless expanse of brown that surrounds this place is stupefying. The city sprawls into the desert like water poured on a tabletop; beyond it, "boundless and bare the lone and level sands stretch far away."

But the main reason I arranged to come to Phoenix in December is that I have visited Phoenix once before—in July.

The local coordinator, a real pro, has brought off the best-attended press conference so far, and arranged for the listening group to be held at her church in the evening. We sit around a folding table on folding chairs in the youth pastor's office, six Phoenix women and me. Marie, who suggests a sturdy Earth Mother in her jeans and thermal knit top, starts us off.

"I was twenty-one when I had my abortion. My husband was going to school and I was home with the two kids; I got pregnant again when Rachel was not yet one year old. When I told Vince he got really upset—he has a pretty controlling personality. He said that only ignorant people have more than two kids. It was the population control idea: Two in, two out.

"I was seeing a Christian therapist for depression, and she told me that I couldn't go through the pregnancy because of my condition. When I said I didn't think abortion was right, she said that was only because of my Catholic upbringing. She told me to listen to my husband.

"So at last I went to the doctor. When he asked me what I wanted to do, I said that my husband wanted an abortion, but the baby...and he interrupted me, saying, 'What have you been reading? It's a *fetus*.' So I scheduled the abortion. I had about a week of waiting, hoping that Vince would turn around and say, 'No, I want this baby!'"

Marie pauses, woeful. "It never took place. He never rushed in and saved me. All the prayers I said—it never happened. It never happened.

"I remember him trying to cheer me up on the way to the abortion. He stopped at an art festival." The circle of women shake their heads in commiseration. "I can remember picking up this vase that was fired with coal; it had black splotches all over it. I bought that thing. Vince said, 'Why did you buy that?' I said, 'This is my soul.' I felt just terrible.

"Finally, on that last stretch of road before the clinic, he turned to me and said, 'Do you think you're smarter than the Supreme Court?'" Here Marie gives a particularly heavy sigh. "That just killed any last maternal instinct that was in me. I thought, how could I be smarter than the Supreme Court?

"I went through it. One of the things that amazed me was

that, when I got there, they would not let Vince come in any further than the front door. I think if he had, it might have made a difference. It was easy for him to push and run, but when it came to doing it, I was by myself.

"The nurse at the clinic said, 'You can have another baby when you're ready.' It was the only time that anyone but me used the word 'baby.' I had a suction abortion, and I can still remember the expression on the nurse's face as she watched."

Marriages break up so frequently after abortion that I am surprised to hear Marie say that she and Vince are still married. The abortion was sixteen years ago.

Carol, the redhead to Marie's left, comments thoughtfully, "It's amazing how something ten or fifteen years ago can still seem like yesterday. I can still feel that pull, feel my stomach cramping."

"How many of you have shared your complete story before?" asks Alice.

"I've shared it a lot," says Marie, "but it took me a long time to be ready. I went through all the rationalizing: the baby wouldn't have lived, I wasn't actually pregnant, all of that. But if you don't share your story and talk about it, your thinking gets messed up," she warns. "When I got pregnant with our next child, I thought, 'Oh, this is the same baby come back.' It was really demented. It was because I never had a chance to talk to anybody about it. Even the therapist didn't talk about it."

"I can relate," says Becky, a wide-eyed beauty of comfortable proportions. "I haven't had any kids at all, just the one abortion, but it's like I've always tried to get something to fill that void the baby left. Sometimes I've wanted to try to get pregnant just to see if I could, but I think that—I know God's not a punishing God, but something would happen. The child would die in a car wreck or something. Payback."

"My third child was really sick," says Marie, "and I thought that was punishment. Not talking about the abortion puts all these weird ideas in your head."

Jane adds, "I had an ectopic pregnancy after the abortion. I thought I would never have kids."

"Has anyone here had more than one abortion?" asks Carol. Heads around the table shake no. "I had four between 1979 and 1981," she goes on. The group is suitably surprised. "Three were with my first husband, who I married at eighteen. When I told him I was pregnant he said, 'There's no way we can have a baby now'—it was inconvenient timing.

"There wasn't a Planned Parenthood in my small town and so I had to drive thirty miles for the abortion. I walked into the clinic and the nurse told me to strip—I don't remember getting a pregnancy test—and they didn't give me anything for pain. I held the nurse's hand like I was going to squeeze it off, feeling that suction.

"The first two abortions were like that; the third time I thought, 'I'm not going through that again.' This time I drove 150 miles by myself to Lubbock, Texas. I did it behind my husband's back because I thought, 'If I tell him I'm pregnant again he'll really beat me up.' That's the kind of man he was, physically abusive, emotionally abusive, pornography, drinking. So I did the third without telling him.

"The kind of counseling I got was limited to, 'Is this pregnancy a problem?' 'Yeah, it's a problem, why else would I be here?' Not very deep. It was easy for me to fall into using abortion as birth control. I was a dancer and thin, so I thought that getting pregnant would ruin my body. Also I just was uninformed about the whole thing. If a counselor had said to me, 'You're eight weeks pregnant, this is what the baby looks like, it has a heartbeat, it is male or female, it would experience pain.' But no, it's 'Give me your $300 and make it cash.'"

Jane asks Carol, "Were you ever afraid after that that you couldn't conceive?"

"Yes," she says, "the first time I got pregnant with my new husband I was so scared I would miscarry. But I went through a lot of healing, and God showed me that he has all those babies.

"Still, when I was in labor and it came time to push, I felt so lethargic. I was thinking, 'How can I give birth to life? The only thing that's passed through my birth canal is death.' Thank God for the pastor's wife who was my coach—she kept saying, 'You're going to push this baby out!'" As Carol smiles, the women begin to chuckle. "I did it! I ripped, and I got hemorrhoids, but I pushed that nine-pound baby out!"

Carol concludes thoughtfully, "During those first pregnancies, I think I would have found myself actually very open to having the baby. Especially with the resources that are available now that weren't then, or were never presented.

"The big deception of the abortion industry is their hiding the fact that they are a money-making business, and they have absolutely no investment in offering alternatives. I just needed someone to have faith in me, to say, 'You *can* be a good mother'— because I thought that by aborting my children I was actually doing them a favor, I was not going to raise my family like I was, raised by alcoholic parents, being sexually molested. If someone had told me, 'There's resources for you, there's financial assistance, you can do it,' if I knew that counselor was going to be there for me, boy, I would have wanted that baby. I did want that baby," she corrects herself. "I just didn't have the resources."

Carol is so insistent that she would have defied her miserable situation to give birth that I want to test the rosy glow of hindsight. "Think about what this was like," I say. "You were living with a husband who was angry and abusive, you were afraid he would beat you up. If you had gone to the best-equipped pregnancy care center there was, could you have gotten what you needed? For example, would you have needed housing? Would you have left your husband to have the baby?"

"Yes, I would have," Carol replies firmly. "That first time, or even the second time I would have."

"I think a lot of women who wind up in this situation are from dysfunctional homes, and suffer from depression or low self-esteem," says Jane, a petite woman in a white cableknit sweater. "I was just fifteen. I thought I was having sex, but I realize now that it was only very heavy petting. I got pregnant anyway.

"My reaction was like it would be if you looked down on your arm and saw a tarantula. Do you think, 'Oh, I'll lift it down carefully, because it's a life.' No, it's panic, 'Get rid of it!'

"I was Catholic and I knew abortion was wrong, but my biggest fear was of getting into trouble with my parents. People had come to school to talk to us against abortion, but I'd only have listened to someone my own age. My parents had told me that premarital sex is wrong, but I'm adopted, so I felt like, 'You're telling me that I am a sin? You wouldn't have a daughter if it wasn't for premarital sex.'

"So I went to the clinic, and they sent me to the government office to get stamps to pay for it. Right after the procedure I was crushed at what I had done. I wrote a letter to my child and gave it to my parents, and that was the beginning of healing for me.

"Now I have three children, and together we pray for this child that died. I believe it was a girl named Sarah. So we pray for Sarah, although my children don't know yet that she was aborted. This whole sex education thing—my parents' generation told us to wait for sex until you were in love. Well, with the hormones and everything, there's times in your monthly cycle when you're in love! So kids need to be taught to use their heads, and to understand what makes a healthy, mutually respectful relationship."

As the moms in the group nod over this insight, childless Becky breaks in a bit nervously. "My situation was a little different. I was fifteen too, and when I found out I was pregnant I kept praying to God that it wasn't true. You talk about choices and alternatives, and I've thought about that a million times. But I was so afraid that, if I lost my parents, I would die. Their abandoning me would be death. I believed that I had to sacrifice my child so I wouldn't lose my parents." Here tears appear on her lashes and her voice is pinched. "They were alcoholics. I never really had a mother—I mothered my mother, and my sisters were 'the babies.' I always took care of the babies, and I had every baby-sitting job in the neighborhood.

"When I found out I was pregnant I ditched school one day and phoned home from a friend's house; I told my mom I needed to talk to her. My dad picked up the extension and right away came around in his patrol car to pick me up. I went up to my room and my mom followed.

"Before this we hadn't talked for a year. I always wanted a mother, but we were in competition; I got a lot of attention from my dad, so she was jealous of me. She came in the room saying, 'What's your problem? What's the matter with you?' Then suddenly she stopped and looked at me and said, 'You're pregnant, aren't you.'

"I just looked at her astonished. She said, 'A mother knows these things.' I told her, 'If you tell Dad, I'll kill you'—I was so afraid he would be disappointed in me. My mom was saying, 'How could you do this to the family, what a disgrace,' and so on. No sympathy there!

"She left the room, then I heard the front door slam, and she said, 'You can come out, your dad's gone.' So I went in the front room and we sat down and watched TV. I was thinking, 'This is crazy, this is totally insane. We're sitting here watching "Wheel of Fortune." Where did my dad go? To get a gun?' Because, another complication here, my boyfriend was Mexican, and my parents were very prejudiced.

"When my dad opened the front door I was so scared. But he just came over to me and gave me a kiss and said, 'I love you.' He said, 'I made an appointment for you to see a counselor at Planned Parenthood this afternoon, and whatever you decide to do we're going to stand by you.'"

Becky grins down at the marred tabletop and shakes her head. "Baloney. They knew exactly what they wanted me to do. 'But your mother and I think that you're not ready to have a child, blah blah blah, but whatever you decide to do.' So I went to Planned Parenthood, and of course they told me exactly what I was supposed to hear. They skipped over that adoption thing pretty quick! They said, you know, 'We're just going to put this little tube up there, and a little vacuum, and it's not going to be that painful...'"

The other women are nodding knowingly. "Liar," one says. "What kind of abortion did you have?" Marie asks. This description sounds like a typical vacuum aspiration abortion, the type done during the first trimester.

"I don't know what it was, but I went in the night before and they did something, and then I went in the next day for the abortion." "They inserted laminaria the night before—put things in your cervix to stretch it?" "Yes," Becky confirms.

This sounds like preparation for something more complicated than a vacuum aspiration procedure; it sounds like preparation for a later abortion. "Did you have a saline injection? You know, where they stick the needle in your stomach?" another woman asks. "I don't know," says Becky, appearing confused, "they put me out for the procedure." The women react in surprise. General anesthesia is also less common in an early abortion.

"How far along were you?" someone else asks. "I think about twelve weeks?" Becky ventures. "It sounds like more than that. This sounds like a later abortion," another woman comments.

At this Becky's face falls. "You see, I don't want to know anything," she says softly. "I didn't allow myself to feel the pain about all this until a couple of years ago. I didn't think I had the right to grieve because, after all, the abortion was my choice. But I spent those fifteen years trying to pay myself back, with drugs, alcohol, you name it.

"I had been clean and sober for four years when I had an emotional breakdown—and it was the anniversary of the abortion! Hello! So I ended up in a treatment center, where the therapist kept telling me that I needed to talk about my child. I fought that, and got worse and worse. Eventually I got into a healing group at church, and they suggested I name my child. I named her Crystal."

Marie says, "I had one tubal and six miscarriages, and I named them all."

Alice has said little so far, but she jumps in at this point. "I thought I'd never have children after the abortion; I thought, 'This will be it, I've ruined my body, and it's my just punishment.' But eventually I did get pregnant and now we have two kids."

Alice goes on. "That's my second marriage; it was in the first marriage that I had the abortion. I was a feminist in college and I didn't have much time for men. Looking back, I think I hurt a lot of people, because I was going to be it and make it in a man's world. I was going to be a doctor.

"So when I got married I was on a low-dose birth control pill for about a year. When I noticed I was gaining weight, I went to my old family doctor for a pregnancy test, and it was negative. Then a month later, when I was *really* gaining weight, I went back, and it was negative again. By the time I figured out that I was pregnant I was too far along, and would have to go out of state for the abortion.

"My husband said, 'Don't worry about it; I've been through this before and it's no big deal.' That didn't sit well with me, but I let him make all the phone calls and set up the appointment. I just didn't feel right about it. Looking back now I can see that was the turning point of our relationship. That very month he started being unfaithful to me. Then soon afterwards we divorced.

"Since we had to go up to the next state, my husband turned it into a vacation. See things and have your abortion and shop! We stayed in this real sexy hotel with mirrors on the ceiling and everything. The contrast was so weird.

"Then going into the clinic," Alice goes on, shaking her head. "That hollow, hollow feeling in the pit of your stomach. I didn't want to look anyone in the eye. All the girls sitting around like statues, trying to talk. The sound of that stupid machine. I'm sure that I had a suction abortion; I was pretty far along, three or four months. I don't remember getting anything for pain. I was crying out—"

"'Be quiet, be quiet,'" Carol whispers, remembering.

"The doctor was rushing, and it seemed like he was tearing

me apart. Afterwards I felt so weak. I think the weakness comes not just from the physical but from the emotional ordeal. In the recovery room the other girls looked white as sheets, and I thought, 'I must look just as pale.' I just felt ugly, having to sit there and wait for a half-hour before we could go.

"Then it was back on vacation! We never talked about it. I guess it was denial; I just pushed it back in my mind. I had been through embryology and knew all the stages; I knew the miracles that come together to make a skull or eyeballs. I have never told my parents and probably never will; I don't think they would ever understand."

Nell is the last woman here to tell her story, and she tells it briefly. "I had two; the first was when I was seventeen. I was raised in a very dysfunctional home, and my greatest fear was of my boyfriend leaving me. After the abortion we got married—in fact, I'm going through a divorce with him now. We never, ever talked about it. I got an infection and an ovarian cyst and had to have surgery afterwards.

"Then, about a year later I had another abortion. They never explained the procedure or talked about alternatives. The first time I was so sedated I didn't remember a thing, but with the second one I kept waking up; I was in a hall with a lot of girls on gurneys and they were wheeling them in and out, in and out. Then I woke up in the room and I knew I'd had the abortion, because I saw the tube and the jar and the baby. Talk about feeling empty inside. The second one was worse than the first.

"I have endometriosis now. I blame this on the abortion; I don't know how clean it was there, the instruments and everything. But I just couldn't forget all those women lying there, in and out."

"Like an assembly line," says Alice.

"I have two children now," Nell concludes.

"Having an unplanned pregnancy is not an unbearable burden," says Carol. "It's a crisis. It's a time of stress, because it's something you didn't expect, like your car breaking down. But it's not a burden, it's a baby. It's alive."

"I am adopted and I feel bad because you think I'd know that an unplanned pregnancy can turn out well. What better example than me?" says Jane. "My mom wasn't married. My father told her to get an abortion, and she said no. She had the guts to stick around and have me; I turn around and have an abortion. You're in such a state of shock you can't think clearly."

"It seems to me that we've lost the idea of children being a blessing," says Carol, returning to her theme. "My grandmother lived on a cotton farm; she had five kids, and she had them all at home. It was beans and cornbread, every day, and a dirt floor. When she got pregnant that fifth time, some people told her they would set her up with an abortionist, but she said, 'No way.' And that fifth child turned out to be the biggest blessing to her."

Jane adds, "Well, you know, society today tells you that if you have a child you have to have that matching crib and car seat and so forth. It's just consumerism."

But Becky takes a more thoughtful turn. "I know that, at the time I had the abortion, I didn't value my own life. How could I value another person's life? I didn't have a relationship with Jesus Christ; it was sex, drugs, and rock 'n' roll. He sure didn't fit in with that."

"The cases like that are hard," says Carol, "but it's almost harder to counsel a woman when there isn't a crisis. You start to probe into it and find out that, well, she can afford the baby. What's really the issue here is an insensitivity to the fact that this is life. You show her pictures of fetal development and ask 'What do you think?'—and you get a blank stare."

Becky recalls her own resistance. "It used to be that anything pro-life just made me furious. I remember one time driving behind a woman with a pro-life bumper-sticker. I just got so angry, I was thinking, 'You fat cow, why would anyone want to have sex with you?'" The women around the table whoop with laughter; the church's parking lot sports plenty of pro-life bumperstickers tonight.

"I'm serious! I'm totally serious!" Becky protests with a grin, "and of course I have my own armor of fat." Even in a sweatshirt, with hair falling tousled from a topknot, Becky's generous form looks more voluptuous than blubbery. "But I had so much resentment. All my growing-up, it seemed like having a baby was presented as just another pain. There was never joy when someone was pregnant—it was almost like a duty thing."

"Well, you had all the old women sitting around talking about their labor and births, all the pain, how much weight they gained..." Marie recalls.

"Look at me now!" Carol sings out in a Granny-Clampett voice. "My breasts used to be so firm, and now they're down to here! I can throw 'em over my shoulder! And the stretch marks! I used to have a nice figure but now I have this belly!"

This out-of-bounds outburst brings on rolling laughter. As it subsides, Carol grows more serious. "Talk about getting angry after abortion—by the time I had my fourth one I was like, 'okay, now I'm *really* angry.' I was out to really hurt men, and got very involved with feminist issues, feminist spirituality. It was funny how we said God had to be a she, but never said the Devil was a she!"

"I'm just coming off of that," says Becky. "It's been a long, hard process. Men and dating—I just don't do relationships. People ask, 'Do you have anyone special in your life?' I say, 'Well, there's my TV...' Because, after the abortion, I was always so terrified that I would get pregnant and lose the guy. Soon after the abortion my family moved to Tucson. One day I got a phone call from my old best friend and she sounded upset. It turned out that the guy who had gotten me pregnant got another girl pregnant. But he *married* her."

We discuss how painful this rejection was for Becky, but also what the process may have been like for the boy. Perhaps he, too, was so hurt by the experience of abortion that he swore he would never do that again. The grief that the fathers of aborted children feel is even more invisible than that of abortive moms.

"Vince was in denial a long time," says Marie. "His healing came when he realized that our baby was thrown away in a garbage can. Remember that case a few years ago, when they found all those plastic garbage bags full of fetuses? He was reading a story about it in the paper and he just started to cry. The kids were coming up to him saying, 'Daddy, what's wrong?' and all he could do was cry.

"So he was picketing outside an abortion clinic a week or two later..."

"A week or two!" someone interrupts.

"When Vince makes a decision, he makes a decision!" Marie smiles. "He saw someone he knew from work going in, and he stopped him and said, 'I put my wife through hell with this. Are you going to do the same thing?' They turned around right then. Later he thanked Vince; he said that they really wanted the baby but just needed someone to help them stop and think about what they were doing."

Becky says, "Before, when I was pro-abortion, I really wanted other people to have abortions too. I supported another family member through an abortion; I was like, 'Oh yeah! I'll take you!' It was like I was still trying to make mine okay. I didn't care about her or her baby or anything else—I was just justifying my abortion."

I return to my original question: What would it have taken for you to have chosen life?

"If Vince had seen an ultrasound of the baby, if someone could have educated him about it. But he didn't want to be educated," says Marie.

Carol says, "If I had some encouragement from a caring person, someone who could have said, 'You're okay, you can be a decent parent.' I needed facts about my body, about everything— I was in total ignorance."

"I would have needed a place to stay," says Alice. "That would have been an important part, because I couldn't stay with my husband. There may have been such places available, but I didn't have the strength to look for them."

"Adoption would have been out of the question," Becky insists. "I was way too selfish and too self centered. I don't know that I could have given up my baby. Thinking it wasn't a baby, and letting it get killed, was so much easier. Maybe if I had seen the stages of fetal development, and if someone had told me, 'We will not leave you alone, you'll have support 100 percent.' My major fear was abandonment, that I was going to be cut off."

Becky concludes, "So many times people have said, 'Well, without the abortion, you wouldn't have had your career, you wouldn't have had this, you wouldn't have had that'—well, so what? I look at this stuff I have, and you know it doesn't fill that void."

"If you could have had a shepherding home, a nice family to live with, the medical bills handled..." suggests Carol.

"Yes, yes," Becky nods.

"A lot of times we find the shepherding home is better, more healthy and loving, than the home the girl comes out of," Carol adds.

"Knowing now how much kids love you," says Alice reflectively. "It's the coolest thing in the world. You can try to describe it to someone who doesn't have children, but you could never really explain it—how much a child loves you, and what a sense of purpose that gives you. It's so much more than I ever imagined. If someone could have shared that with me, when I was thinking about having the abortion, it might have gotten into my brain."

The night is growing late, and these words set most of the participants thinking about their little ones at home. In our discussion tonight we have resurrected the ghosts of aborted children, and their shades have haunted us through many words of regret. But the siblings of these ghosts are real, hearts thumping with life, shouting now in that final blaze of bedtime energy, splashing in the tub and scampering down the hall. It seems good to close now and let these moms try to beat the sandman home for a goodnight kiss.

Becky lingers as the others leave. We share a few words about men and dating; how can she learn to trust again? Is it a matter of just diving in and taking that chance?

As she departs, I think about how her story seems the most unfinished of all the tales tonight. I wonder, when she enters her empty apartment and snaps on the TV, if the screen will bloom with lovers embracing. They will not be moms and dads passing a hug over the toddlers' heads. Instead the glass will glow blue with a glittery lie: young singles passing a steamy night in the land where no one gets sick or pregnant, no babies go out in the trash, and no teenager with wide, beautiful eyes gets her heart frozen for the next twenty years.

SCHOOL AND CAREER:
Making it Work

W hen pregnancy care center directors were asked which problems clients reported most often, two of the top five items had to do with conflicts at school or on the job. Problems arising after the baby's birth were listed slightly more frequently than those present during pregnancy. For the sake of chronology, however, we'll look first at how pregnancy itself impacts a woman's school or job situation.

Public high schools (and even, in some cities, junior highs) have become accustomed to pregnant girls in the classroom. At one point in history, the occasional girl who got pregnant might have been tutored at home; now she is usually mainstreamed, probably because the ranks have grown so dramatically. In Baltimore, an entire school is set apart for pregnant girls, with an average student population of three hundred.

At Christian schools the story may be different. These institutions face a tough riddle: how to support and encourage the girl in her decision to choose life, without appearing to condone premarital sex? One impulse is to call her "very brave" in light of the tough road that lies ahead; another is to flee any appearance of normalizing, or worse "heroicizing," sinful behavior. Also, what about the boy? If he is attending the same school, will he share the public shame the girl feels? Or might this backfire, highlighting him among all the boys as the stud that scored?

For these reasons, girls in Christian schools may feel unusual pressure to hide the problem by aborting. Not just their schools, but their entire environment—parents, church, youth group— may be scandalized by the pregnancy. Among all women having abortions nationwide, one in six says that she is an evangelical or born-again Christian.[1]

The college situation differs slightly. On secular campuses, sexual activity has become less of a scandal than virginity, so pregnancy is not seen as shameful. It is, however, seen as stupid. A student at an Ivy League college told the author that the campus health center refers about fifty women every year for abortions; yet in the previous five years the number of students who continued their pregnancies totaled zero.

Mary Cunningham Agee founded her organization, The Nurturing Network, specifically to help the woman most at risk for abortion: one who is in her late teens to early twenties, with a middle-class background, and planning a career. (Despite the image of clinics crowded with barely adolescent girls, 89 percent of aborting women are age eighteen or older.)[2] These women told Agee that the pressure they faced in their situation was of a social, not material nature. The woman's college was not threatening to expel her for pregnancy, but "everybody" was telling her she should have an abortion. Over four hundred colleges participate in The Nurturing Network, offering the student an alternative campus for the duration of the pregnancy. She can be sitting in a new classroom within three weeks.

The situation for a pregnant woman on the job is somewhat more difficult. A pregnant student can usually, with some finagling, take a year off with little harm done. (College scholarships, particularly for athletics, can complicate this.) But a pregnant employee cannot tell her boss she's going to stay with Aunt Minnie for a few months. Agee's Network includes over five hundred employers who are willing to provide meaningful employment for the woman who needs a fresh environment to complete her pregnancy. All The Nurturing Network's services, which include housing with families and medical and legal resources as well, are free (see Appendix E).

It is illegal for a boss to fire a woman because she is pregnant; nevertheless it is not impossible for him to do so, by finding fault with her punctuality or some other aspect of her work. "We offer legal recourse in those situations, but the woman usually doesn't want to take it," says Terry Weaver, president of USA Birthright.[3] Such suits can succeed; Margaret Bonnell was awarded $84,000 by a Tampa jury that decided her boss fired her after she refused to have an abortion.[4]

The problems that pregnancy causes in school and job situations appear to be somewhat vague and occasional, and chiefly social in nature. The power of social pressure should not be underestimated, but it is a general human constant, not elicited by the specific obligations of school or job.

That picture turns upside down once the baby is born. The headaches and heartaches of raising a child while continuing full-time work or schooling outside the home are extraordinary, and have been selling magazines and filling air time for over twenty years.

Recently, however, a revolution has begun to brew. For twenty years, only about 30 percent of mothers said that, if financial circumstances permitted, they would quit their jobs and stay home with their kids. In 1989, the figure had grown to 38 percent. By 1991, it had leapt to 56 percent.[5] The fact that mothers love and long for their kids was not one that could be suppressed forever.

If there is a recurrent flaw in feminist ideology, it has been the tendency to assume that whatever men had was what women wanted, a tendency to be deaf to unique feminine needs. The sexual revolution was one such example. Feminist doctrine scoffed at the notion that women wanted commitment in return for sex, and now does not know what to do with the male tendency toward sexual opportunism. Women used to be taught to expect that men's sexual impulses were different from their own, and schooled in tough-minded resistance to seduction. Today's victims of unisex sexuality can do little more than cry a surprised "date rape!" after the fact.

That codes deeply written in our genes should disobey feminist doctrine never fails to surprise movement leaders. Maggie Gallagher describes the disappointment of female *Washington Post* reporters when they discovered that male colleagues had enjoyed a stripper at a stag party: "Men were behaving like men when they had *promised* to behave like people."[6]

The feminist movement made a similar mistake in assuming that women would gladly place careers ahead of children. The movement grew from a larger counter culture that, ironically, rejected careerism and materialistic success. Through the late sixties, the life of the Man in the Gray Flannel Suit was described as one of "quiet desperation"—a "rat race." Groovy Aquarians wanted no part of it, and early feminism was marked by sartorial choices (bralessness, hairy legs) which did not lend themselves to a successful power-suit-and-pearls image.

Somewhere in the early seventies this was reversed. Feminism broke from the gentle-people-with-flowers-in-their-hair mold and began pursuing power. If men want it, women must want it too. The world of office politics, martini lunches, ulcers, and early heart attacks was a wonderland from which women had been excluded too long. One feminist of the era proclaimed that a paycheck was more fulfilling than an orgasm.

Another expected advantage to entering the workforce was thought to be escape from the burdens of child care. It was presumed by young, mostly childless feminists that childrearing was doltish work, mind-numbingly dull, and better turned over to those who were paid to endure it. In contrast, a career offered multiple rewards and fulfillment.

One problem with this scenario was a peculiar blindness

brought on by its elitist roots. Most women—and most men—don't have careers. They have jobs. A job does not fill your life with meaning and tell you who you are; a job just gives you the financial ability to do the things that do so in the scraps of time left over. A celebrated feminist writer, living childless in Manhattan and preaching the redemptive splendor of a career, was having a very different life from the teenage single mom who rolled her cilantro over the checkout laser beam each week.

The feminist writer loves her job. The checkout girl may or may not love her job, but she loves her baby with an intensity that surprises and almost frightens her. Her passion for the baby's father never led to thoughts that, without hesitation, she would die to save his life; this is a love more vast and imperious than she ever expected to feel. Somewhere at the end of her checkout line a baby lets out a wail and she feels her breasts respond with the aching, plummeting release of milk. Her own baby may be crying now in his box on the crib-wall at Teeny Care. He may have been crying quite a while.

The children of the power-suit feminists were raised to want to have it all; these are now twenty- to twenty-four-year-old new parents, and they are beating it back to the homefront, eager to raise their own kids. "My mother worked; my husband's mother worked; we want our child to have more parental guidance at home," says one Generation X'er. "The two-paycheck family is on the decline. The traditional one-paycheck family is now the fastest-growing household unit," reports the business and financial weekly *Barrons*. Mothers twenty-five to thirty-four are returning to the home at a slower pace, and even older women, "those hard-core careerists," are slowing their workforce participation. But it is the parents in their early twenties who are leading the charge.[7]

Says William Mattox of the Family Research Council, "In some ways, this group of young men and women feel cheated. They believe their parents weren't as available to them as they should have been. In fact, in one study 62 percent said that they intend to spend more time with their children than their parents did with them."[8]

Only a few years ago these high school students were parroting back the supermom myth. One girl told sociologist Ruth Sidel: "I want to be smart. I want to be somebody. I want to make money. I want to be a successful lawyer, but my personal life comes first. I want to be a lovely wife, do my husband's shirts, take Chinese cooking lessons, and have two children. I want my children to be two angels and I want to have a great relationship with my husband. I want to be thin and gorgeous and have a spectacular Bloomingdale's wardrobe. I want to have a briefcase in my hands. I want to look good and feel good and be happy in what I'm doing. Happiness comes first."[9]

Sidel says that girls' responses to her "What do you want to do when you grow up?" question were so formulaic, so identical to the above, that it reminded her of the chanting statements of loyalty and devotion yielded by young Chinese in the throes of their Revolution.

When women choose to stay home—especially women who leave the workforce to do so—they provoke bitter reactions from women who choose to work outside the home. Since most professional female journalists fall into the latter category, media treatment of at-home moms has not always been kind. Alecia Swasy, in a *Wall Street Journal* article, described the surge in full-time motherhood as "downright chic," "fashionable...because it is a luxury that so few families can afford—the equivalent of, say, a BMW a decade ago." Swasy sympathizes with working moms who feel "the pressure to be 'maternally correct.'"[10] This article led, predictably, to another outbreak of shelling in what is usually termed "the Mommy Wars," bitter and inconclusive exchanges between employed and home-based moms.

One way to deal with the conflict between career and child-rearing is to forego children. One study showed that 90 percent of male business executives had children by age forty; the figure for female executives was 35 percent.[11] But childlessness takes its own toll. A Canadian study that examined 1123 women in the professions of medicine, law, engineering, and accounting found that levels of psychological well-being were highest for married mothers, lower for married childless women, and lowest of all for single women without children. Nor were childless women earning more. "Childless women don't really get much out of giving up having children," said researcher Ethel Roskies.[12]

Do women with children get much out of giving up being at home? There's an assumption that the mother's second income is vital; without it the family cannot get by. But a sizable proportion of families break that expectation every day. Of all married women with children under the age of six, 41 percent are outside the paid labor force. Women who are paid for even one hour's work a week are not represented in that figure.[13]

Many women who are employed outside the home are shocked to discover that, when taxes and work-related expenses are deducted, they're working for less than minimum wage. Jonathan Pond of Financial Planning Information, Inc. invites us to imagine a wife's income of $25,000.[14] Federal, state, local, and social security taxes take about 40 percent off the top, knocking us down to $15,000 at one blow. At $150 per week, child care expenses cut that figure in half. (In Baltimore, child care for two children takes a bigger bite out of a median income than housing.)[15] Commuting, clothing, and meal expenses can deduct another $2500. At the end of the year, then, her full-time job has netted the family $5,000.

"The rule of thumb is 20 percent ," says Pond. "You can pretty well assume that, for salaries that go as high as the $60,000 range, about 20 percent will be left over." One woman had told him, "What you are telling me is that, at the end of the day I have gone absolutely nuts and am exhausted and all I have is $20 to show for it?"

Fortunately for the Internal Revenue Service, on paper the employed mother's salary looks enticing indeed. The median income for two-earner families is $45,266, and for single-earner married couples it's $28,747.[16] For some families, that ephemeral extra income is just what they need to be boosted into a higher tax bracket.

Many reformers recommend tax relief as the best way to help all families. Proposals are made regularly to raise the tax exemption for kids, many citing the startling fact that, if the 1948 per-child exemption of $600 had kept pace with income growth, it would stand at over $8000 today. The 1948 family paid 2 percent of its income in taxes; the 1989 family paid 24 percent .[17]

The $16,500 difference in on-paper income between one- and two-earner families would also appear to debunk the idea that a stay-at-home mom is an ornament displayed to flaunt a family's wealth. Far from tooling around in a BMW, the stay-at-home mom is likely to drive an older car, live in a smaller home, and celebrate with pizza, not steaks. She is also likely to spend much more time with her children, the whole point of the exercise. The amount of time parents spend with their children has dropped 40 percent since 1965.[18] In that area, if no other, stay-at-home moms are trying to "turn back the clock."

There's another fallacy at work here, that of categories. We tend to imagine two entrenched camps glaring at each other across the barricades: working moms and non-working moms. The truth is that women scamper back and forth across the line all the time, sometimes sitting down for a picnic in the middle.

A woman can be in her home raising children "full-time" and still be earning varying levels of income. She can be self-employed, doing traditional "women's work": typing, making quilts, or baking bagels. Or she may bring home professional skills that previously earned an income in an office, establishing herself as boss of a home-based business.

Even if she opts to forego earnings for awhile, the childrearing years don't last forever. She will not need to spend her day caring for her children when they are twenty years old. Her life may "sequence" naturally, as she prepares for a career and is employed before parenthood, raises children, then returns to work when she feels the kids are old enough to spare her. Those years are irreplaceable in children's lives, and even if mom gives fifteen years to childrearing between the ages twenty and sixty-five, thirty years still remain for a career.

There are a number of ways for women to be employed, not just self-employed, while her children are young. The least preferred option is traditional nine-to-five office work with the children in day care. The Child Care Employee Project of 1989 found that children in care centers spent a third to a half of their time "wandering aimlessly."[19] Are home-based child care services, or care by relatives, any better? A study by the Families and Work Institute found that only 9 percent of these caregiving situations could be rated as "good." Fifty-six percent were described as "at best, custodial," while 35 percent were actively harmful to children's development.[20]

"A Search for Child Care—One Mother's Story" is an essential essay on the subject, written by Linda Burton, founder of the group Mothers at Home. When she had her first child at the age of thirty-three, Burton was a professional fund-raiser for a public-interest law firm. After the birth she took a job as a writer for a public TV station, and began a quest for child care that was eventually to consume two years.

An initial decision to have a nanny in the home brought candidates who were too expensive, too under-qualified, and too transient. Day care in other mothers' homes was similarly disappointing; the care provided was of uneven, occasionally horrifying quality. Even the best provider would be nature-bound to love her own children best; Burton's child would grow up feeling like the kid "mom" loves less.

Lastly, Burton turned to institutional day care, where she found "under-paid, under-educated, and under-interested" personnel. The best directors at the best centers pleaded with her not to place her children there. Burton reluctantly concluded that "it is impossible to have quality controls over the capacity of one human being to love and care for another." She and her friends had been telling each other that their minds were too good to waste raising kids; now she began to ask whether she really wanted her kids raised by minds of lesser caliber.

"My carefully worded advertisements for child care literally came back to haunt me," Burton writes. "I was looking for someone 'loving, tender, reliable, responsible, nurturing, intelligent, and resourceful.' I had wanted someone with a driver's license, good English, a sense of fun, and an alert, lively manner. I wanted someone who would encourage my children's creativity, take them on interesting outings, answer all their little questions, and rock them to sleep. I wanted someone who would be a 'part of the family.'

"Slowly, painfully, after really thinking about what I wanted for my children and rewriting advertisement after advertisement, I came to the stunning realization that the person I was looking for was right under my nose. I had been desperately trying to hire me."[21]

These thoughts may seem a long way from the frightened girl sitting in the client's chair at the pregnancy care center. Can she really opt to stay home with her child? Only if, to return to an earlier theme, she marries the baby's father, a choice that should be carefully weighed. Full-time at-home mothering requires a full-time husband and father to be economically viable.

Failing that, she should be encouraged to consider placing the child for adoption. Single parenting can be a disaster; to choose it is to choose hardship for herself and problems for her children for decades to come.

A great many women will still choose single parenting. Few of them will be able to earn enough as self-employed, home-based workers to support their small families. Some pregnancy care centers run job-training programs; others are able to connect women with actual jobs through sympathetic employers. The Rockville (Maryland) Pregnancy Center does both: a "Computer Moms" program trains clients in word processing and spreadsheet software, then a temporary-placement agency sends her to her first job. The center even stocks a closet of "career woman" clothing so that, as center director Gail Tierney says, "When she goes for her interview, nobody has to know she's poor."

There is a middle ground between full-time work outside the home and unemployment; it's a type of work usually termed "flexible." Flexible work varies widely. It can mean "flextime," wherein employees have some leeway in determining when to begin and end their workdays. Jobs described as having "shortened hours" are salaried professional positions without the stigma of the term "part-time." "Job-sharing" is a variant on this, whereby two people share one full-time position. A "compressed work week" might mean, for example, covering forty hours in four ten-hour days.

The most intriguing, and one of the fastest-growing, categories of flexible work is variously called "telecommuting," "telework," "flexiplace," or most plainly "work-from-home." It is, just as the last term hints, employment which allows the worker to fulfill at least part of her duties from home. The advantages are manifold: less commuting, less spent on office clothing, less wear-and-tear on the employee generally. Many find they can work more creatively from home as well. Estimates of Americans doing some or all of their work from home range from 2.6 to 7.6 million.[22]

Whereas the industrial revolution removed dad from the home, and the feminist movement tried to remove mom as well, the telework revolution may enable both parents to return and earn a living in the midst of childrearing. It suggests a return to the cottage workshop. There's an added bonus: people don't have to leave their small towns for the big city in order to work for a high-tech firm. An office high-tech enough to satisfy can be set up in any room that has wall outlets. This is good news for America's small towns and rural communities, which have long been losing their young citizens to big cities. It is good news as well for big cities, which are testing the limits of overcrowding.

Some small communities will even help underwrite a central "telecottage" for citizens to share, a community center with phone lines, computers, and fax machines. The idea is already at work in Europe and Australia. The government of France is investing forty million francs in telecommuting programs, in hopes of strengthening smaller communities: "In a sense, the government is using high-tech telecommunications capabilities to support and preserve the rural lifestyle that gives France much of its charm and priceless character."[23]

Flexible work variations are an idea that is becoming more appealing to major American corporations, as they listen to employees' desires to create more family time. Corning Glass was losing women employees at twice the rate of white males; that trend was reversed when the company began encouraging job-sharing, home working, and part-time management jobs. Aetna Life and Casualty has a full-time consultant on family issues available negotiate similar arrangements.

At Honeywell, Inc., a parent who needs to stay home with a sick child can take as many paid days off as her supervisor permits—there is no set limit. Or the parent can take advantage of an in-home sitter service; Honeywell pays 80 percent of the cost.

IBM offers employees three years unpaid parental leave, with full benefits, and does their best to give a returning employee a job comparable to the one she left. At *Time* magazine, an employee might choose to work three fourteen-hour days a week. US Sprint communications allows employees leeway in setting their workday hours, as long as everyone's on board from 10:00 A.M. to 2:00 P.M.[24]

While many different problems with school or job may confront a pregnant woman, the most daunting of them all will probably be the difficulty of holding on to a job while caring for a child. She is right to view that as a steep mountain to climb, and we do her no good when we pep-talk her up the lower slopes.

Single parenting and dreary institutional day care can be the worst choice for both her and baby. If she cannot marry the baby's father, and if she will not consider adoption, that may be the only choice she has left. But as pregnancy care-givers canvas their communities for sources of support for these women, they should also look carefully for mom-friendly employment opportunities. Some employees understand that a kid needs her mom, and are willing to bend the edges of the work contract as long as the job gets done. Pregnancy care centers need a list of these employees as urgently as they need lists of obstetricians, pastors, and maternity homes.

1. The Alan Guttmacher Institute, *Facts in Brief,* March 15, 1993. AGI goes on to report that Catholic women are as likely to have abortions as all women nationally; Evangelical women are half as likely.
2. Stanley K. Henshaw, "Abortion Trends in 1987 and 1988: Age and Race," *Family Planning Perspectives,* March/April 1992, 86.
3. Interview with author, May 23, 1994.
4. Roy Maynard, "Mommy Track Leads Back Home," *World,* April 2, 1994, 16.
5. Elena Neuman, "More Moms are Homeward Bound," *Insight,* January 10, 1994, 18.
6. Maggie Gallagher, *Enemies of Eros* (Chicago: Bonus Books, 1989), 5.
7. *Barron's,* March 21, 1994.
8. Maynard, "Mommy Track."
9. Ruth Sidel, *On Her Own: Growing Up in the Shadow of the American Dream* (New York: Viking, 1990). Quoted in book review by Florence King, *The Washington Post,* January 16, 1990.
10. Alecia Swasy, "Stay-at-Home Moms Are Fashionable Again," *The Wall Street Journal,* July 23, 1993.
11. Ellen Debenport, "En Route to the top, diaper brigade folds," *Washington Times,* March 24, 1993.

12. Associated Press, "Career Women with Families Happiest," *Washington Post*, November 27, 1992.
13. William Mattox, "The Mother of All Myths," *Washington Post*, August 3, 1991.
14. Charles Jaffe, "Two incomes do not necessarily contribute to a very happy family," Newark NJ *Star-Ledger*, February 13, 1994.
15. Laura Lippman, "Child care system falls short," *Baltimore Sun*, April 7, 1994.
16. US Census bureau data cited by William Mattox Jr., "The Mother of All Myths," *Washington Post*, August 3, 1991.
17. Robert Rector, "How to Strengthen America's Crumbling Families," The Heritage Foundation Backgrounder, April 28, 1992.
18. "Data collected at the University of Maryland," cited by the Family Research Council, "Family Time: What Americans Want," February 1991.
19. Sara Engram, "Honor Thy Toddler," *Baltimore Sun*, April 17, 1994.
20. Ibid.
21. Linda Burton, Janet Dittmer, and Cheri Loveless, *What's a Smart Woman Like You Doing at Home?* (Vienna, Va.: Mothers at Home, 1992).
22. Robert Moskowitz, "Telecommuting: Bringing the Work Home," *Hemispheres*, April 1994.
23. Ibid.
24. Susan Bacon Dynerman and Lynn O'Rourke Hayes, *The Best Jobs in America for Parents* (New York: Rawson Associates, 1991).

Listening in Tampa

man is sitting tonight in the front room of the University Pregnancy Center, reading a magazine. He is a volunteer; his job is to be a visible male presence that can be glimpsed through the glass door, so that the women who come here at night won't feel uncomfortable.

But this suburban dad doesn't look entirely comfortable himself. A pregnancy care center is as thoroughly a woman's world as the beauty parlor or girdle department. The dusty-rose and floral decorating scheme that mark these centers from Maine to Mexico has not been used sparingly here. He sits on the fluffy, rose-strewn sofa looking like an auto mechanic confronted with a tea-party crumpet.

Down the hall we enter the conference room, which is set up with a ring of twenty chairs and plenty of juices and cakes. However, this evening's meeting could have been scheduled for the broom closet. Lisa, the post-abortion counselor who organized the hearing, expected seven or more participants tonight, but all afternoon they have been calling to cancel. Lisa thinks it's because of the weather, the windy rain of early Spring; my local coordinator thinks it's cold feet. The coordinator's assistant holds the theory that these gals wanted to spend the evening protesting Pat Ireland; the president of the National Organization of Women is giving a speech in Tampa tonight. Earlier today Ireland herself was out protesting Rush Limbaugh, who is also in town; Limbaugh's supporters are videotaped gleefully hauling orange juice out of the supermarkets, seven or eight gallons at a time. The usual charges of insensitivity to women's needs hover in the air.

At any rate, the only people to show up tonight are Lisa and one other invitee, Cheryl. However, Cheryl will turn out to have a story complex enough for a roomful.

Lisa is bright-eyed and animated, and her pink turtleneck gives her a rosy glow. Her story is more sordid than her clear good looks could foretell. She gives me the most complete description of an abortion experience that I have heard so far.

"I was seventeen when I had my abortion," she says—or asks. Her warm Southern accent turns every statement into a question. "I had been real promiscuous since I was about fourteen, although I was from a Christian family and had become a Christian when I was thirteen. I led two lives: I was in youth group and real spiritual, but I led this other life that nobody knew about. Yet I really wanted to be a Christian!

"Meanwhile, my family was going downhill: my dad had gone bankrupt and my parents were close to divorce. No one was asking me what time I came home and I didn't have a curfew—nobody cared. But we still went to church every Sunday.

"I guess just 'looking for love' was the main issue. I didn't care about sex—I hated sex. I *hated* it. But what led up to it, the first things— I just didn't know how to say no.

"So I was pregnant at seventeen. We didn't have pregnancy care centers, and didn't have an abortion clinic nearby—the closest was an hour and a half away. The guy I was dating couldn't handle the situation; after all, the baby wasn't his. The man whose it was told me he didn't believe it was his either. He would only give me half the money, so I had to borrow the rest from people at work and at church. One of our youth ministers at church was a social worker, and she convinced me I was doing the right thing. She even drove me to the clinic.

"It was a big, big butcher shop, because it was the closest place you could go—people drove in from all over the state. I got to meet some of the girls in the waiting room." With Lisa's bouncy friendliness, I can imagine that she could indeed have seen the waiting room of a vast abortion clinic as a great opportunity to "get to meet" new people. "Black women, white women, college students; some had their boyfriends, some had their husbands, some had their moms.

"The staff took us in, did another pregnancy test, and told us all about birth control. Then they took us in groups, eight at a time, and moved us from room to room. In one room there was a plastic model of a uterus with a little red blob in there. They told us that was what we would abort. I didn't know any different; I believed them.

"Then we went into a room where you change into the gowns. It was a big room with wooden benches on each side. The walls were concrete block and there was a big drain in the middle of the floor. I ask everybody I know, what was the drain for? Maybe it used to be a big shower or something. But I kept thinking about how they shoot cows and stuff? And wash the blood down the drain? I saw a movie about the Holocaust on TV the other day, and when I saw that gas chamber room, it reminded me so much of that room. It just gave me the chills."

Even these parts of the story Lisa tells with energy and hand gestures, and her smile is never far away. "So then we had to wait for our names to be called. You know how you feel scared to death and sick, terrified at something you know is going to hurt? I had decided I did not want to be put out; I knew I was going to want to remember what I had done.

"So when they herded us into the table room—I think they might have had two rooms going at the same time—they sent this girl in and told me to hold her hand. She wasn't a nurse, but maybe an administrator of the clinic. They don't want you to be loud because you're going to upset the others—that room of women is right there.

"I'll always remember what this girl looked like. For every woman there's one person she remembers from her abortion, and this girl was mine. She was beautiful, with long, straight, dark hair, and she looked like she might be part Indian; she was gorgeous. If I saw her today I would recognize her.

"I held that girl's hand and listened, and I heard the whole thing. I heard the vacuum; it sounded just like a vacuum cleaner. I guess they had things covered up so I wouldn't see anything, but it hurt. It hurt so bad. I could feel him scraping inside. I held that girl's hand so tight that afterwards there were red nail marks in her hand.

"And I cried and cried. I wanted my mom really bad, even though my mom would have *beaten my butt,*" she laughs, "if she found out I was in there. When we got through and I got in the wheelchair I was crying still. The girl was saying, 'It's over, why are you still crying?' She was getting frustrated with me. I said, 'I just killed my baby.'

"I was the only one in recovery crying, except for the little college student who had been in the other room with me, and she didn't stop crying. We were there for five hours, and she cried for five hours. When we went into the room to drink the orange juice and stuff, the other girls were all laughing and having a party with their cookies. I could tell that some of them had been there quite a few times before.

"Then the woman came to pick me up. When I got in the car this jubilation came up in me: There's no more problems. It's great. I got home and called the guy, and he said, 'Glad you called, 'bye.' Then I got down on my knees by the side of the bed and just bawled and begged God to forgive me. I knew it was wrong. I knew what I had done, there was never a doubt."

The advocates of abortion routinely insist that post-abortion grief is a myth, that the primary emotion women feel after abortion is relief. Perhaps that is all they see before the woman walks out the clinic door. "The jubilation only lasted a few hours, then?" I ask.

"Yeah, it wasn't long," she laughs. "I guess it was the relief of coming through it alive, because you're so scared, and because the problem is gone." I talk about the almost-hysterical surge of laughter that can rise after extreme tension; it is not the same thing as joy. "Yeah, it was probably more a physical manifestation than a real deep emotion," Lisa agrees.

"About three days later my mom found these little pills in my purse. My mom had been given the same pills after her miscarriage, so she knew what it was. I tried to deny it, but she was so angry, she called me a whore. I found out later that she had been pregnant with me when they got married—she could have shared that with me and been a comforter. I went in to my Dad and I just cried and cried, and he cried and cried; I said 'Dad, you know what I did.' We were always real close, but my mom was not a real good comforter."

I have to interrupt here again. "But when you were having the abortion, it was your mother you said you wanted."

"I've always wanted my mother, and I've always wanted her to be like that, but she was never able to be. She always said the right things, but there was never any warmth in it or hugs." It strikes me that several women have said this to me in these hearings; that their mothers were cold, and that they desperately longed for maternal warmth. I wonder if such deprivation predisposes a woman toward abortion—if the lack of trust in mother-love damages her own ability to picture herself as a loving mother.

I ask Lisa to picture again the chaos before the abortion; what was the main reason she made that decision?

"Probably that I had such an unstable home life. With the bankruptcy, and having to move out of our mansion house and sell the Cadillac, and my mom freaking out because she was going to have to drive a Datsun, I was afraid that the pregnancy would be just too much."

I now ask, "What would have helped you have the baby?"

"Well, it would have helped if someone could have gone with me to tell my parents. But I never really knew the answer to that question until I saw a James Dobson tape. It shows three cases: a girl who had an abortion, a girl who keeps her baby, and a girl who chooses adoption; they talk to them before and after. If there had been a pregnancy center, and if I had had some support, I would have placed my baby for adoption. Because if I had seen how that girl on the tape loved her baby enough to pick out a Christian family for it, I would have done the same thing.

"But there were no other options ever offered, not one time, in all the people I met. Even though I could get money for the abortion from half the people in town!"

Lisa winds up her tale with the emphatic verve that has marked it throughout. I notice her earrings: sizable, flashy numbers with rhinestones of pink and white, and she is wearing them, in my opinion, backwards. It is charming. As we turn our attention to Cheryl, I see a quieter backdrop to Lisa's sparkle. Cheryl's eyes are gray-green, and her long dark hair is pulled back in a ponytail; she wears a black sweater and silver jewelry. She speaks in a calm, measured voice as she unrolls an extraordinary story.

"I need to give a little background. I've actually had three pregnancies, two full-term and one abortion. Lisa and I are very similar in our backgrounds, except that my mom and dad divorced when I was ten. So it was just my mom who was in charge, and she let me be pretty promiscuous; as long as she was happy with a boyfriend she didn't care. She was very promiscuous herself, and so I learned that from her. My dad wasn't around much before the divorce either, so I was always looking for that love in all the wrong places.

"When I was about eleven or twelve my neighbors moved back from living a while in Texas, and they had gotten wise with all the worldly wisdom. And I was just innocent, a churchgoing girl. Well, that girl next door started showing me the ways of the world. By the time I was fifteen she wanted to move out on her own, and I went with her. I don't know how I never got killed, but we got by; we had some pretty wild friends.

"So we slept around wherever, and I ended up getting pregnant. I went home to my mom and she took me to the doctor and confirmed I was pregnant. My mom wanted me to go to the home for unwed mothers and give the baby up for adoption, but I didn't want that. I wanted the guy to marry me; I always wanted to get married and have a big family."

When I ask a question about the "boy" in this story, Cheryl corrects me—he was a "man," ten years older than her. But surely a grown male who preys on girls barely fifteen deserves some more fitting epithet than being called "a man".

"But my boyfriend got some pills from somewhere and gave them to me to abort the baby. They didn't work and I carried the baby full term, still living with this man. I had the baby just three days before my sixteenth birthday, and gave it up for adoption. I wasn't supposed to find out the sex, but when I went to sign some papers I found out it was a boy. He would be twenty-something years old now.

"That was the hardest thing. Leaving the hospital and not bringing home a baby, leaving to go with this man that really didn't love me but was going to—*tolerate* me. I begged him to let me continue living with him—'Take me home with you'—I didn't want to go back home to my mom. I found out years later that my dad said, 'Let me kill him'—he wanted to blow him away. But my mom was still pretty much 'Well, you can come home if you want, whatever you want to do.'

"So I was still living with him and I got pregnant again. He was the father of both these pregnancies, but he didn't want to admit it—he said I'd been sleeping around. Right away he didn't want me to keep it. He already had six kids—" Lisa and I react in surprise—"and he didn't want to have any more. But I wanted that baby, I wanted to be pregnant, I wanted to have a family. And he made me go get an abortion. I remember that it was just the horriblest thing I ever went through in my life. From the moment he told me he wanted me to have the abortion until it was over, it was just like a nightmare. It was like something you would see on Shock Theater. I just felt like I was being dragged through something I didn't want to do.

"I don't remember the details like you do," she nods toward Lisa, "but I remember just feeling so scared and alone, and the pain and the agony afterwards. He was supposed to go out and get me some pills to help the pain, and instead he went and got drunk! For hours I lay in bed just dying, bleeding and feeling so alone. I didn't know the Lord so I didn't cry out to him. It was just total devastation. And then I just wanted to forget it."

Something jogs Cheryl's memory at this point and she takes an emphatic side-tack. "When I became a Christian and heard people talking about abortion, anti-abortion people, I thought, 'These people don't know what they're talking about. They have no idea. They're arrogant'—I mean, I had some choice words for people who talk about it but have never been through it. You don't want to even let anybody know what happened to you, because they're already speaking out of ignorance. If you bring it up you're an open wound. I didn't talk about it—it was a part of my life that happened, that didn't happen."

I ask if Cheryl was still pro-choice at that point in her journey.

"No, I never thought abortion should be an option. I just thought it was a horrible thing to do. I love babies, I love big families, and I never would have thought of abortion; I just followed what the man wanted. When I had the baby the first time I was pregnant, he dropped me off at the hospital and didn't even stay with me. That was a lonely experience too, going into the hospital to have a baby all by myself."

"What a horrible human being," Lisa bursts in. "This is one of *the* worst—I won't say the worst—men stories I've ever heard. And I hear *bad* men stories."

"I have a real bitter taste in my mouth," Cheryl admits.

I ask Cheryl what sort of comments from pro-lifers made her angry.

"When they say that women just lie when they say they don't know about birth control; they say that women get pregnant out of laziness and abortion is just an easy out. But there is such a thing as ignorance about sexuality. I was a kid; this man envelopes you and you're not thinking about getting pregnant. I didn't even know about birth control."

"Well, listen to this!" Lisa bursts in. "I had convinced myself—now I do not know *where* in the world, I just got this out of the *air*—I had convinced myself that I was sterile and I couldn't get pregnant. I do not know why I said that! Because I knew I could get pregnant. See, *that's* one for therapy," she grins.

"I guess I can see how that could be," says Cheryl, "because I started probably younger than you did. I don't think I thought about pregnancy at twelve or thirteen."

"I had my first experience when I was twelve," says Lisa, "and I didn't even know what had happened. I didn't even *know*. So I didn't even do it again until I was fifteen."

"The first time I had sex was like a nightmare for me, too," says Cheryl. "All of them have been bad. I feel the same way you do"—she gestures to Lisa and chuckles—"It's like, 'Sex, yuck. Don't touch me.' But anyway, when I would listen to a pro-life speaker, or walk up to a group of people talking about abortion, I just thought that they don't understand that there are people who aren't educated. I mean, my mother never talked to me about hygiene or sexual intercourse or getting pregnant. She was so embarrassed; she threw me a menstrual pack one night when I was taking a bath. I just thought, 'Sex must be awful.'

"But like Lisa, if I had one person rallying on my side, I could have made it. Like with the first baby. I felt good about that, because I prayed for that child, and wherever he may be he has a good life. With the next baby if I had had one person say, 'Cheryl, don't do that. Do like you did with the other baby. Leave this jerk. Go ahead and give it up for adoption.' I would have done it in a minute. But this man was my life.

"I tried to share the Gospel with him, but he thinks he was

the best thing that ever happened to him. That's the kind of man he is. He's blinded by sin. One of the times he did get in contact with me he said, 'I found my thing in life, I know what's going to make me happy, and I want you to be part of it.'" Cheryl pauses. "'I need two women.'" Lisa and I register amazement. "I was, like, 'This man has gone over the edge.'"

"You ought to tell her about Savannah," Lisa prompts.

Cheryl smiles. "I was a church secretary, teaching Sunday School, and taking care of an elderly couple all week. On the weekends I would go to my mom's house for meals, but this time she and her girlfriend were going to a barbecue for dinner. I thought I would just go for dinner and then leave, but this guy came up and tapped me on the shoulder. I danced with him one time and it was all over with; he swept me off my feet. So we got involved, and I got pregnant, and it was another nightmare situation. He professed to be a Christian and wasn't, and left me beaten and bruised and battered and torn, about five months pregnant.

"The church picked me up right where he left off. They said, 'Whatever you need, financially or otherwise, we'll take care of you.' I went to the Alpha Pregnancy Center here in Tampa and decided to keep the baby. I didn't know if it would be a boy or girl, but all I could think of was the name 'Savannah,' because I saw the movie, *Savannah Smiles*. And I thought, 'If this is a boy, what am I going to do? I'll end up calling it Sylvester or something.'

"So I got through the pregnancy and had a natural birth, and one of my girlfriends from the church was my coach. She'd come over and rub my legs and play these beautiful tapes for relaxation. And Savannah will be ten in June."

"And she is beautiful!" Lisa exclaims.

"And she came out smiling, so she fit her name," Cheryl concludes.

I ask, "That middle pregnancy, the baby that was aborted— do you think you could have continued that pregnancy if you'd had the support of your church?"

"The help I got the last time made the difference," Cheryl nods. "When there's a hard situation like this in our congregation, my pastor has just the committed members of the church stay after service. Then he has the person who's in need stand up and tell their story, or have somebody read it for them. So I went before the church, and it was just like a mob of love being poured on me. Savannah has never lacked for anything. It's a good way of handling situations, because it stops the rumors."

Lisa adds, "And it keeps you from being fearful to come back to church; how can you walk in there pregnant? One family had a daughter who got pregnant, but she wouldn't go before the church. They asked her to, but she wouldn't. And she's never been back to church because she can't face anybody."

The conversation has come to a natural end, and we stand up to begin packing away the barely dented cakes and bottles of juice. I observe that, with Cheryl's unusual story, she could have played all three parts in the Dobson video; they'd only have had to change the wig. We make our way back to the front of the building and go out under the watchful eye of the man on the sofa. We have heard tales of a couple of bona-fide jerks tonight, yet here is a guy who, after putting in a long day at work, donates his evening sitting guard so women can talk in safety.

Tomorrow the papers will be full of the controversial figures appearing on the local stage. We will hear what a threat Limbaugh-ite conservatism constitutes to women, how women must overthrow the oppressors and protect their rights. There won't be a photo of this guy; the actual work of protecting women is not that glamorous. In a couple more hours he can go home.

Welfare and Faring Well

T
he poor, unmarried pregnant woman sitting in the client's chair at the pregnancy care center is in the crosshairs of a bazooka. Welfare reform has state and federal governments in a frenzy, and she is the favored target. They've figured out that her maternity is the source of too many problems.

Unfortunately, they are right. Her pregnancy, per se, is not the problem, nor will her squirming baby be once it is born. The problem lies solely in the way she plans to raise the child. She intends to do it without a husband. The results can be devastating for us all.

Welfare reformers want to stop paying her to do this. Robert Rector of the Heritage Foundation explains that welfare payments constitute a contract with single mothers; the government promises her a "paycheck" as long as she meets two conditions. First, she must not get a job; second, she must not marry a man with a job.[1] As the adage goes, you get more of what you subsidize. Over the last thirty years, Americans have bought lots and lots of single moms and fatherless kids.

The amount of money spent on buying this dysfunction is

astounding. Since President Johnson's War on Poverty began in 1965, we have spent over *$5 trillion*, an amount greater than the national debt. If this rate continues, 1998 welfare spending will outstrip defense spending by two to one. Despite this "the official poverty rate has remained largely unchanged since the War on Poverty began," says Rector, "while the problems of family break-up, welfare dependency, eroded work ethic, and crime all have gotten dramatically worse."[2] The War on Poverty is over. We lost.

Even a math-impaired person might wonder why the nation's poor aren't the nation's millionaires after having their pockets filled so relentlessly. In fact, the $225 billion spent in federal, state, and local welfare programs in 1990 was more than twice enough to give every American an income above the poverty threshold.[3] But, of course, the money doesn't go to poor people; it goes to a poverty program.

Welfare systems, says *Washington Post* columnist William Raspberry, "grow in direct proportion to their failure to accomplish their mission." The more welfare clients are strengthened and enabled to be self-sufficient, the more welfare caseworkers fear for their jobs. Raspberry quotes Sharon Morris-Billotti, a thirty-year employee of the Illinois public welfare system, as saying that she and her colleagues "know that we need a continual flow of people needing us...[yet] to continue to suppress America's underclass, to foster their dependency, to render them powerless over their own lives, is the antithesis of empowerment."

Morris-Billotti points out that the maze of programs has grown so dauntingly complex that it takes specially trained case workers with college degrees to maneuver clients through. "Shouldn't that tell us something?" she says. "Special people to manage the services and resources needed by the consumer, and ultimately their lives, because we have created such a rat maze that no one but a pro can get through it. How can the underclass possibly escape dependency?"[4]

William Bennett writes that there is "acknowledgment

among experts in the field that a strong link exists between social pathologies, exploding rates of illegitimacy, and welfare payments to single mothers."[5] Keep that spinning triangle in mind: unwed motherhood and fatherless childhood cause social ills; social ills cause illegitimacy; welfare money keeps the whole process going.

This has, of course, been used as an argument in favor of abortion: bump off the kids before they show up to eat our tax dollars and kill us in the streets. The racism lingering beneath the surface here is usually expressed only in whispers, but sometimes it emerges in thrillingly hideous form. Famed California abortionist Edward Allred says, "When a sullen black woman of 17 or 18 can decide to have a baby and get welfare and food stamps and become a burden to us all, it's time to stop. In parts of south Los Angeles, having babies for welfare is the only industry the people have."[6]

Allred meant, of course, that it was "time to stop" her baby from living; he went on to express a desire to set up a free abortion clinic in Mexico to protect us from immigrants who lack "respect for democracy and social order." Many assume that the only solution to the welfare-baby problem was to kill the baby. Few realize that it might be just as efficient, and markedly more agreeable, to kill welfare.

Recently, the idea of cutting welfare payments to single mothers has become popular, even among left-wing policy jockeys. One of the reasons seems to be resentment brewing among working moms; why should she have to work to pay taxes so another woman can stay home with her kids? "I think a lot of women, even the most liberal, have turned around and said, 'Excuse me, something's wrong with this picture,'" says Rep. Joan Menard of the Massachusetts state legislature. Menard recently voted for welfare cuts, something that would have been anathema to a liberal not long before.[7]

The cutting of welfare payments is not without controversy. The hope, of course, is that when the bonus for unwed childbearing disappears, women will be less likely to engage in the practice.

Pro-lifers hope that these women will return to requiring marriage before sex, and form healthy two-parent families to raise the next generation. Pro-choicers would, for the most part, just as soon she be promiscuous but contracepted, and abort any unexpected arrivals. Either way, the cycle of single parenting is broken. But the risk is that the woman will just go on having babies without an in-home father, and the poverty the family struggles with will be deeper than ever.

The debate over these cuts can be glimpsed in miniature in the state of New Jersey. In August 1993 the state's Family Development Act went into effect, which halted giving increased payments to welfare mothers for each additional child. Because a law like this caps payments to expanding families, they are generically referred to as "family cap" laws. In New Jersey, typically, a second child had brought a $102 per month increase, while a third brought $64. Will the new law decrease the birth rate of unwed mothers? That's the $64 question.

Mothers on public assistance in the city of Camden, where 80 percent of the population receives welfare payments, gave the policy mixed reviews. Some embraced it enthusiastically. "The government has to get tough on us," said Cookie Horta, a twenty-five-year-old with three children, on welfare since tenth grade.[8] "It shouldn't be so easy to sit home, have babies, and collect a check." Others scoffed at the negligibility of the amount. Maxine Dorsey, a mother of four and welfare recipient for fourteen years, said, "What is $64 gonna do? That's not even a pair of shoes!"

Dorsey is not alone in her estimation of the law. The National Organization of Women and the American Civil Liberties Union have filed a complaint seeking to block the family cap; they believe it is "discriminatory, punitive, dangerous to children, and an invasion of constitutional rights." Strange bedfellow Rita Martin, of the pro-life Citizens Concerned for Life, agrees. "We feel that denying a mother an additional $64 a month...is a coercive move...that could push her into having an abortion she wouldn't otherwise have."

When Maryland considered a similar law, Pro-Life Maryland attacked it as "eugenics:" "The family cap is deliberate government pressure on vulnerable women to abort their babies...Welfare reform shouldn't be confused with welfare abuse, coercing mothers and killing dependents."[9] Pro-choice forces in Maryland played into this scenario by asking that the family cap be tied to expanded public funding of abortion (which already stood at over $3 million annually). The 1994 state legislative session ended before any of these proposals could pass.

Presidents of pregnancy-care center chains are watching these changes closely. Terry Weaver of USA Birthright agreed that cutting welfare payments won't stop the pregnancies, but merely reduces the resources that young mothers have to cope. "If you take this away from my moms, what will you give back?" Weaver asks. She fears that if welfare tinkering and public-funded abortion don't stop single parenting, the next step will be compulsory sterilization: "We're going fast back to Hitler." She also doesn't believe that the family cap will make any difference. "I don't know any woman who deliberately got pregnant to get $60 a month," she says.[10]

But Peggy Harschorn of Heartbeat International confessed to "mixed feelings. I hate to see any disincentive to continue a pregnancy, but we do need some disincentive to unwed mothering."[11] When asked whether a $60 per month increase swayed a woman's decision to get pregnant, Hartschorn responded, "It's not the primary reason for getting pregnant, but it does make a difference. These women sometimes have *no* idea of the value of money. All they know is that their check will go up."

Harschorn also commented on women's savvy concerning the welfare system. "We had a client living with us once whose mother was on welfare in another state. Every time her mother had gotten pregnant, the state had showered her with baby furniture and equipment. Our client was complaining about our state in comparison: 'Your system doesn't do *anything*!' There are people out there who know how to work the system."

This kind of street-wisdom in itself is not cause for disapproval. Women in all ages have used their wits in gathering the things they need to survive and feed their children. Today's coupon-clipping, comparison-shopping mom is using the same innate skills that her ancient forebear did when she determined that the large red berries are good but the little purple ones give you heartburn. Welfare payments invite women to hone these skills in a different arena, one which is almost a parallel universe to the rest of the American economy. Here she must negotiate her way through Morris-Bellotti's "rat maze," and the better she does it the larger her prize. Sixty dollars is not a king's ransom, but it is a nice, if small, reward.

Will welfare cuts cause a rise in abortion rates? Human behavior is notoriously unpredictable. It would be reasonable to brace for at least a temporary rise. On the other hand, the closest parallel suggests that when doors to sexual heedlessness close, women change their behavior.

A dozen years ago, when the Hyde amendment first restricted public funding of abortion, the question was not whether cutting off welfare funds would cause more abortions, but the reverse. *The Wall Street Journal* headlined the answer: "Cutoff of Abortion Funds Doesn't Deliver Welfare Babies." Economics professor Jacqueline Kasun had analyzed pre- and post-Hyde statistics for abortion and birth, and had discovered that both categories dropped. There were not just fewer abortions, there were fewer conceptions—in Ohio, 15 percent less, for example.[12] The increased abortions we fear may simply not materialize.

Welfare reform that simply takes a broad swipe at payments is an innovation born of frustration; the previous round of reform was aimed at moving people from welfare to employment, a concept called "workfare." Traditionally these programs have begun with lengthy periods of job training, but "job training is a crock," says Marvin Olasky, author of *The Tragedy of American*

Compassion, which analyzes a century of American approaches to poverty-fighting. Olasky criticizes job programs for taking kids who are already suffering from parental deprivation—no father—and separating them from their mothers as well. "Why deprive those poor kids further?" he asks.[13]

The National Organization for Women agrees, after a fashion—or did at one time. The NOW Bill of Rights, adopted at the organization's first national conference in 1967, demands the right of poor women to have welfare and job rights equal to men's, but "without prejudice to a parent's right to remain at home to care for his or her children."[14]

The second problem with job training, Olasky says, is that "the [placement] records are abysmal. Job training only provides jobs for social workers; it's middle class welfare." When long-term welfare recipients finally get jobs, 66 percent of them quit during the first three to six months.[15] Olasky quotes Mickey Kaus: "Only work works." One welfare reform proposal, from a group of moderate and conservative Democrats calling themselves the Mainstream Forum, calls for directing welfare applicants to jobs immediately; the newly employed can get whatever training they need on the job.[16]

The problem with a proposal like the above is its price tag, $18 billion, making it the "most expensive" and "most comprehensive" of the welfare bills, says proud sponsor Rep. Dave McCurdy. Workfare is costly because moving five million unskilled, uneducated single mothers into the workforce will require immense amounts of remedial education, transportation vouchers, job placement services, and hours and hours of child care. Some proposals even include fallback-position "community services" jobs, with salaries supplied by taxpayers. Robert B. Carleson, leader of the Welfare Crisis Group, warns, "Does it cost more than the current system? If so, it's going in the wrong direction."[17]

Others worry that workfare moves people, not toward independence, but toward new entitlements: job training, guaranteed jobs, and child care. "Workfare could be used as an excuse for a national day care bill," says Rep. Jim Talent.[18]

Pregnancy care services have long relied on welfare to help their clients make ends meet; they may have had mixed feelings about the ultimate effect of these handouts but, as long as they were there, they would be used. As this resource begins to end, we can hope that the numbers of crisis pregnancies will drop. Unlike welfare bureaucracies, pregnancy care centers can afford to see their client load lighten as problems are solved.

This is a good opportunity, too, for us to think through the distinction between problems caused by poverty and problems caused by behavior. A few years ago George Graham, a professor of nutrition and pediatrics at Johns Hopkins University, caused some scandal with an article attacking the WIC program (Special Supplemental Food Program for Women, Infants, and Children).[19] First, Graham criticized the dairy-heavy program as being less than healthful: "Future generations could have good reason to accuse this one of dumping these unwanted surplus foods on the poor, contributing to the high incidence among them of obesity, diabetes, and degenerative vascular disease."

But Graham also made the more significant point that poor nutrition is not the cause of low-birth-weight infant mortality in America—prematurity is. And prematurity is associated with "smoking, drug abuse...previous abortions, stress and infec-tions...which often result from sexual promiscuity." Peru has a lower prematurity rate than the US; Jamaica has a better infant mortality rate than Washington, D.C. (even though Washington has one of the nation's highest WIC-participation rates). WIC can't solve the problem because malnutrition is not its cause, says Graham. Babies' lives are saved only when their mothers' lives, and behaviors, are changed.

Graham uses another startling example: Mexican-American women born in Mexico have healthier babies than Mexican-American women born in the U.S. Ronald David of the Kennedy

School gives a little more insight into this phenomenon. Mexican-American women overall are poorer than African-American women, and have less access to medical care, yet their infant mortality rate is equal to, or better than, that of European-American women. To explain this, "you must look at the different ways in which the community mobilizes around the pregnant woman...Typically, other Mexican-American women who have had childbearing experience gather round, embrace, and support the pregnant female. The African-American mother-to-be, in contrast, is often isolated from nourishing social relationships."[20]

The theme emerges again that it is not material resources so much as loving support that makes the difference. The loss of an extra $64 a month does not threaten poor pregnant women as much as their own self-destructive behavior, friendlessness, and isolation. Pregnancy care centers are in a position to offer individualized, long-term friendship that can lift them out of this despair. And when our government stops paying these women's tuition in the School of Hard Knocks, we may have less despair to deal with.

1. Robert Rector, "How to Strengthen America's Crumbling Families," The Heritage Foundation Backgrounder, April 28, 1992.

2. Roy Maynard quoting Rep. Jim Talent, "Rhetoric and Reality," World, April 23, 1994; also, Larry Burkett, "The Not-so-great Society," World, May 21, 1994.

3. Marvin Olasky, "Wealth and Welfare in Biblical Perspective," paper delivered at the Wilberforce Forum, April 23, 1994.

4. William Raspberry, "Why the Welfare System Will Never Work," New Dimensions, June 1991.

5. William Bennett and Peter Wehner, "End Welfare for Single Women Having Children," AFA Journal, March 1994.

6. Quoted in Joseph Sobran, "Arguing Abortion Ethnically," Washington Times, November 2, 1989. Sobran attributes the quotes to an interview in the San Diego Union.

7. "Inside Politics," *Washington Times*, May 24, 1994.

8. Cheryl Wetzstein, "Mixed reviews from recipients greet assault on welfare trap," *Washington Times*, April 6, 1994.

9. "Eugenics is Back," paper distributed by Pro-Life Maryland, Spring 1994.

10. Interview with author, May 24, 1994.

11. Interview with author, May 25, 1994.

12. Jacqueline Kasun, "Cutoff of Abortion Funds Doesn't Deliver Welfare Babies," *The Wall Street Journal*, December 30, 1986.

13. Interview with author, May 24, 1994.

14. The NOW Bill of Rights appears in the Historical Documents section in Robin Morgan, ed., *Sisterhood is Powerful* (New York: Random House, 1970), 512. It is followed by another Historical Document, the SCUM (Society for Cutting Up Men) Manifesto.

15. Study cited by *Boston Globe*, reiterated in "Inside Politics," *Washington Times*, May 19, 1994.

16. Cheryl Wetzenstein, "Welfare 'declaration' proposes more radical reform," *Washington Times*, May 12, 1994.

17. Cheryl Wetzstein, "Private Panel Creates Welfare Reform Plan," *Washington Times*, May 13, 1994.

18. Maynard, "Rhetoric and Reality."

19. George E. Graham, "Mothers, Not Malnutrition, Cause Infant Mortality," *The Wall Street Journal*, April 2, 1991.

20. Interview with Dr. David in *Harvard Magazine*, March/April 1993, quoted in "Notable and Quotable," *The Wall Street Journal*, March 15, 1993.

## CHAPTER FOURTEEN

Listening in Boston

T he spring afternoon is sunny but not without a chill. We are meeting today in an old stone school building, elaborately appointed in the manner of the previous century, before aesthetics were crowded out by values like "bullet-proof." I follow worn wooden floors down twisting hallways to a conference room, and arrive no longer sure which direction the windows face. But I know which end is up: the ceiling's plasterwork frames a deep skylight, and a rectangle of brilliant blue creeps across the glossy mahogany table top.

The room has a very high ceiling, massive cabinets, and the table is proportionately huge. The five of us sit clustered around one end. I ask each woman to sign a release form, giving me permission to use her story in this project. The form specifies that I will not use her real name.

Rita Ann, seated immediately to my right, surprises me by doing something that no other group participant has done. She takes out her pen and carefully draws a line through the last sentence of the release.

I look over and ask her, "You don't mind if I use your real name?" "I want you to use my real name," she corrects me. "I'm ready to tell my story." She looks at me with calm confidence, a woman well into middle age, her straight auburn hair cut short, no earrings, pale blue eyes. I know that she has never participated in a group like this, never told her story before. As of today, she is ready to sign her full name to it: Rita Ann Albertelli.

Marion Syverson, across the table, looks up at this exchange. "I sure don't have anything to hide," she laughs. "Go ahead and use my name too."

"Well, I'm not ready for that," says brown-eyed Kathy with a smile. Colleen just looks down, a little uncomfortable. She is telling her story for the first time today, too.

As I finish describing the project I invite a volunteer to begin. Marion asks, "May I start?"

She is a tiny, effervescent brunette whose every fiber seems to proclaim "Kiss Me, I'm Italian." She begins by describing a chaotic childhood. Her father beat his wife and kids with a belt; at the age of thirteen Marion, the eldest, broke up a fight and commanded her dad to leave, which he did. After the divorce, Marion's mom embarked on a new life: promiscuity, bars, and drugs. She treated her daughter to explicit descriptions of her sexual activities and tokes of marijuana. Marion says, "I thought she was *awful* cool— and at the same time I thought, 'This is really stupid. I hate this.'

"When I was 15, I started being really desperate for affection that was more normal," Marion goes on. "I discovered that I was able to get it from a boy, if I wanted to. I got pregnant; I had made a decision to do that. I wanted to get out of the house, but I couldn't leave my younger brothers and sisters in the hands of a lunatic, with our abusive dad still living up the street. The only noble way was if I had my own baby to take care of. So, although my mother had given me birth control pills when I first got my period, I didn't take them. I knew exactly how to get pregnant, because she'd told me. Actually, she'd told me how not to, but I wasn't stupid. I figured it out," Marion grins.

"I went to Planned Parenthood because they gave a free test; I didn't know about any crisis centers. I blurted out my story—'My dad's a jerk, he beats us up'—and not in pretty language.

"The counselor ripped off a sheet of paper and wrote on it the address of an abortion clinic. But as I was going home on the bus I was thinking, 'I don't want to do this.' Abortion was killing. I wanted to give the baby up for adoption. But who would pay for everything? What about school? Who'll tell my parents?

"So I decided to go to a church for help. I thought, 'Okay, I'm going to get yelled at, and then they'll help me take care of it.' I picked this church because it was pretty; it had stone and vines and window boxes and I thought, 'If God lives, he'd live here.' So I went in, sat down in the minister's office, and blurt, blurt, blurt.

"Well, he hit the roof. Got up and started like Jimmy Durante, 'what's-this-generation-coming-to' kinda thing. Then he sits down, opens the bottom drawer of his desk, and hands me $150 in greenbacks.

"I'm fifteen, I don't ask any questions. That would imply that I don't understand, and that would be not-adult. So I took the money, put it in my pocket, and he shoves me out the door. I was standing outside the church thinking, 'What does he want me to do with this?' Then I realized." Marion's voice grows quiet. "God wants me to have an abortion.

"I was surprised that this was what God wanted. But it was what every adult I talked to told me was best. I was sad and I couldn't go home right away. So I walked by the river and sat on the bridge. I swung my feet and talked to my baby."

Marion now speaks quietly, intensely, and her eyes drill the tabletop. "I think about that little girl sitting there and I get upset. In my high school there were two thousand people, but nobody told me about God. I was the whore, I was the girl they called when the football team wanted to have a party. Nobody told me about God; it was going to take more than $150 given to me in five minutes to solve my problem. I was going to be a problem for a long, long time. And we don't want to deal with people like that. We care about people getting saved, but we don't care that much. Not enough to inconvenience ourselves."

She straightens, and tears are in her eyes. "So I sat there and swung my feet and told my baby, 'I've wanted to have you since I was five years old. I wish I could have you—but I can't. 'Cause there's *crazy* people at my house, and they'll hurt you.'" There's a catch in Marion's throat. "'And I wonder if you're a girl, or a boy, and I'm really sorry—that I have to kill you—but God wants me to.'"

She wipes her eyes and manages a smile. "Now I'm going to look like Bozo. Let me drop these tears right here for a minute." She takes a breath. "This is not a matter of me not being healed. I'm thirty-eight now, I have my own life, nobody victimizes me like that anymore. Just try it!" she laughs. "I'll be right in your face! But somebody's doing it to *somebody* today. So we each have to do our part."

Her story is long, but so fascinating that no one makes a move to cut it shorter. She patters along at a rapid pace, covering paragraphs in a single bound. "So a friend drove me into Manhattan for the abortion. It was in a converted house; I don't remember anybody wearing medical whites or gloves, and they didn't mention anesthesia. I was *screaming*. They're going in with something like the jack to put up your car"—she makes jacking noises—"Unbelievable! What, are you going to drive something in there? Afterwards I was bleeding and I hurt, but I was still walking and talking, so they gave me orange juice and put me out the door.

"On the way home I started feeling sad about my mom and thinking about how I wanted to make up. So when I came in she was lying on the couch in her Sarah Bernhardt pose, and I came around to her face—always a dangerous place to be—and I said softly, 'Mommy, I'm so sorry. I killed my baby.'

"She jumped right up screaming, 'You've been nothing but trouble since the day you were born; you're a slut, you're a this, you're a that—' and I went -click- 'Mom, you're a jerk, I hate you, I hate you.' I went up to my room and got high, wrote in my diary holding the pen like a knife, slashing through pages, 'I hate you, I hate you.'" Marion seems close to tears again as that old fury surfaces fresh. Her present relationship with her mother is not much better, though twenty years have passed.

"Everything went downhill from there. A year later my mom brought guys home from the bar for me, guys ten years younger than her and ten years older than me. She told them what a slut I was, how I'd sleep with anybody. And by this time it was true. They raped me, and the school psychiatrist said there was nothing I could do about it because of my reputation. I was taking drugs, too. I went to school carrying wine in a bottle shaped like grapes—this was the expensive stuff—and I'd sit out in the parking lot, taking barbiturates and drinking wine. The only friend I had was a dealer who wouldn't let me have acid because he was afraid I would go out a window.

"When I was seventeen I decided to try again to get out of the house by getting pregnant. I told my mom, 'I'm pregnant and you can't do anything about it—Tom is going to marry me.' She didn't say anything, and I thought that was alarming. She usually had something to say immediately, with her hand moving at the same time.

"So she had Tom meet her at the bar, and he told her 'I love her, I want to marry her, [singing softly] she's having my baby; what a lovely way to say how much,' and all that. So my mom says, 'You don't even know if it's your baby. You see those guys in the corner? It could be their baby.' She had him sitting there in the bar crying. He called me up sobbing, 'I can't marry you, sorry, I can't marry you, 'bye!'"

Marion is clenching her fists now. "I just sat there going, 'I'm going to kill her. I'm going to kill her.' Writing in my diary, 'I hate you, I hate you.' Everything was fine till he met with her.

"So it was back to the Manhattan abortion clinic. What else was I going to do? Who could I turn to? The minister who didn't have the time of day for me? Somebody at my school? There's nobody. So my mom takes me to the clinic. When it's time for me to sign the form I whisper to the nurse, 'I don't want to have the abortion—my mother's making me, she's somewhere in the building, but please don't make me have the abortion.' The nurse just said, 'Look, there are people waiting. Do you want it or don't you? Make a decision or get out.' The thoughts were flying through my head: Where would I live? Who would pay the doctor? Who could I turn to?

"I couldn't think of any answers. So I said, 'Okay. I'll have the abortion.' And I did.

"A year later I got pregnant by Tom *again*. This time he contacted his priest and they decided to get me to a maternity home in Illinois where I would be safe. But before I left I tried one night to stop my dad from beating my brother. I said bad words to my father, and he came right after me, and pounded the tar out of me. I was swinging back—I don't recommend you try this at home—and he banged my head into the front door and gave me a concussion. He threw me in the street and a car stopped right before hitting me. I did make it to Illinois, but it was too late; I ended up having a miscarriage."

The rapid-fire story is not quite over. "My life didn't get a lot better soon. I got pregnant again, this time by Mort. At first he thought that maybe it wasn't his baby. He told me to have an abortion and I said, 'Are you kidding? Do *this* with *that* body part.' So he came to his senses and we got married. I was taking Quaaludes all the time, and got in the habit of just dropping the baby into the crib so he'd cry and need me.

"Then one day two people came to the door, and said they were doing a Campus Crusade survey. They told me about Jesus and showed me in the Bible that he loved me. I said, 'Well, he couldn't love *me*.' They said, 'Sure! He forgives everybody.'

"I bought it hook, line and sinker, and so did Mort. We were saved together, and that was fifteen years ago."

This whirlwind tour is over, and it looks like a hard act to follow. But not for Kathy, seated to Marion's left. She is in her early thirties, with a clear, open face and a robust, almost farm-girl glow. Kathy has a natural poise and confidence that suggests she is both an eldest child and a high achiever. There is a twinkle in her eye, an air of reserved amusement.

"Well, I'm just bowled over!" she says to Marion with a grin. Marion looks down modestly. "In my case," Kathy goes on, "I met my husband when I was fifteen and he was sixteen. He told me that he was going to marry me, so I said, 'All right, let's go to bed!' I got pregnant within a year; we used birth control very sporadically.

"My parents were not in a good situation; they fought violently, although only with each other. And they were very, very pro-choice. I had been raised that there was nothing wrong with abortion, and so when I found out that I was pregnant, I assumed that was what I would do."

I ask why the boy didn't make good on his promise to marry her then.

"At that age? I was sixteen!" Kathy says. "Kids in suburban Boston don't get married at sixteen. We thought we'd marry someday. Marriage wasn't something that I would have ever considered then.

"And of course I didn't think of telling my parents. I was smart and mature and I was going to handle it all by myself. Except that Bob was going to do all the important parts, like find out where to go, and get the money, all of which he did. The only adult I told was the director of our school play; I wrote him a note saying that I was going to miss a rehearsal because I was going to have an abortion. Looking back at this now, I realize that I was really looking for some adult input.

"So I told the play director and he looked a little shocked. The next day at school he came up to me with his wife, whom I knew as a substitute teacher, and said, 'Look, I hope you don't mind, but I told my wife about this and I think you ought to talk to her.' She took me aside and said, 'Kathy, have you thought about this? Are you sure about what you are doing? Do you have any concerns?' And I said, 'No, no, no. I know what I'm doing.'" Kathy bursts into laughter at her own blind bravado.

"So Bob and I skipped school together and went to the abortion clinic, and it was all over quickly. I had the good fortune to be completely anesthetized, so I have no recollection of the procedure itself." She adds an odd afterthought: "Although I still hate vacuum cleaners."

Marion chimes in, "I can relate. I didn't have enough money to be put under."

Kathy says, "It's funny, but they didn't charge extra around here."

Marion responds, "Well, in New York they charge extra for mustard on your hotdog."

Marion and Kathy sit side by side across the table from me. They look reasonably alike in their professional outfits and jewelry, though Marion is small and slight and Kathy is sturdy, glowing with health. Both women were pregnant in their teens. But Kathy, who had a loving boyfriend, supportive parents, and teachers offering help, plus an extra dose of native self-confidence, walked into an abortion clinic without a backward glance. Marion, the battered waif, wept over her baby and begged for help to save it, but ended up hopeless and alone.

Kathy resumes her story. "Three years later I got pregnant again, and my parents pressured me to have an abortion. There was no way that I was going to do that again."

"Why not?" I ask.

"First of all," Kathy says, "I had gone back to church. Not to my parents' church—I figured that if they belonged to it, it wasn't much good. Also I'd developed a sort of a romanticized image of the Catholic church. I was a bookworm and had read books by Maria Von Trapp and others that led me to think of the Catholic church as a *family* church, a church where your religious beliefs are part of your daily activities. Bob's family was Catholic, and I thought I saw them living out what I had been reading. So I said, 'This is for me,' and I started to investigate becoming a Catholic.

"So when I went back to college that fall I confided in a nun that I was pregnant (she said, 'Well, I didn't figure you were the

Virgin Mary') and she and the priests were very, very supportive.

"The tough part had been getting through that summer. My father's attitude was, if you're pregnant, you get married or you have an abortion. And my mother's attitude was that you have an abortion or you have an abortion. They sent me to three different psychiatrists to persuade me to have an abortion. But I really didn't want to do it; I wanted to give the baby up for adoption. I had the feeling that I wanted to do it *right* this time. I wouldn't have told you that I got pregnant on purpose, but I got pregnant on purpose. I wanted to do what I should have done the first time.

"Five years after that pregnancy, Bob and I got married. At that point we had known each other nine years. We now have three kids, seven, five, and one."

It strikes me that this is another one of the rare cases, like Cheryl in Tampa, where a woman has taken all three paths: abortion, adoption, and parenting. The difference in Kathy's case is that her husband was father to all the children. The three kids at home have, not a half-sister, but a full sister, out there somewhere, fifteen years old. "Do you know where your first daughter is now?" I ask.

"I know where she *was*," Kathy says. "I was going to college in New Haven, and that's where she was adopted." Recalling her college town prompts Kathy to tell me something more. "I don't say this out of pride, but sometimes it makes a difference to people. I went to Yale College and Harvard Law School. Not that it matters, but sometimes it makes people listen harder."

I am impressed, though not really surprised. Marion looks down and deadpans, "Well, *I* did *drugs* in high school." This brings on laughter, which doubles when Kathy says, "So did I!"

When order returns, I ask Kathy, "Can you compare the grief of the abortion and the adoption?"

Kathy states, "There wasn't any grief with the adoption."

"Really?" I'm surprised. But throughout her story Kathy has shown herself to be unusually strong-minded.

"Well, the hard part," she says, "was having to face for the first time that I wasn't quite as capable as I had thought. And realizing that the right thing for my baby wasn't me. I came to see that wishing I could keep this baby was like wishing the sky was green—and I'm just not the kind of person who goes around thinking, 'If only the sky was green.'"

I ask Kathy what would have helped her not have an abortion. She says, "I definitely needed more information, to help me visualize the baby. In today's climate you can't get near a clinic without there being pro-lifers outside; I think that probably would have made a difference to me. But whether it would have made me more determined or whether it would have made me waiver—I don't know. Partly, I was just numb."

Colleen pipes up now to add her experience. She is a small, appealing woman with a round freckled face framed by dusty-brown curls. Her Boston accent is strong enough to pucker gabardine. "If you think numb is something, I was *anesthetized.* I didn't even know I had an abortion. This is true. I had forgotten about it.

"When I had my abortion, I too was sixteen. I'm from a very strict family. And for me to get pregnant—I was a fabulous princess, I was the one who never gave them any problems. I was in fear of my father; even though I knew he loved me, I wouldn't tell him."

I ask if he was violent or yelled at her.

"No, no, he loved us," Colleen says, surprised. "He loved us and he never—no, he wasn't abusive. He was a moral authority. I'm from a tough city and I grew up in a tough neighborhood, and my father was always trying to protect me somehow. So I'm growing up with all this morality, and I meet this boy and he's got the morality too. I had not a *clue* to sex or anything. I'm not kidding you. I don't know who is going to believe this because I can't believe it."

Rita Ann says, "I believe it." Others agree.

"Not a clue," says Colleen. "I got pregnant. He had me skip school with him, and I was thinking 'I can't believe I'm doing this, but I'm doing it.' My parents were fighting at home, no one was paying enough attention to me. I knew that they loved me, but they had their own problems, you know? I said, 'I'll just have sex,' and the boy said 'Sure.' I was so stupid!

"I'm sixteen years old, I'm a senior at a girl's high school. The boy was at a public school, and I thought he was a doll. At a private school we never see boys. He really loved me, honestly; we really loved each other. So sex was like a natural thing to do at this point. We went home and, believe it or not, we told his parents. His parents loved me, absolutely. Everyone is going to protect me, it's this little round face. They haven't got a *clue* what's going on up here.

"His parents were absolutely furious at him—not me. It was, 'How could you do this to her?' And I started thinking, yes, how could you do this to me? He was a good guy, and I would have married him.

"So I thought, I'm going home and tell my mother. My mother and I are best friends now, but at that time in my life, I totally was deserted by her—totally. I think she was in so much fear of what my father would do—I really think that she was afraid he would," Colleen's voice drops, "have the guy bumped off. Yes, that's it exactly."

I recall her previous description of her dad and comment, "That's a high moral standard."

She says, "Yes, that's pretty high. My father is very pro-life today, and that is what kills me. I think if we had given him a chance, he would have supported me and I could have had the baby. I feel a lot of regret about that. But we just did not give him a chance. He never had a chance, this guy." She is genuinely sad.

Marion says, "When it comes to remembering our parents' responses, their initial reactions aren't necessarily the ones we should keep in mind. Can you imagine the shock?" This strikes me as generous, coming from one who still feels such rejection from her own mother.

"So anyway," Colleen goes on, "my mother planned to dissolve this. That's the word they used. It was never a baby. It was a dissolvement.

"Now this is the sad part. I was four and a half months pregnant, so figure it out. They bring me to my uncle's apartment, where I used to go for dinner. There were two abortionists there. I was on the kitchen table. And it didn't take. Then they told me they were going to give me a pill and it was going to dissolve.

"Did I know what was going on? It's really sad, it's very pathetic. So I thought it was all done. They said no, do you have any pains in your stomach? I went through two days of labor all by myself with not a clue of what was going on. And then I actually flushed that baby down the toilet. I was scared to death. And then I started getting milk in my breasts and I didn't know what was going on.

"My mother never saw me, she never once came in, but she stayed in bed for almost two days while I was going through that. That was what she used to do." I think about the forms a mother's grieving can take, and about the phenomenon called the "couvade syndrome" wherein the husband of a woman in labor will take to his bed with sympathetic pains.

Colleen concludes, "I actually went through a healing where I asked God to forgive me of this. And he really healed me and also showed me hope, and he showed me that his children would not be forgotten. And we will not have to be so secretive."

Rita Ann has been sitting quietly, serenely all this time. It is at last her turn to speak. "The part I feel sad about, Colleen, is that both of my parents died before I admitted to having an abortion. I never got a chance to talk about why it happened, to say to them, 'I'm sorry I took your grandchild away.'" I encourage her to go on.

"I had a storybook romance abortion," she says with a wry smile; it's quite a phrase. "I was the youngest of four, three older brothers in an Italian family. Talk about princess, I was a *queen*. I could do no wrong.

"I was twenty-two years old, but I was a baby twenty-two. It was 1965, and I had been going with Tom for a couple of years. When we made plans to marry, we went away for Labor Day—

how appropriate—and I got pregnant. When I realized it I told the youngest of my brothers.

"Then he said, 'What are you telling me for?' I said [whisper], 'Because now *you're* going to tell mom and dad.'" There is a burst of laughter from the group.

"Ronnie told my dad, and then I went in to talk to him. He took it well enough; he said, 'We'll just have a smaller wedding, and you won't get as much money and you won't get as many gifts.'

"Then I told Tommy. His reaction knocked me for a loop. 'You're pregnant? We can't get married with you pregnant. I can't do that to my family,' he said. I said, 'What choice do we have?' I was bewildered. I told him, 'I already told my family, everything is fine, we'll just get married in February instead of May.' But he was adamant; he wanted me to have an abortion."

"His family was backing him on this?" I ask.

"His family still does not know," Rita Ann says. "His family still thinks, to this day, that I had a ruptured appendix. They didn't ever learn I was pregnant.

"So I was between a rock and hard place. And I'm saying God, what did I do? Where are you? I became almost like a zombie. Tom arranged for me to have an abortion in Canada."

I ask, "Did you see this as a choice between Tom and your baby? You had the support of your family. Did you consider giving up Tom and having the baby?"

"No, it never crossed my mind," Rita Ann says. "He promised me that if I had the abortion, I would get pregnant on my honeymoon. We would have a child right away. As I look back it seems like I was there but I wasn't there, like I was going through the motions but I had already shut down. So he sent me to Canada with my best friend, Evelyn. We stayed at a hotel and came back and I was still pregnant. We never left the room. I mean, there was no way I was going to do this.

"Tom picked us up in Springfield and gave me a hug and asked me how I was. I said 'I'm fine, I'm pregnant.' 'You're what?!'" We laugh again. "'I sent you to abort it!' 'I can't do it, I won't do it, I didn't do it,' I told him.

"And yet I still didn't know what else I could do. All the avenues were open except this one, this guy who didn't want to shame his family. I think about what would have happened if I'd told my family, 'This is what Tommy wants me to do.' My father or my mother or one of my brothers would have kicked his butt! They would have called his family and said, 'Look, our daughter is pregnant. Never mind this crap about protecting your family's image—this is our daughter.'"

After a sigh, she goes on. "He couldn't hurt his family, but he could risk my life. So time went by, we got formally engaged at Christmas—I got my diamond and was still going through the motions. And then on January 22—yes, every year when January 22 comes I remember, because that's the anniversary of *Roe v. Wade*—he took me to the Hotel Madison. Anybody from Boston remember it? Well, they tore it down; it used to be over by the Boston Harbor, a real pit stop.

"He took me into a coffee shop on the ground floor, and handed me over to two men." Here Rita Ann slows her story, reduces it to broken bits. "Two men took me into a room. I was five months pregnant. They injected me with saline—I hemorrhaged. I left there looking like Ghandi in a sheet, with it wrapped around my legs. I ended up at the hospital in a coma with peritonitis...septicemia..." (she draws it out slowly) "106.7 temp...and...sterile."

"And sterile?" someone breathes. "Wow."

Rita Ann goes on. "So I was in the hospital, hanging on to life. The police became involved. My dad had connections. People say Tommy never left the hospital all the time I was in there; but it wasn't because he was concerned for me. It was because he feared for his life."

Marion says, "Thank goodness your father had connections."

Rita Ann nods. "Had he left the hospital, he would have been dead."

"Well then, thank God," says Marion. "Somebody made him do something right."

I'm thinking, boy, they play rough in Boston. This is the second time today I've heard this dad-with-connections angle.

Rita Ann goes on. "So he stayed at the hospital until I came out of the coma. They thought I would have to have dialysis or have brain damage. Well, nobody is too sure about the brain damage," she laughs, "but I don't have a kidney problem.

"The doctors decided that there was no way to save the baby. The septicemia and the peritonitis were so rampant that they had to take my baby cesarean just for me to survive. Years and years later I had a doctor look up those old medical records. There were photos. My baby was nothing but a burnt black mass. I stayed in the hospital for a couple of weeks, came home for a couple of days, and then went back into the hospital for another month and a half with complications.

"I did marry Tom. Being raised as I was, Italian, I was thinking if I couldn't have children, what purpose did I serve on God's green earth? I pictured myself: I can't have children, I've got two huge scars. Who can I show those to? Nobody else would have me. So I kept with the only man who knew it all.

"I told my family I was going to marry him. Since I was the real queenie, they just thought, 'If this is what she really wants.' But nobody understood where I was coming from; I'm not sure I did even.

"Part of it was that I had hoped that when we got married, I could adopt a child and life would go on. Well, I married in October. For Christmas he asked me what I wanted, and I said adoption papers. For my birthday in May, he asked me what I wanted, I said adoption papers. For Valentine's Day, for Easter, for Columbus Day, you name it. That went on for five years. And we had everything: a house in Belmont, a new car, a van, a truck, cruisers. We had a great life on the outside. If only they knew.

"My family and I never discussed it. His family, of course, thought I'd had a ruptured appendix. But when I finally discussed it with my brothers, they said that the fact that I lived was far more important to them than the abortion.

"After five years, I left him. And then for ten years I lived with another man, a childhood development therapist. He would come home and talk about the kids in his practice, and I would run in the bathroom and cry. He was a good man, but it was hard on him. Finally I came home one night and he'd left me a letter saying, 'I can't give you what you need.' I felt run into the ground. I went into crisis therapy and everyday saw a man in the morning and a woman at night, but still I wasn't talking about the abortion.

"That August, 1987, I was just falling apart," Rita Ann goes on. "I was dysfunctional at work, I lost weight (it was wonderful!). I walked into St. Joan's Church and met a priest; he had just said mass and he was still all draped. I said, 'I want to go to confession.' Less than five minutes later I was saying, [a blurting rush of words] 'It's been twenty-two years since my last confession and I had an abortion!' I walked out of that church like I was in a first communion dress, and it has been with me ever since.

"Then I got together with my doctor and we got my old medical records and went through them together, slowly. I found out that there was a nurse at the hospital, a black woman in the maternity ward. I remember her telling me for some reason to be quiet and not say anything. What I found out from the records, and this was the ultimate for me, is that she had baptized my baby. She named him Michael."

Rita Ann's smile is blissful, marked by her habitual deep quietness.

To round off the session, I ask what anyone could have done to help them continue their pregnancies.

Marion says, "Just if someone could have provided me with the same kind of help that we give in pregnancy care centers. I couldn't look myself in the mirror if I didn't stand by those women and walk them all the way through."

Rita Ann has obviously been thinking this over. "Sometimes I think we post-abortion women need to reach out and let people know what's on the other side for you if you have an abortion. You should know what you're going to live with. I thought there could be an ads in papers saying, 'Thinking of abortion? Talk to me first,' and an 800 number. The line would be answered by women like me who are comfortable talking about it.

"Not religious, not our faith experience," she goes on, "just a frank description of the impact, the self-destructiveness. Tell her she's killing herself too. Women counselors like me, without the anger, without the hatred of men, just one woman to another saying, 'I did it, I went through this pain.'" Rita Ann would call this project SAGE, for Sharing Abortion's Grief Experience.

We stand up to leave; some have long drives ahead. As the others depart, Colleen lingers behind. She has done so for a reason. She comes up to me, takes my hand, and looks me in the eye. "I have to tell you, Frederica, I almost didn't do this today. I almost backed out. Over and over again I thought, 'I just don't know if I'm ready.'

"But when I saw you, I knew it would be all right. I knew it would be safe to tell you my story." Her eyes are a tender blue.

As I look at her I see the dozens of other women this year who have made that decision, who have risked revealing some of their most painful memories to the ears, and the tape recorder, of a stranger. The Real Choices hearings are over now, and soon all the stories will be frozen in type and stacked between book covers. From there they may provoke tears from the sympathetic, or sneers from those who believe only immature women reject their abortions. Or they may be ignored.

But dozens of women across the country, strangers to each other and to me, decided, like Colleen, to take a chance. All they ask is that we listen.

Summary and Recommendations

I sure thought it would be easier," said Jeannie French, Director of Executive Affairs for the National Women's Coalition for Life. When NWCL took on this research project, we had an expectation that the problems in unexpected pregnancy would be easy to identify, even if the solutions were not. We thought that by surveying pregnancy care centers, talking to post-abortion women, and reviewing previous research we could readily come up with a rank-order list of the most pressing problems. Finding solutions would be the next step.

It turned out that the first step was a doozy. The Alan Guttmacher Institute study which we used as our springboard had listed "Woman is concerned about how having a baby could change her life" as the most common reason; our pregnancy care center directors pegged it as number six, behind concerns about work, school, finances, adoption, and her relationship with the baby's father. Women in our post-abortion listening groups put their relationship with the baby's father first, and pressure from their parents second. Pregnancy center directors had parental pressure in thirteenth place.

Looking at others' research did not clarify the picture. The Open Arms Survey echoed our listening groups' insistence that the reasons for abortion are overwhelmingly social, not practical, while David Reardon's work in *Aborted Women, Silent No More*, showed social pressures accounting for less than half. Mary Cunningham Agee insisted that in The Nurturing Network's experience problems with college or career head the list; these are fourth and fifth on the pregnancy care center survey.

Part of the problem, of course, is that unplanned pregnancy creates a nest of interlocking problems not easily separated. They are of different categories: financial problems coexist with relational problems, with concrete worries and vaguer emotional undercurrents. We are comparing, not apples and oranges, but apples and sneezes and telephone poles. What's more, a relational problem may be overcome, indirectly, by a practical solution, and vice versa.

Even the apparently simple task of listing potential problems is more difficult than it seems; redundancy and overlap are hard to sort out. We wished, for purposes of consistency, to build on the Alan Guttmacher Institute study, but in so doing perpetuated some of its problems. What is the difference between "concerned about how having a baby could change her life" and every other item on the list? Between "too young to have a child" and "unready for responsibility"? What hidden overlap between "can't afford baby now" and "wants to avoid single parenthood"?

Differences between women factor in too. Those who are strong-willed and self-reliant will make soup out of stones; others, more aimless and dependent, will drift unresisting where the tide carries. For some the sense of shame at the pregnancy is so overwhelming that other problems and solutions are irrelevant. Each woman is a case unto herself.

For this reason, as the Alan Guttmacher Institute study recommended, attempts to help women continue pregnancies must be individualized. We would add that they be personalized, that is, that they involve a strong component of one-to-one personal friendship. This, then, leads off our list of recommendations:

1. Fight isolation with friendship. Abortion grows from a woman's sense that she is alone and unsupported. Abortion-rights rhetoric tries to turn her isolation into a virtue by proclaiming her autonomy: it's her right, her body, her decision alone. But the experience of pregnancy is about human inter-connectedness at its most profound levels. We reverse the fall into loneliness by ringing the woman with circles of support.

Women in our post-abortion groups said consistently that what they needed most was a steady friend to stand by them through the days ahead. Be that friend. There are no "public policy" implications here; this is not an item for bureaucracy. Pro-lifers who wish to turn the tide of a million and a half abortions a year can tackle them one at a time, by volunteering personally to befriend women in their community. If you are not already so involved, check your local Yellow Pages for groups offering "Alternatives to Abortion", or phone the national office of an organization listed in Appendix I.

2. Encourage natural bonds. The need for the friendship and support of a stranger is a sign that connections with more natural sources of support have broken down. Seek ways to rebuild these. Explore carefully the possibility of marriage to the baby's father, the person intended by nature to meet the woman and child's continuing needs. The widespread expectation that these dads are disposable—or, even worse, contemptible—damages us all in myriad ways. When men are offered a parental role that is urgently needed and worthy of respect, they may be moved to accept it; the alternative of single parenting damages mother and child too deeply.

For a young woman, her parents are another obvious source of encouragement. That relationship may have been shaken by storms of adolescence even before the pregnancy began. An impartial third party, especially one who knows from experience what it is to be a parent, may be able to help mend fences.

3. Encourage consideration of adoption. Adoption is a choice which benefits both baby and mother far more than does single parenting. It may be painful for a woman to imagine placing her child for adoption, but it may be a source of less pain over the years than the poverty, frustration, and blighted dreams of premature child-rearing or the guilt of abortion. Assure women that adoption delays for older, foster children do not extend to babies, and their children will not be rejected. Help her make adoption plans that take into account her need to move through stages of grief to healing; wide-open adoption may backfire in this department, keeping wounds wide-open for decades.

4. Help build employment plans that allow her to mother her child. Develop leads for employment locally with businesses that allow some work from home, flexible hours, job-sharing, compressed work-weeks, or other innovations developed with parents in mind. Keep on hand books suggesting ideas for home-based businesses and self-employment. Explore opportunities for alternative ways of earning income before she is pushed into the dreary McJob/day care cycle.

5. Prepare for a phasing-out of welfare benefits to single mothers. Pregnancy care centers have always used any help they could get, and welfare was no exception. The tide is now turning against single parenting, however, and we can expect to see those benefits reduced in the years ahead. The hope is that this will, ultimately, cause centers to have fewer clients, as women make wiser choices about sex, marriage, and pregnancy.

Where needs still remain the gap should be filled by help from churches. Marvin Olasky points out that the church is charged to care and suffer with the needy, and full-scale welfare interfered with hearing that call. "A system that increases the tendency to aid the least of these brothers is a good one; a system that decreases that tendency is doing Satan's work."[1]

6. Take courage. Abortion is the tail attached to the double-kite of careerism and sexual revolution. It does not soar on its own, but is lifted by these behaviors. Indeed, they make abortion almost inevitable. A woman who places workplace competition before all other goods will find herself seriously impeded if she has a child. On the other hand, the expectation that she will have sex with a variety of men as often as she wants, maybe more, means that she is exposed more frequently to conceiving a pregnancy in situations where there is insufficient commitment to raise a child. Simultaneous pursuit of behaviors that cause children and that are hampered by children finds its resolution on the abortion table. As long as these values—careerism and sexual revolution—were ascendant, abortion could not be contained. Now there are some signs—faint but encouraging—that that double-kite may be preparing to plummet:

• The youngest generation of parents, the twenty- to twenty-four-year-olds, are refusing to put job ahead of family. "The one-paycheck family is now the fastest-growing household unit," intones the financial weekly *Barrons*. Majorities of these young parents say they're going to give their kids more attention than their parents gave them. Even the older generation of parents, the ones who pioneered the mom-at-work experiment, are following the younger parents home.

• Liberal as well as conservative thinkers over the last few years have been daring to propose that two-parent families are better for children than any alternative family innovation. The April 1993 cover of the *Atlantic Monthly*, which stated in sizable block letters, "Dan Quayle Was Right," signaled the turning of this tide.

• Welfare reformers are paying heed to what conservatives have been saying for years—that the broken family is the mainspring of poverty and a school for criminals. Politicians across the political spectrum are more willing to vote for reforms that cut subsidies for unwed childbearing.

• Abstinence, once the laughingstock of social theories, is making a comeback. Even liberals are beginning to be willing to say that the youngest adolescent girls, if no one else, should be taught to say "no" to sex. *Washington Post* columnist Judy Mann writes, "Is there anyone who would argue that a 12-...[to] 16-year-old-child—yes, I said child—ought to be having sexual intercourse? Can we not agree that, raging hormones or not, this is simply too young?"[2]

Mann has company. President Clinton's domestic policy advisor, William Galston, wants a teen abstinence education campaign as aggressive as anti-smoking efforts. Maryland already has an abstinence campaign, which includes billboards that read: "Virgin—Teach your kid it's not a dirty word." The project has seen a 5 percent drop in teen births every year. When a national pro-choice/pro-life dialogue network recently choose topics for working groups, the one concerned with teen sexuality framed its task as, not sex-ed-and-contraception, but "postponing sexual involvement."

Judy Mann's counterpart at the *Baltimore Sun*, Susan Reimer, exemplifies the bind liberals endure here. She believes that "sexual liberation...[was not] a bad idea,"[3] yet sees the need for abstinence education, since "sex education is not enough...providing information on contraceptives does not increase the likelihood that [teens] will use them." Unwilling to ask anyone to "renounce pleasure," she suggests that girls be told instead to wait and grow up because older men are "better lovers" (an idea that falls under the category of "not completely thought through"). Reimer's column the next day was headed "Painfully concluding having babies out of wedlock is wrong." Rough times for the Daughters of the Sexual Revolution.

Pro-lifers began the fight against abortion some twenty-five years ago, expecting that most reasonable people would instinctively recoil from the idea of killing unborn children, and that they would readily agree it should be illegal. Attention was focused on the political battle, with strategists confident that the majority of Americans shared the pro-life view.

That confidence was unwarranted. The political playing field was swept by a hurricane of cultural change, change for which abortion was a necessary enabler. While the majority of Americans would still tell a pollster that they disliked abortion, they were reluctant to make it illegal; it had become a cultural necessity. The battle wasn't, at root, a political one after all.

In this project we have tried to identify and seek solutions for the cultural pressures that lead toward abortion. Readers used to the polarized, political terms typical of this issue may not immediately realize that nothing in these pages concerns strategies to make abortion illegal. The present, legal status has been assumed. We have not gloated over ways to restrict "a woman's choice"; instead, we have sought ways to expand her choices with adoption, marriage, shelter, employment, and every other resource available.

Pro-choice leaders have long said, "No woman wants to have an abortion." Pro-lifers agree. But if women are doing something they don't want to do forty-four hundred times a day, they are further from freedom than ever. If a woman is to make a life-affirming choice, one both she and her baby can live with, she needs more than the one miserable alternative of abortion.

It's time to have another cultural revolution. It's time to give her Real Choices.

1. Marvin Olasky, "Wealth and Welfare in Biblical Perspective," paper delivered at the Wilberforce Forum, April 23, 1994.
2. Judy Mann, "What's So Bad About Abstinence?" *Washington Post*, April 24, 1992.
3. Susan Reimer, "No Putting Off New Way of Saying Sex Must Wait," April 6, 1994.

APPENDIX

A P P E N D I X   A

Membership of The National Women's Coalition for Life

National Headquarters
Jeannie French, Executive Director
PO Box 1553
Oak Park, IL 60304
708-848-5351

Members

American Victims of Abortion: educating the public about abortion's devastating effects on women and families.

Olivia Gans, President
419 7th Street NW, Suite 402
Washington, DC 20004
202-626-8832

Capitol Hill Women for Life: uniting women working in the legislative sector to advocate for the unborn and their mothers.

Jennifer Larkin
c/o Congressman Dornan
US House of Representatives
Washington, DC 20515
202-225-2965

Feminists for Life: continuing the tradition of pro-life feminism, condemning abortion as another victimization of women.

Serrin M. Foster, Executive Director
733 15th Street, NW Suite 1100
Washington, DC 20005
202-737-3352

Fortress International: assisting women who have become pregnant through rape or incest, as well as children conceived through sexual assault.

Julie Makimaa, President
PO Box 2562
South Bend, IN 46680-2562
219-288-3688

International Black Women's Network: motivating and strengthening black women to address the various needs in the black community, including spiritual and familial.

Pastor Jean Thompson, President
3308 Dodge Park Road
Landover, MD 20785
301-322-3311

Life After Assault League: offering Christian victim-to-victim assistance to sexually abused adults and children.

Kay Zibolsky, President
1336 W. Lindbergh
Appleton, WI 54914
414-739-4489

National Association of Pro-Life Nurses: seeking to nurture all life and to protect the rights of the nurses to refuse to participate in unethical medical procedures.

Jodie Breakiron, President
PO Box 82
Elysian, MN 56028-0082
904-724-1581

National Coalition of Catholic Women: acting through its affiliated organizations to educate and organize Catholic women in spirituality, leadership, and service.

Annette Kane, Executive Director
1275 K Street, NW Suite 975
Washington, DC 20005
202-682-0334

Professional Women's Network: representing women from a variety of professional and business fields who respect the sanctity of human life.

Rose M. Walsh, National Director
PO Box 31965
Chicago, IL 60631
312-362-1620

Victims of Choice: providing support for women who have suffered as a result of the deceit of the abortionists and their proponents.

Elizabeth Verchio, Executive Director
PO Box 815
Naperville, IL 60566
708-378-1680

Women Affirming Life: voicing the commitment of Catholic women in supporting women and the dignity of life and motherhood.

Gerri Holland, Executive Director
PO Box 35532
Brighton, MA 02135
617-327-7626

Women Exploited By Abortion: working to expose the horror and trauma of abortion and supporting women who mourn the loss of their children.

Kathy Walker, Executive Director
PO Box 268
Venus, TX 76084
817-578-1681

Women for Faith and Family: affirming the intrinsic sacredness of all human life, consistent with the teachings of the Catholic Church.

Helen Hull Hitchcock, Director
PO Box 8326
St. Louis, MO 63132
314-863-8385

Women for Women: a Marian organization assisting women in the transition between the workplace and the home.

Janice Weber, President
PO Box 937
Kings Park, NY 11754
516-269-0844

A P P E N D I X   B

REAL CHOICES - PREGNANCY CARE CENTER DIRECTOR'S SURVEY

Name _____

Center Name _____

Address _____

City, State _____   Zip _____

Phone_____

I. Resources:

Here is a list of resources you might offer women in a difficult pregnancy. As you read over the list, please put an X over the number of any resource you do not offer (e.g., 19. Parenting classes). Then, please circle the number of the four resources that you most urgently need more of (e.g., 4. Donated legal assistance).

1. Hot-line/Crisis counseling
2. Ongoing support counseling
3. Donated (in whole or part) obstetric care
4. Donated legal assistance
5. Maternity/baby clothes, equipment
6. Adoption assistance
7. Housing during pregnancy
8. Housing after birth
9. Job training or placement
10. Peer group support
11. Support fighting job discrimination
12. Specialized services for young teens
13. Assistance in continuing education
14. Training in handling finances/ budgeting
15. Child care for school/work hours
16. Mother's Day Out (occasional child care)
17. Assistance accessing public benefits
18. Childbirth/breastfeeding education
19. Parenting classes
20. Transportation to services
21. Assistance receiving child support payments
22. Monetary aid with bills, groceries, etc.
23. Rape or family violence counseling or referral
24. Miscarriage/stillbirth counseling
25. Post-abortion grief counseling
26. AIDS/sexually transmitted disease referral
27. Aiding communication with partner/parents
28. Substance abuse treatment referral
29. Experienced-mother/new-mother mentorships
30. Other_____
31. Please estimate how many clients you serve per year_____

32. Please estimate, as best you can, the profile of the clients you serve:

Under 18	_____%	Married	_____%
18-24	_____%	Single	_____%
25-29	_____%		100%
30-40	_____%		
over 40	+_____%		
	100%		
Black	_____%	First pregnancy	_____%
White	_____%	Previous abortion	_____%
Latino	_____%	Previous birth	+_____%
Asian	_____%		100%
Am. Indian	_____%		
Other	+_____%		
	100%		

II. Problems: When a woman is having difficulty continuing a pregnancy, how often are the following problems involved? How easy are they to solve? What resources, from the list in Section I above, might you use in solving them?

PROBLEM	RARE	COMMON	EASY	DIFFICULT	RESOURCES
Example: Woman's parents want her to have abortion	1 2 3 ④ 5		1 2 ③ 4 5		7, 19, 27
33. Woman apprehensive about physical experience of pregnancy/birth	1 2 3 4 5		1 2 3 4 5		_____
34. Woman doesn't want others to know she has had sex or is pregnant	1 2 3 4 5		1 2 3 4 5		_____
35. Husband or partner absent, undependable, or insufficiently supportive	1 2 3 4 5		1 2 3 4 5		_____
36. Husband or partner wants woman to have abortion	1 2 3 4 5		1 2 3 4 5		_____

PROBLEM	RARE	COMMON	EASY	DIFFICULT	RESOURCES

37. Woman has problems with relationship or wants to avoid single parenthood

1 2 3 4 5   1 2 3 4 5   _____

38. Woman at risk for being battered/abused

1 2 3 4 5   1 2 3 4 5   _____

39. Woman tempted to batter/abuse

1 2 3 4 5   1 2 3 4 5   _____

40. Woman's parents want her to have abortion

1 2 3 4 5   1 2 3 4 5   _____

41. Pregnancy will interfere with school or job situation

1 2 3 4 5   1 2 3 4 5   _____

42. Child-rearing will interfere with school or job situation

1 2 3 4 5   1 2 3 4 5   _____

43. Woman says she can't afford baby now

1 2 3 4 5   1 2 3 4 5   _____

44. Woman or partner has AIDS or sexually transmitted disease

1 2 3 4 5   1 2 3 4 5   _____

45. Adoption appears too difficult (practically or emotionally)

1 2 3 4 5   1 2 3 4 5   _____

46. Woman is concerned about how having a baby could change her life

1 2 3 4 5   1 2 3 4 5   _____

PROBLEM	RARE	COMMON	EASY	DIFFICULT	RESOURCES
47. Woman needs assistance with obstetric care	1 2 3 4 5		1 2 3 4 5		_____
48. Woman is worried about what others will think (family, friends, co-workers, teachers, etc.)	1 2 3 4 5		1 2 3 4 5		_____
49. Woman says she is unready for responsibility	1 2 3 4 5		1 2 3 4 5		_____
50. Woman needs housing during pregnancy	1 2 3 4 5		1 2 3 4 5		_____
51. Woman needs housing after birth	1 2 3 4 5		1 2 3 4 5		_____
52. Woman has all the children she wants or has all grown-up children	1 2 3 4 5		1 2 3 4 5		_____
53. Woman needs child care after birth	1 2 3 4 5		1 2 3 4 5		_____
54. Woman says she is not mature enough, or that she is too young to have a child	1 2 3 4 5		1 2 3 4 5		_____
55. Woman has habits complicating care (drugs, alcohol, prostitution, etc.)	1 2 3 4 5		1 2 3 4 5		_____
56. Woman has health problem	1 2 3 4 5		1 2 3 4 5		_____

PROBLEM	RARE	COMMON	EASY	DIFFICULT	RESOURCES

57. Fetus has possible health problem

1 2 3 4 5   1 2 3 4 5   _____

58. Woman was victim of rape or incest

1 2 3 4 5   1 2 3 4 5   _____

59. Public benefits are inadequate

1 2 3 4 5   1 2 3 4 5   _____

60. Other_____

1 2 3 4 5   1 2 3 4 5   _____

61. In your opinion, which are more influential in discouraging a woman from continuing a pregnancy:

_____ emotional concerns or   _____ practical problems? (Check one)

62. Would you be willing to work with pro-choice activists to alleviate these problems, if beliefs about abortion were not raised as an issue?

Yes _____   No _____

63. Further comments. Are there problems we have not named, or solutions that we have not seen? Other factors that should be considered? Comments on the survey or the project as a whole? Please use reverse sides as necessary.

_____

_____

_____

_____

_____

_____

_____

_____

A P P E N D I X   C

REAL CHOICES-PREGNANCY CARE CENTER DIRECTOR SURVEY FINAL REPORT

Return Rates

1980 surveys were mailed according to the following schedule:

Christian Action Council (Care Net):	460	June
Birthright	200	June
Birthright (2nd set)	700	August
Alternatives to Abortion Int'l	50	May
Bethany	50	June
Heartbeat	300	August
Andy Merritt (for independent centers)	60	June
Maryland centers	40	June

194 surveys were returned between June 7 and November 8, 1993, resulting in an overall return rate of 10.4%.

Resources Most Often Not Offered

RESOURCE	NO.	PERCENT
#16. Mother's Day Out (occasional child care)	169	87.1 ± 1.6
#9. Job training or placement	165	85.1 ± 1.8
#11. Support fighting job discrimination	164	84.5 ± 1.8
#15. Child care for school/work hours	163	84.0 ± 1.9
#21. Assistance receiving child support payments	136	70.1 ± 2.9
# 3. Donated (in whole or part) obstetric care	124	63.9 ± 3.2
#12. Specialized services for young teens	112	57.7 ± 3.4
# 4. Donated legal assistance	109	56.2 ± 3.5
#19. Parenting classes	108	55.7 ± 3.5
# 8. Housing after birth	107	55.2 ± 3.5
#22. Monetary aid with bills, groceries, etc.	106	54.6 ± 3.5
#29. Experienced-mother/new mother mentorships	104	53.6 ± 3.5
#13. Assistance in continuing education	102	52.6 ± 3.5
#10. Peer group support	100	51.5 ± 3.5
#24. Miscarriage/stillbirth counseling	89	45.9 ± 3.5
#14. Training in handling finances/budgeting	86	44.3 ± 3.5
#18. Childbirth/breastfeeding education	73	37.6 ± 3.3
# 20. Transportation to services	69	35.6 ± 3.2

RESOURCE	NO.	PERCENT
# 7. Housing during pregnancy	30	15.5 ± 1.8
#26. AIDS/sexually transmitted disease referral	23	11.9 ± 1.5
#1. Hot-line/Crisis counseling	20	10.3 ± 1.3
#23. Rape or family violence counseling or referral	20	10.3 ± 1.3
#6. Adoption assistance	20	10.3 ± 1.3
#28. Substance abuse treatment referral	19	9.8 ± 1.2
#27. Aiding communication with partner/parents	14	7.2 ± 0.9
#17. Assistance accessing public benefits	13	6.7 ± 0.9
#25. Post-abortion grief counseling	11	5.7 ± 0.8
#2. Ongoing support counseling	7	3.6 ± 0.5
#5. Maternity/baby clothes, equipment	6	3.1 ± 0.4

Resources Most Often Needed

	NO.	PERCENT
#3. Donated (in whole or in part) obstetric care	70	36.1 ± 3.2
#7. Housing during pregnancy	65	33.5 ± 3.1
#8. Housing after birth	60	30.9 ± 3.0
#4. Donated legal assistance	41	21.1 ± 2.3
#22. Monetary aid with bills, groceries, etc.	35	18.0 ± 2.1
#15. Child care for school/work hours	32	16.5 ± 1.9
#29. Experienced-mothers/new-mother mentorships	28	14.4 ± 1.7
#9. Job training or placement	28	14.4 ± 1.7
#1. Lot-line/Crisis counseling	27	13.9 ± 1.7
#10. Peer group support	27	13.9 ± 1.7
#2. Ongoing support counseling	26	13.4 ± 1.6
#19. Parenting classes	23	11.9 ± 1.5
#12. Specialized services for young teens	18	9.3 ± 1.2
#20. Transportation to services	18	9.3 ± 1.2
#25. Post-abortion grief counseling	16	8.2 ± 1.1
#5. Maternity/baby clothes, equipment	13	6.7 ± 0.9
#27. Aiding communication with partner/parents	12	6.2 ± 0.8
#14. Training in handling finances/budgeting	11	5.7 ± 0.8
#16. Mother's Day Out (occasional child care)	9	4.6 ± 0.6
#23. Rape or family violence counseling or referral	9	4.6 ± 0.6
#26. AIDS/sexually transmitted disease referral	9	4.6 ± 0.6
#6. Adoption assistance	8	4.1 ± 0.6
#13. Assistance in continuing education	7	3.6 ± 0.5
#17. Assistance accessing public benefits	7	3.6 ± 0.5
#24. Miscarriage/stillbirth counseling	7	3.6 ± 0.5
#28. Substance abuse treatment referral	5	2.6 ± 0.4
#18. Childbirth/breastfeeding education	4	2.1 ± 0.3
#21. Assistance receiving child support payments	3	1.5 ± 0.2
#11. Support fighting job discrimination	2	1.0 ± 0.1

Demographics

Average NO. OF CLIENTS served per year per center = 763

Reported Demographics
>   weighted by No. of clients seen in center per year:
>   (note: reported percentages will not always add up to 100%)

Estimated distribution of clients by AGE:

< 18	18-24	25-29	30-40	> 40
27.9%	43.3%	17.3%	9.5%	2.0%

Estimated distribution of clients by MARITAL STATUS:

MARRIED	SINGLE
25.9%	73.2%

Estimated distribution of clients by RACE:

BLACK	WHITE	LATINO	ASIAN	AM. INDIAN	OTHER
19.9%	63.9%	14.2%	3.0%	2.9%	3.1%

Estimated distribution of clients by PREGNANCY HISTORY:

FIRST PREGNANCY	PREVIOUS ABORTION	PREVIOUS BIRTH
59.7%	15.7%	28.9%

Please be aware that these data are merely estimates.

Most Common Problems (IN ORDER)

1. #45. Adoption appears too difficult (practically or emotionally)
2. #35. Husband or partner absent, undependable, or insufficiently supportive
3. #43. Woman says she can't afford baby now
4. #42. Child-rearing will interfere with school or job situation
5. #41. Pregnancy will interfere with school or job situation
6. #46. Woman is concerned about how having a baby could change her life
7. #37. Woman has problems with relationship or wants to avoid single parenthood
8. #34. Woman doesn't want others to know she has had sex or is pregnant
9. #47. Woman needs assistance with obstetric care
10. #49. Woman says she is unready for responsibility
11. #48. Woman is worried about what others will think (family, friends, co-workers, teachers, etc.)
12. #36. Husband or partner wants woman to have abortion
13. #40. Woman's parents want her to have abortion

14. #54. Woman says she is not mature enough, or that she is too young
to have a child
15. #53. Woman needs child care after birth
16. #59. Public benefits are inadequate
17. #51. Woman needs housing after birth
18. #50. Woman needs housing during pregnancy
19. #52. Woman has all the children she wants or has all grown-up children
20. #33. Woman apprehensive about physical experience of pregnancy/birth
21. #55. Woman has habits complicating care (drugs, alcohol, prostitution, etc.)
22. #38. Woman at risk for being battered/abused
23. #56. Woman has health problem
24. #44. Woman or partner has AIDS or sexually transmitted disease
25. #57. Fetus has possible health problem
25. #58. Woman was victim of rape or incest
26. #39. Woman tempted to batter/abuse

Most Difficult Problems (IN ORDER)

1. #45. Adoption appears too difficult (practically or emotionally)
2. #51. Woman needs housing after birth
3. #40. Woman's parents want her to have abortion
4. #58. Woman was victim of rape or incest
5. #35. Husband or partner absent, undependable, or insufficiently supportive
6. #55. Woman has habits complicating care (drugs, alcohol, prostitution, etc.)
7. #36. Husband or partner wants woman to have abortion
8. #57. Fetus has possible health problems
9. #38. Woman at risk for being battered/abused
10. #44. Woman or partner has AIDS or sexually transmitted disease
11. #39. Woman tempted to batter/abuse
12. #37. Woman has problems with relationship or wants to avoid single parenthood
13. #42. Child-rearing will interfere with school or job situation
14. #59. Public benefits are inadequate
15. #41. Pregnancy will interfere with school or job situation
16. #34. Woman doesn't want others to know she has had sex or is pregnant
17. #56. Woman has health problems
18. #52. Woman has all the children she wants or has all grown-up children
19. #54. Woman says she is not mature enough, or that she is too young
to have a child
20. #53. Woman needs child care after birth
21. #43. Woman says she can't afford baby now
22. #49. Woman says she is unready for responsibility
23. #46. Woman is concerned about how having a baby could change her life
24. #48. Woman is worried about what others will think (family, friends,
co-workers, teachers, etc.)
25. #50. Woman needs housing during pregnancy
26. #47. Woman needs assistance with obstetric care
27. #33. Woman apprehensive about physical experience of pregnancy/birth

Most Useful Resources

PROBLEM RESOURCE	NO.	NTOT*	PCT	ERROR

#33. Woman apprehensive about physical experience of pregnancy/birth

	NO.	NTOT*	PCT	ERROR
#18. Childbirth/breastfeeding education	110	155	71.0	±3.2
# 2. Ongoing support counseling	77	155	49.7	±3.9
#29. Experienced-mother/new-mother mentorships	44	155	28.4	±3.2
# 3. Donated (in whole or part) obstetric care	20	155	19.4	±2.5
#10. Peer group support	27	155	17.4	±2.3

#34. Woman doesn't want others to know she has had sex or is pregnant

	NO.	NTOT*	PCT	ERROR
# 2. Ongoing support counseling	106	147	72.1	±3.3
#27. Aiding communication with partner/parents	82	147	55.8	±4.0
# 7. Housing during pregnancy	46	147	31.3	±3.5
# 1. Hot-line/Crisis counseling	43	147	29.3	±3.3
#10. Peer group support	29	147	19.7	±2.6

#35. Husband or partner absent, undependable, or insufficiently supportive

	NO.	NTOT*	PCT	ERROR
# 2. Ongoing support counseling	93	144	64.6	±3.7
#17. Assistance accessing public benefits	64	144	44.4	±4.0
#21. Assistance receiving child support payments	53	144	36.8	±3.8
#27. Aiding communication with partner/parents	53	144	36.8	±3.8
# 7. Housing during pregnancy	44	144	30.6	±3.5

#36. Husband or partner wants woman to have an abortion

	NO.	NTOT*	PCT	ERROR
# 2. Ongoing support counseling	104	145	71.7	±3.3
#27. Aiding communication with partner/parents	99	145	68.3	±3.5
# 1. Hot-line/Crisis counseling	54	145	37.2	±3.8
# 7. Housing during pregnancy	25	145	17.2	±2.3
# 6. Adoption assistance	15	145	10.3	±1.5

#37. Woman has problems with relationship or wants to avoid single parenthood

	NO.	NTOT*	PCT	ERROR
# 2. Ongoing support counseling	100	145	69.0	±3.5
#27. Aiding communication with partner/parents	68	145	46.9	±4.1
# 6. Adoption assistance	57	145	39.3	±3.9
#10. Peer group support	27	145	18.6	±2.5
# 1. Hot-line/Crisis counseling	26	145	17.9	±2.4

* Total number of respondents answering question with one or more resource numbers.

PROBLEM RESOURCE	NO.	NTOT*	PCT	ERROR
#38. Woman at risk for being battered/abused				
#23. Rape/family violence counseling/referral	114	140	81.4	±2.0
# 2. Ongoing support counseling	82	140	58.6	±4.0
# 7. Housing during pregnancy	47	140	33.6	±3.7
# 1. Hot-line/Crisis counseling	40	140	28.6	±3.4
# 4. Donated legal assistance	23	140	16.4	±2.3
#39. Woman tempted to batter/abuse				
#23. Rape/family violence counseling/referral	94	131	71.8	±3.5
# 2. Ongoing support counseling	76	131	58.0	±4.2
#19. Parenting classes	48	131	36.6	±4.0
# 1. Hot-line/Crisis counseling	36	131	36.6	±3.4
#29. Experienced-mother/new-mother mentorships	24	131	18.3	±2.6
#40. Woman's parents want her to have abortion				
#27. Aiding communication with partner/parents	107	141	75.9	±3.0
# 2. Ongoing support counseling	96	141	68.1	±3.6
# 7. Housing during pregnancy	63	141	44.7	±4.1
# 1. Hot-line/Crisis counseling	43	141	30.5	±3.5
# 6. Adoption assistance	23	141	16.3	±2.3
#41. Pregnancy will interfere with school or job situation				
# 2. Ongoing support counseling	77	139	55.4	±4.1
#13. Assistance in continuing education	70	139	50.4	±4.2
#15. Child care for school/work hours	37	139	26.6	±3.2
# 9. Job training or placement	36	139	25.9	±3.2
#17. Assistance accessing public benefits	35	139	25.2	±3.1
#42. Child-rearing will interfere with school or job situation				
#15. Child care for school/work hours	69	140	49.3	±4.1
# 2. Ongoing support counseling	59	140	42.1	±4.0
#13. Assistance in continuing education	51	140	36.4	±3.8
#17. Assistance accessing public benefits	38	140	27.1	±2.4
# 6. Adoption assistance	25	140	17.9	±2.4
#43. Woman says she can't afford baby now				
#17. Assistance accessing public benefits	102	143	71.3	±3.4
# 5. Maternity/baby clothes, equipment	75	143	52.4	±4.1
#14. Training in handling finances/budgeting	58	143	40.6	±4.0
#22. Monetary aids with bills, groceries, etc.	51	143	35.7	±3.8
# 2. Ongoing support counseling	49	143	34.3	±3.7

PROBLEM RESOURCE	NO.	NTOT*	PCT	ERROR

#44. Woman or partner has AIDS or sexually transmitted disease

	NO.	NTOT*	PCT	ERROR
#26. AIDS/sexually transmitted disease referral	125	137	91.2	±1.3
# 2. Ongoing support counseling	53	137	38.7	±4.0
# 3. Donated (in whole or part) obstetric care	19	137	13.9	±2.0
# 1. Hot-line/Crisis counseling	12	137	8.8	±1.3
#17. Assistance accessing public benefits	11	137	8.0	±1.2

#45. Adoption appears too difficult (practically or emotionally)

	NO.	NTOT*	PCT	ERROR
# 6. Adoption assistance	117	140	83.6	±2.3
# 2. Ongoing support counseling	92	140	65.7	±3.7
#10. Peer group support	40	140	28.6	±3.4
# 1. Hot-line/Crisis counseling	14	140	10.0	±1.5
# 4. Donated legal assistance	10	140	7.1	±1.1

#46. Woman is concerned about how having a baby could change her life

	NO.	NTOT*	PCT	ERROR
# 2. Ongoing support counseling	106	140	75.7	±3.0
#29. Experienced-mother/new-mother mentorships	60	140	42.9	±4.1
#19. Parenting classes	47	140	33.6	±3.7
#10. Peer group support	45	140	32.1	±3.6
# 6. Adoption assistance	23	140	16.4	±2.3

#47. Woman needs assistance with obstetric care

	NO.	NTOT*	PCT	ERROR
# 3. Donated (in whole or part) obstetric care	94	134	70.1	±3.5
#17. Assistance accessing public benefits	72	134	53.7	±4.2
# 2. Ongoing support counseling	18	134	13.4	±2.0
#20. Transportation to services	14	134	10.4	±1.6

#48. Woman is worried about what others will think (family, friends, co-workers, teachers, etc.

	NO.	NTOT*	PCT	ERROR
# 2. Ongoing support counseling	117	139	84.2	±2.2
#27. Aiding communication with partner/parents	70	139	50.4	±4.2
#10. Peer group support	52	139	37.4	±3.9
# 1. Hot-line/Crisis counseling	24	139	17.3	±2.4
# 7. Housing during pregnancy	17	139	12.2	±1.8

#49. Woman says she is unready for responsibility

	NO.	NTOT*	PCT	ERROR
# 2. Ongoing support counseling	101	141	71.6	±3.4
#19. Parenting classes	59	141	41.8	±4.0
# 6. Adoption assistance	58	141	41.1	±4.0
#29. Experienced-mother/new-mother mentorships	48	141	34.0	±3.7
#10. Peer group support	45	141	31.9	±3.6

PROBLEM RESOURCE	NO.	NTOT*	PCT	ERROR

#50. Woman needs housing during pregnancy

# 7. Housing during pregnancy	131	139	94.2	±0.9
#17. Assistance accessing public benefits	24	139	17.3	±2.4
# 2. Ongoing support counseling	23	139	16.5	±2.3
# 8. Housing after birth	13	139	9.4	±1.4
# 6. Maternity/baby clothes, equipment	6	139	4.3	±0.7

#51. Woman needs housing after birth

# 8. Housing after birth	96	126	76.2	±3.2
#17. Assistance accessing public benefits	37	126	29.4	±3.6
# 2. Ongoing support counseling	24	126	19.0	±2.7
# 7. Housing during pregnancy	8	126	6.3	±1.0
#14. Training in handling finances/budgeting	8	126	6.3	±1.0

#52. Woman has all the children she wants or has all grown-up children

# 2. Ongoing support counseling	100	137	73.0	±3.3
# 6. Adoption assistance	67	137	48.9	±4.2
#10. Peer group support	26	137	19.0	±2.6
# 1. Hot-line/Crisis counseling	24	137	17.5	±2.4
# 6. Experienced-mother/new-mother mentorships	12	137	8.8	±1.3

#53. Woman needs child care after birth

#15. Child care for school/work hours	84	125	67.2	±3.9
#17. Assistance accessing public benefits	36	125	28.8	±3.6
#16. Mother's Day Out (occasional child care)	27	125	21.6	±3.0
# 2. Ongoing support counseling	23	125	18.4	±2.6
#29. Experienced-mother/new-mother mentorships	9	125	7.2	±1.2

#54. Woman says she is not mature enough, or that she is too young to have a child

# 2. Ongoing support counseling	97	139	69.8	±3.5
# 6. Adoption assistance	59	139	42.4	±4.1
#19. Parenting classes	56	139	40.3	±4.0
#10. Peer group support	46	139	33.1	±3.7
#29. Experienced-mother/new-mother mentorships	38	139	27.3	±3.3

#55. Woman has habits complicating care (drugs, alcohol, prostitution, etc.)

#28. Substance abuse treatment referral	123	137	89.8	±1.5
# 2. Ongoing support counseling	55	137	40.1	±4.0
#26. AIDS/sexually transmitted disease referral	26	137	19.0	±2.6
#17. Assistance accessing public benefits	18	137	13.1	±1.9

PROBLEM / RESOURCE	NO.	NTOT*	PCT	ERROR
#56. Woman has health problem				
# 3. Donated (in whole or part) obstetric care	83	125	66.4	±3.9
# 2. Ongoing support counseling	53	125	42.4	±4.3
#17. Assistance accessing public benefits	37	125	29.6	±3.7
#20. Transportation to services	8	125	6.4	±1.1
# 1. Hot-line/Crisis counseling	6	125	4.8	±0.8
#57. Fetus has health problem				
# 3. Donated (in whole or part) obstetric care	76	125	60.8	±4.2
# 2. Ongoing support counseling	59	125	47.2	±4.4
#17. Assistance accessing public benefits	32	125	25.6	±3.3
#10. Peer group support	12	125	9.6	±1.5
#24. Miscarriage/stillbirth counseling	9	125	7.2	±1.2
#58. Woman was victim of rape or incest				
#23. Rape/family violence counseling/support	123	137	89.8	±1.5
# 2. Ongoing support counseling	72	137	52.6	±4.2
# 1. Hot-line/Crisis counseling	20	137	14.6	±2.1
# 6. Adoption assistance	19	137	13.9	±2.0
#10. Peer group support	18	137	13.1	±1.9
#59. Public benefits are inadequate				
#17. Assistance accessing public benefits	60	118	50.8	±4.5
#22. Monetary aid with bills, groceries, etc.	44	118	37.3	±4.2
# 5. Maternity/baby clothes, equipment	34	118	28.8	±3.7
#14. Training in handling finances/budgeting	34	118	28.8	±3.7
#17. Assistance accessing public benefits	28	118	23.7	±3.3

Answers to Questions 61 & 62

#61. In your opinion, which are more influential in discouraging a woman from continuing a pregnancy: _____ emotional concerns or _____ practical problems?

Answer	Frequency	Percent
Emotional	105	58.5 ± 3.6
Practical	74	41.5 ± 3.6

Frequency Missing = 15

#62. Would you be willing to work with pro-choice activists to alleviate these problems, if beliefs about abortion were not raised as an issue? Yes   No

Answer	Frequency	Percent
Yes	127	79.2 ± 2.5
No	34	20.8 ± 2.5

Frequency Missing = 33

A P P E N D I X   D

Alan Guttmacher Institute Study

"Why Do Women Have Abortions?" by Aida Torres and Jacqueline Darroch Forrest, *Family Planning Perspectives,* July/August 1988.

"Percentage of abortion patients reporting that a specific reason contributed to their decision to have an abortion, [breakdown by age eliminated here]..., and percentage saying that each reason was the most important."

REASON	TOTAL	% MOST IMPORTANT
Woman is concerned about how having a baby could change her life	76%	16%
Woman can't afford baby now	68%	21%
Woman has problems with relationship or wants to avoid single parenthood	51%	12%
Woman is unready for responsibility	31%	21%
Woman doesn't want others to know she has had sex or is pregnant	31%	1%
Woman is not mature enough, or is too young to have a child	30%	11%
Woman has all the children she wanted, or has all grown-up children	26%	8%
Husband or partner wants woman to have abortion	23%	1%
Fetus has possible health problem	13%	3%
Woman has health problem	7%	3%
Woman's parents want her to have abortion	7%	less than 0.5%
Woman was victim of rape or incest	1%	1%
Other	6%	3%

A P P E N D I X   E

Open Arms, Reardon, and Agee Surveys

Open Arms Abortion Information Survey Project

The post-abortion organization, Open Arms, has been gathering information from abortive women since 1986. These items from their ongoing survey reflect data up to March, 1993.

Reason for abortion

Social:	82%
Economic:	8%
Health:	5%
Life:	1%
Rape:	1%
Incest:	<1%

Would have liked
pro-life information then

Yes:	63%
No:	20%
Not Sure:	7%

Did the relationship
with the father of the
baby end soon after
the abortion?

Yes:	52%
No:	45%

Would they have this
abortion again?

Yes:	9%
No:	83%
Not Sure:	3%

Aborted Women, Silent No More by David Reardon.
Crossway Books, Westchester, IL, 1987.

David Reardon has become one of America's leading experts on post-abortion grief. In his research for his landmark book, Reardon distributed a lengthy survey (57 questions) to 252 women in 42 states through the organization Women Exploited By Abortion, a member of the National Women's Coalition for Life. The following are the questions from this survey which relate to the reasons for the abortion.

	N/A OR UNSURE	NOT AT ALL				VERY MUCH
	0	1	2	3	4	5
Was the decision made for reasons of:						
mental health?	40%	34%	4%	6%	6%	11%
physical health?	41%	48%	2%	3%	1%	6%
financial limits?	32%	27%	5%	9%	5%	23%
social acceptance?	20%	12%	3%	7%	10%	47%
family size?	42%	48%	1%	2%	1%	6%
career goals?	41%	30%	4%	7%	5%	13%
long-term needs?	43%	22%	4%	7%	6%	18%
short-term needs?	41%	14%	2%	5%	9%	28%
other	54%	2%	0%	3%	2%	39%

Do you feel you were "forced" by outside circumstances to have an abortion?

	4%	12%	10%	10%	10%	54%

Were you encouraged to have an abortion by:

parents?	43%	35%	2%	6%	2%	21%
other family members?	41%	39%	3%	3%	2%	12%
husband?	54%	33%	1%	1%	2%	9%
boyfriend?	27%	27%	2%	4%	7%	33%
social worker?	52%	32%	2%	0%	4%	10%
abortion counselor?	39%	20%	2%	4%	8%	27%
doctor?	41%	27%	3%	6%	5%	18%
friends?	38%	28%	2%	7%	6%	18%
other	77%	5%	0%	2%	3%	13%

	N/A OR UNSURE	NOT AT ALL				VERY MUCH
	0	1	2	3	4	5

Would your choice have been different if any or all of the above had encouraged you differently?

	8%	4%	2%	3%	7%	76%

Do you feel you were "forced" by others to have an abortion?

	4%	23%	10%	10%	14%	39%

Other questions indicate that majorities of women felt that their decision was rushed, poorly thought out, and made with insufficient information. Respondents indicated a fairly even spread when asked if their decision was firm when they arrived at the abortion clinic, but are emphatic that clinic personnel did not help them explore the decision, offered biased opinions, and misinformed or under-informed them.

Did you consider adoption?

	4%	62%	13%	7%	6%	8%

Under better circumstances, would you have kept the baby?

	10%	1%	2%	3%	3%	81%

Mary Cunningham Agee Survey

Between January and March of 1984, Mary Cunningham Agee (Executive Director, Founder, and full-time volunteer for The Nurturing Network) held phone conversations with 100 women who had had abortions. These women were recruited through a dozen different sources, including abortion clinics, friends, and various service agencies. The phone interviews were done anonymously; neither Agee nor the respondents knew each other's identities.

Agee asked each woman, "If you had been presented with a positive alternative to abortion, would you have chosen it instead?" Of the 100 women, 91 responded "yes."

Some would ask, "What do you mean by 'a positive alternative'?" Agee would return, "Could you tell me what a positive alternative would have looked like to you at the time?" The answers were consistent: "I was under tremendous peer pressure to have an abortion; I needed to get out of there without jeopardizing my career/education plans." The women needed to transfer to either another job or another college, at least for the duration of the pregnancy.

Out of these responses grew Agee's plan for The Nurturing Network, which today includes well over 400 colleges that can transfer a woman within three weeks, and over 500 employers willing to provide a meaningful employment alternative. The Nurturing Network also offers shelter in the homes of over 1200 families, emotional counseling, and medical and legal resources. These resources are provided by 18,500 volunteers across the country, all available free via their toll-free number: 1-800-TNN-4-MOM.

The Nurturing Network has now assisted over 5000 women, of whom roughly half have had previous abortions. Those 2500 women have been asked the same question that Agee asked her initial 100-woman sample. The response remains at over 90% "yes."

A P P E N D I X   F

Listening Groups Summary

Listening groups were held in the following cities between May 1993 and April 1994. Participants were recruited through local post-abortion counseling services, and in the small groups were invited to tell the reasons that they had abortions, and what would have been necessary to solve those problems.

The following is an attempt to isolate the main reason cited by each participant, and to group those under common headings, identifying which reasons recurred most frequently. This is a frustrating undertaking, since the reasons are not always clear-cut (there are shades of gray between "boyfriend pressured" and "boyfriend unsupportive"), several reasons may be implicated in a single case, and from woman to woman there are differences in style of storytelling that make it difficult to compare the relative weight of problems. The summary chart of results, therefore, must be taken as a reasonable but not definitive conclusion.

Despite these limitations, there is one striking overall pattern: these women say they had abortions because of their relationships. Each made that choice either to please or protect her parents, or to please the father of her child. Practical problems—housing, career, finances, and so forth—were cited rarely, and never as the prime cause.

	CLASSED AS REASON #
LOS ANGELES	
Deb—boyfriend threatened to leave	1
Becky—mom would kick out of house	2
Paula—mom said, "you have a choice between family and baby"	2
Jill—afraid of hurting parents	3
Martha—"convenience" (relationships with men involved not strong enough)	4
CLEVELAND	
Kate—husband's health "couldn't take raising another kid"	1
Cathy—afraid for dad to find out pregnant by black man	5
Rose—"wasn't ready to give up having fun"	6
Lee—"how could I do this to Mom?"	3
Eunice—husband said, "I don't want it"	1
Anna—afraid boyfriend would leave	1
Annette—mom said, "your father would leave me"	2
Rochelle—didn't say	Not counted
Ruth—no memories	Not counted

CHICAGO

Martha—mom said, "you have to have an abortion"	2
Sally—boyfriend unsupportive	4
Libby—chaotic family life	6
Cindy—embarassed to tell parents didn't know who father was	5
May—boyfriend unsupportive	4

WASHINGTON, D.C.

Elizabeth—mother pressured	2
Kelly—protect dad (afraid would die of heart attack)	3
Bette—boyfriend pressured	1
Barbet—boyfriend encouraged abortion, variety of reasons	1
Sandi—boyfriend encouraged abortion, discouraged adoption	1

PHOENIX

Marie—husband pressured (population control)	1
Carol—husband pressured	1
Jane—didn't want to get in trouble with parents	5
Becky—parents pressured, afraid parental rejection	2
Alice—husband pressured	1
Nell—afraid boyfriend would leave	1

TAMPA

Lisa—didn't want to upset parents	3
Cheryl—boyfriend pressured	1

BOSTON

Marion—adults directed her toward abortion	6
Kathy—too young to marry	6
Colleen—mother pressured	2
Rita Anne—boyfriend pressured	1

Reason	NUMBER	PERCENTAGE
1. Husband/boyfriend pressured her to have abortion	13	38.2%
2. Parents pressured her (in 6 of 7 cases, her mother)	7	20.5%
3. Woman wanted to protect parents	4	11.7%
4. Husband/boyfriend weak and unsupportive	3	8.8%
5. Woman afraid of parental disapproval	3	8.8%
6. Other	4	11.7%

A P P E N D I X   G

Reardon Case Study Project

In the course of his research into post-abortion grief, David Reardon (*Aborted Women, Silent No More,* 1987), has collected hundreds of first-hand abortion stories through his Abortion Case Study Project. The case study form asks five questions, of which only the first ("1. How did you come to have an abortion and who was involved?") is relevant to the present study.

We reviewed 566 Case Studies, attempting to isolate the most pressing reason for the abortion and correlate it with the reasons listed on the Pregnancy Care Center Director's Survey. In some cases, strict correlation was impossible, so some of the categories have been altered.

	Reason	NUMBER	PERCENTAGE
1.	Husband or partner wants woman to have abortion	67	11.8%
2.	Confused/misinformed/lack of information	66	11.7%
3.	Woman's parents want her to have abortion	55	9.7%
4.	Lack of alternatives	49	8.7%
5.	Woman says she is not mature enough, or that she is too young to have a child	45	8%
6.	Woman has problems with relationship or wants to avoid single parenthood	44	7.8%
7.	Woman doesn't want others to know she has had sex or is pregnant	42	7.4%
8.	Woman says she is unready for responsibility	35	6.2%
9.	Pregnancy or child rearing will interfere with school or job situation	33	5.8%
10.	Woman says she can't afford baby now	29	5.1%
11.	Everyone—family, friends, co-workers, etc.— wants her to have an abortion and she feels rushed into it	25	4.4%
12.	Woman is concerned about how having a baby could change her life	24	4.2%
13.	Husband or partner absent, undependable, or insufficiently supportive	13	2.3%

Reason	NUMBER	PERCENTAGE
14. Woman has health problem	11	1.9%
15. Fetus has possible health problem	9	1.6%
16. Woman has habits complicating care (drugs, alcohol, prostitution, etc.)	5	.88%
— Woman was victim of rape or incest	5	.88%
— Woman has all the children she wants or has all grown-up children	5	.88%
17. Adoption appears too difficult (practically or emotionally)	3	.53%
18. Woman apprehensive about physical experience of pregnancy/birth	1	.18%

The following reasons netted zero responses:

> Woman at risk for being battered/abused
> Woman tempted to batter/abuse
> Woman needs child care after birth
> Woman needs assistance with obstetric care
> Woman needs housing during pregnancy
> Woman needs housing after birth
> Woman or partner has AIDS or sexually transmitted disease

A P P E N D I X   H

Pro-Choice Contacts

I. The following letter was mailed to the National Abortion Rights Action League, as well as six other pro-choice organizations: the National Abortion Federation, Catholics for a Free Choice, Planned Parenthood Association of America, the Religious Coalition for Abortion Rights, the Feminist Majority Foundation, and the National Organization for Women. No responses were obtained.

November 3, 1993

Ms. Kate Michelman
National Abortion Rights Action League
1101 14th Street, NW
Washington, DC 20005

Dear Ms. Michelman,

As a pro-life advocate who was once pro-choice, I am heartened by a shift in recent years in both movements. Pro-choice people are more likely to insist that they are not pro-abortion, and hope to make abortion rare. Pro-lifers are more likely to talk about "saving babies" by helping pregnant women with housing, medical care, and loving support. As both sides turn away from intractable legal battles, we discover that pregnancies are not political tokens, but intimate realities borne in the bodies of women for whom abortion is usually a last, and reluctant, choice.

While our sides are probably widely divided on how to prevent these pregnancies, we may share unexpected stretches of common ground when it comes to helping a woman who is already pregnant. Reducing the demand for abortion means understanding her experience and examining the problems that most often occur. We must consider how those problems might be solved, and see what resources we have, or need to improve, in order to help her.

I am writing to invite your input into the Real Choices research project. During this year, I will be listening to women who have experienced difficult pregnancies, and the people who care for them, hoping to answer the questions above. There are probably pieces of this puzzle that pro-choice people best understand, and so I seek whatever advice and direction you can share. The broader our research now, the better we can help women tomorrow.

Please phone or write me at the above address. I look forward to hearing from you.

Sincerely,
Frederica Mathewes-Green

II. Likewise, there was no response to this letter to the White House.

November 8, 1993

The President and Mrs. William Clinton
The White House
Washington, DC 20500

Dear President and Mrs. Clinton,

While pro-life and pro-choice forces remain deeply divided over many aspects of the abortion issue, sometimes they seem to be saying close to the same thing. When you, for example, speak of making abortion rare, or of helping women to feel it is unnecessary, you express a sentiment that many pro-life people share.

Real Choices is a project designed to answer some of the questions that surround the experience of abortion. In it we hope to discover why so many women feel that that tragic choice is their only hope. By identifying the reasons women have abortions, we can begin to work on solutions to those problems. We can review the resources we already have at hand—maternity homes, adoption services, and so forth—and see where improvements need to be made. Real Choices is not about laws, politics, or making abortion illegal. It is about helping women who are pregnant and in need.

To this end we are extending an invitation to pro-choice advocates to contribute to our research. We would like to know, from their side of the fence, what the causes of abortion are, and how best to remedy those problems. For this project, we can set aside our differences, and look together for ways to reduce the demand for abortion.

I am inviting you to lend your support to this project, and to contribute whatever input you may have to share. I hope thereby that we can give women more hopeful alternatives than abortion; and that abortion will indeed become increasingly "rare."

Thank you for your interest.

Sincerely yours,
Frederica Mathewes-Green

III. In scattered cities across the country—San Francisco, Buffalo, Denver, St. Louis—pro-life and pro-choice people have attempted to hold meetings in order to understand each other better or, in some cases, to tackle projects that are mutually agreeable (such as encouraging teens to embrace abstinence). This spontaneous movement is usually called "Common Ground." A Washington, DC organization called Search for Common Ground, usually concerned with international peace dialogue, inaugurated a project to unite and support these various local efforts. The Common Ground Network for Life and Choice is the result.

In December 1993 I was invited to join the Steering Committee of the Common Ground Network for Life and Choice. I sent the following letter to other members of the Steering Committee.

December 9, 1993

To: Members of the Steering Committee
Common Ground Network for Life and Choice

Thank you for making room for me on the Steering Committee; I just got the news from Mary yesterday. I hope I have the opportunity to meet you soon.

In talking with Adrienne yesterday she encouraged me to send you the enclosed information. As you see, I am working on a research project that seeks to discover why women have abortions, and how those problems can be solved. I have had good response from two of the three groups I wanted to hear from—pregnancy care centers and post-abortion women—but have not been able to establish any useful contact with pro-choice people. Hesitation is understandable, of course, in such uncharted waters, but I keep trying. As you look over the attached information, think about whether you would be willing to help with it in any way, or if you could connect me with someone else who might be interested.

A word on method: the survey, as you see, incorporates the items listed in the 1988 Alan Guttmacher survey, but adds to them in an effort to get more detail. (Of course, the pregnancy-care-center survey also looks for ways to solve the problems, which the AGI study did not attempt.) Survey results are being tabulated by professional statisticians—Jim Rogers (whose work has been published in the American Journal of Public Health and the Encyclopedia of Psychology, and presented at the American Psychiatric Association conference, the International Conference on AIDS, etc.) and his assistant Amy Miller.

I am facilitating the listening groups myself, not as focus groups seeking "hard" data, but as a source of "soft" information to put flesh on the bones of the survey results. Women are recruited for these groups through friends-of-friends in each city. I was stymied in my attempts to figure out a way to get a scientifically pure sample (eg, place an ad in the paper?) without compromising the participant's confidentiality, exposing the group to disruptive zealots or the media, and growing beyond an intimate size where vulnerability is possible. While most of the women in these groups are now pro-life, they weren't at the time of their abortion, so since my goal is to listen to the factual history of their decision (not their present feelings about it) I believe the results are useful for my anecdotal purposes. If you would like to see more, I'll gladly send you a copy of the book's chapter 1, which describes the listening group in Los Angeles.

The 500 case studies were gathered by David Reardon for his book, *Aborted Women, Silent No More*. Reardon's interest was in post-abortion stress, a controversial subject which my project does not encompass. I'm looking at pre-abortion stress—the pressures that caused her to choose abortion. The autobiographical case studies submitted to Reardon begin by recounting how the decision was made, and that is the only part of them useful for my purposes.

Sorry to subject you to such a long letter on first meeting. Please let me know what you think. Looking forward to meeting you soon.

Sincerely,
Frederica Mathewes-Green

In a few other cases, letters or face-to-face meetings did initially lead to encouraging dialogue, although no lasting connections were made. Because these contacts sometimes put people who wanted to be helpful in awkward positions, it seems best to leave those exchanges confidential.

A P P E N D I X   I

Pregnancy Care Organizations

Care Net (Christian Action Council)
101 W. Broad Street, Suite 500
Falls Church, VA 22046
703-237-2100

USA Birthright
PO Box 98363
Atlanta, GA 30359
404-451-6336

Alternatives to Abortion International
2606 1/2 W. 8th Street
Los Angeles, CA 90057-3810
213-382-2156

Bethany Christian Services
901 Eastern Avenue
Grand Rapids, MI 49503
616-459-6273

Heartbeat International
1213 1/2 So. James Road
Columbus, OH 43227
614-239-9433

The Nurturing Network
910 Main Street, Suite 360
Boise, ID 83701
208-344-7200

National Institute of Family and Life
Advocates
PO Box 42060
Fredricksburg, VA 22404
703-785-9853

National Life Center/1st Way
686 N. Broad St.
Woodbury, NJ 08096
609-848-1819

255

INDEX

ABOUT THE AUTHOR

As a feminist in the early seventies, Frederica Mathewes-Green advocated abortion as an essential element of a woman's control over her own life. When she read an article describing a second-trimester abortion, however, she realized that another life was at stake. She came to view abortion as an act of violence against unborn children, and one which hurts mothers as well. She has spent years speaking, writing, educating, and dialoguing on this subject.

Frederica directed the Real Choices research project, which was commissioned by the 1.3 million member National Woman's Coalition for Life; she is currently NWCL's Director of Communications. She also served as vice president of communications for Feminists for Life of America and as public affairs associate for Americans United for Life. She earned a B.A. degree in English from the University of South Carolina and a master's degree in theological studies from Virginia Episcopal Theological Seminary. Frederica was also a certified childbirth educator and prepared over four hundred women for their birth experience.

Frederica is a seasoned writer and speaker. She is a nationally syndicated columnist and a national correspondent for *World* magazine. Her writing appears in many national periodicals. Frederica speaks regularly about abortion issues at universities, conventions, and appears on radio and television programs across the country.

After years of agnosticism and Eastern religions, Frederica became a Christian in 1974. She and her husband, Gary, a priest of the Eastern Orthodox Church, live in Baltimore and homeschool their three teenagers.